In Search of Civil Society

Nicholas Deakin

First published 2001 by
PALGRAVE
Houndmills, Basingstoke, Hampshire RG21 6XS and
175 Fifth Avenue, New York, N. Y. 10010
Companies and representatives throughout the world

PALGRAVE is the new global academic imprint of
St. Martin's Press LLC Scholarly and Reference Division and
Palgrave Publishers Ltd (formerly Macmillan Press Ltd).

ISBN 0–333–91278–0 hardback
ISBN 0–333–91279–9 paperback

This book is printed on paper suitable for recycling and
made from fully managed and sustained forest sources.

A catalogue record for this book is available
from the British Library.

Library of Congress Cataloging-in-Publication Data

Deakin, Nicholas.
    In search of civil society / Nicholas Deakin.
        p. cm.
    Includes bibliographical references and index.
    ISBN 0–333–91278–0
        1. Civil society. I. Title.

JC337 .D43 2001
300—dc21   2001032786

10   9   8   7   6   5   4   3   2   1
10 09 08 07 06 05 04 03 02 01

Printed in China

For Phoebe, Adam and Stanley

Contents

Acknowledgements

As a compulsive reader of other people's acknowledgements, I have found that they are becoming less solemn these days, sometimes even flippant. This must have something to do with the new technology. Gone are the cringing references to illegible handwriting, laboriously deciphered by the faithful secretary. I also detect fewer signs of another and more fundamental purging of guilt: the apology to the neglected spouse and abandoned children. Has feminism finally altered the consciousness of the academy? (About time too, some would say). One author – a good friend, as it happens – complements her husband on his domestic management and cooking. Or perhaps writers – even academic ones – have become more efficient in the allocation of their time. Might that even have something to do (perish the thought) with the research regime under whose tyrannies we in Britain now groan? Certainly there seem to be less references to the endless aeons of labour devoted to the masterwork now at last being placed before readers – indeed, I found one case in which the writer boasted about how he had written his eighty thousand words in a matter of weeks (it showed). I have even come across acknowledgements specifying what the author used by way of musical accompaniment to composition and another set composed in verse: more accurately, doggerel. Here, and more soberly, are mine.

First to the Leverhulme Foundation, who by electing me to an Emeritus Fellowship, made this book possible and to Jean Cater at the Foundation, for the light touch with which it was administered (I wish other grant-giving bodies could emulate her). Second to my hosts for the duration of the Fellowship, the Local Government Centre at the University of Warwick, the Director, John Benington and his congenial colleagues. Third, to those who helped with the two research visits funded by the Leverhulme grant: Dr Susan Saxon-Harrold at Independent Sector, Washington and Dr Eva Kuti at the Hungarian Central Statistical Office, Budapest. I was greatly helped, on both visits, by discussions with academics and practitioners too numerous to name – I hope those I pestered with questions will accept a collective gesture of thanks for their generosity with time and trouble.

In writing this book I had the benefit of comments on drafts from a number of friends and colleagues: specifically, Stephen Yeo, Alan Deacon, John Benington (my fellow Jessica Williams fan), and Zsuzsa Ferge. Catherine Jones Finer heroically read the entire text, gave much helpful advice in her customary finely honed editorial manner and refused point-blank to travel to Utopia. Marilyn Taylor did the same job for my publishers, in her own style. My thanks to all of them: the usual disclaimer applies (though I notice some of my less scrupulous fellow authors expressing a wish to implicate their advisors in the consequences of error). Finally, Judy Scully acted as my research assistant for the project and commented on the text; I am grateful for her helpful contribution to the project. I did my own typing and deciphering; Sue Gilbert, who performed that office for many previous projects, was not called upon this time but thanks to her anyway for her good humoured tolerance over all the years.

Domestically, my wife Lucy Gaster has carried on with her own work and left space for me to do mine. My children and stepchildren and their partners made a capital contribution through the arrival of our joint grandchildren. On previous occasions I have chosen to dedicate books to friends and family now departed: as authors grow older there is a risk that the title page becomes a branch of the obituary column. There have been other losses since I last did so (I especially mourn my dear friend the sweet polymath Bill Anderson, with whom I would have particularly enjoyed arguing about connections between the ideas in his books and mine). I also owe an unpaid debt to my late stepfather, Donald Hodson. But on this occasion I would like to salute the future, not the past – a preference that I am sure he, as an excellent grandfather, would have been the first to understand.

Nicholas Deakin
Birmingham

Preface

Anything to declare?

It may help readers to understand the approach that I have adopted if I explain at the outset the reasons that led me to tackle the subjects covered in this book in the way that I have done.

My interest in these subjects is in the first instance a personal one. So I'll start by dropping the mask of social science for a moment and explain how this comes about. This is in part an attempt to come to terms with past experience in my own life and set out why, for someone of my background and generation, the world at the millennium is a particularly confusing place.

Napoleon once said: to understand a man properly, you have to know what the world was like when he was twenty. In my case, that means 1956, which – contrary to subsequent ignorant stereotypes – was a year of high drama internationally and hyperactivity in domestic politics. The world in which I grew up had been dominated by armed conflicts: one that actually took place (the Second World War, which was also a European civil war), and a second which was perpetually imminent (the cold war). I have very clear memories of bombing and evacuation in the first and an especially sharp recollection of that October day in 1962 when the Cuban missile crisis took the world to the brink of mutually assured destruction, from which we were rescued by the cool nerves of John Kennedy (for which he should be forgiven all his many excesses).

The constraints that resulted from the costs of fighting the first and preparing against the possibility of the second governed our lives and cramped our lifestyle. At the same time, even within those constraints we could consider ourselves fortunate, compared with the generation before us. I wore uniform for two years but never heard a shot fired in anger and left the services (aged twenty) a month before the last British imperial adventure at Suez.

By that time, Britain had already achieved a degree of prosperity; the post-war years were kind to the professional middle classes in most Western European countries and better for the skilled working class than any they had previously experienced.

Much of the earlier part of my own professional life was spent as a footsoldier in a campaign in which I had consciously enlisted for the long haul: the attempt to build a New Jerusalem. I was not seeking to play a commanding role – far from it – but extremely anxious to be on the side of the angels (as I and many others saw it). The main instrument for construction was to be the state – for me, that meant first central government and later one of the 'strategic' local authorities created by political consensus in the 1960s. The declared objective was to create the just society, with equal opportunities underpinned by high quality education for all – one in which poverty and unemployment were footnotes in history books. All civilisation's discontents, we well knew, couldn't be cured that way; but (as Freud had shown) there was a reasonable expectation of turning 'hysterical misery into common unhappiness'. However, as time passed the journey began to turn into a route march with the destination always over the next horizon: a case of 'next decade in Jerusalem'.

The good years ended messily with the oil price fiasco of 1973 and the arrival of the International Monetary Fund (IMF) in London in 1976. I observed and played a modest part in attempts to address the consequences – the struggle to keep the ship of state afloat (only pumping out and sailing it in circles, said the cynics). But I deserted the ranks of the public services in 1980, taking with me a vivid sense of increasing limitations on the capacity of the state and turned to exploring other perspectives and alternative approaches to the same set of issues, this time as an academic.

This led speedily to involvement in voluntary action. As a child of the 1950s, I brought a bundle of prejudices to that encounter and many preconceptions about those involved. Closer acquaintance did not entirely disperse them: but offered real possibilities of new avenues for action – alternative routes to the destination I had originally marked out. In particular, the claims of feminism, and particularly the assertion that the political must include the personal began to make better sense. (As a candid friend observed, I had my sixties two decades late).

Some other influences from this period included observing the impact of the policies of Margaret Thatcher at first hand, in the heartland of British manufacturing industry in the West Midlands.

At the time, perceptions of what was happening were distorted by the impact of her personality, but what was always clear was that she had unleashed forces which were producing a fundamental transformation, the full effects of which are still working their way through. The attempt to organise some resistance to the inhumanities that this process of change, whether necessary or not, had brought about was instructive and not wholly futile. God came into it, or at least the Church of England did; my first encounter, as an unbeliever, with that church in a militant frame of mind.

Next came a close encounter with the European project, which seemed to some of us to offer the opportunity to escape from the trap of nationalism which had devastated the continent twice in a century. But closer acquaintance with the flawed reality of a multi-national bureaucracy in stasis quickly banished illusions.

Then after 1989 the barriers that had divided the world since my childhood were lifted and released a flood of all sorts of astonishing events I had never thought to see in my lifetime. I was in hospital under strong drugs on the day the Berlin Wall fell: and believed for some while that the images I was seeing on the inescapable television set could only be hallucinations. Since then, I have spent much time in East and Central Europe travelling and discussing. No dramas to report, no heroic encounters with tyranny; but plenty of incident. From that experience came another message – the importance of civil society, as a concept which had sustained opponents of the regime by providing an alternative perspective, offering the possibility of a different future. These encounters helped me to a better understanding of some of the issues with which this book is concerned.

Another five years and another previously virtually inconceivable event: the arrival of democracy in South Africa (which I'd only seen under apartheid). The long queues in the hot sun, all citizens together, waiting to cast their votes were a humbling lesson in the importance of an act so often taken for granted elsewhere – the essential, though only the first step in a long and complex process.

In 1995, I was offered the opportunity of reviewing the state of the voluntary sector in England, as chair of an independent commission set up by the National Council for Voluntary Organisations (NCVO) . To be exposed over a year to the activities and personalities of voluntary action in its almost infinite variety was a stroke of great good fortune for me: but after the job was done, the experience left me with a number of unresolved questions, to which this book represents at least in part an attempt to find answers.

Finally, and in a different way just as transforming, I have experienced the liberating power of the new information technology – not, by the way, originally the product of commercial enterprise, whatever may now be asserted – so that I can with a single keystroke communicate with friends and relatives in California, Mozambique and Budapest.

Already, memories of what the twentieth-century world was like – the one that I inhabited for all my adult life so far and whose restrictions, personal, professional, and technological, I took for granted – are beginning to fade. For a new generation, the new world that has succeeded it presents new opportunities: they would be right not to be inhibited in the ways that they address them by idle reminiscences from the day before yesterday. Nevertheless, the experiences of the twentieth century, which started so gloriously, with a sunburst of artistic creativity and economic expansion; fell into the catastrophe of the First World War, accelerated progressively downwards through the devil's decade of the 1930s to the abyss before beginning its gradual uneven recovery, are not irrelevant. That century tested the grand theories of social and economic management to destruction, so that by the end there was only one contender left standing.

The twenty-first century will be the assize of the survivor, liberal capitalism. (I shall be using the term 'neo-liberalism' to describe this bundle of beliefs and practices.) Now that the first irrational exuberance of the period of transformation is over, we will be in a better position to draw up a balance sheet – to assess the costs as well as the material benefits of the New World Order.

In these debates, the two linked but separable concepts on which I have chosen to focus, civil society and voluntary action, have a potentially crucial function to perform. The retreat of the state (a universal phenomenon in developed countries) has left spaces to be filled, where the functions that it previously performed and still need to be discharged are located. There are rival candidates for the task of taking on these responsibilities, among whom voluntary bodies are only one plausible contender. And at the same time, such bodies have other roles to play: critical scrutiny as well as development of new initiatives; campaigning as well as provision. To what extent are these roles compatible?

Another related question: should the space in which these bodies operate – that is, the area customarily designated as 'civil society' – be organised and on what basis should the various individuals and groups who occupy that space participate in activities there? This might be called the issue of 'terms of engagement' – the balance between spontaneity and organisation, individual and community-based action, legal and commercial conditions for operating.

In exploring these and other related themes I have tried to preserve a degree of detachment: but it is idle to pretend that my analysis is not coloured by my 'intellectual formation' – the experiences through which I have passed – which is why I have declared them at the outset. Like Dr Johnson reporting parliamentary debates from his garret in Fleet Street, I cannot always allow the Whig dogs (or in my case, conservatives of all parties or none) to have the best of it.

Finally, I have permitted myself a Utopian excursion – not as a luxury but because I believe it essential to stimulate imagination and escape from the limits of my own experience. For I also want to explore possibilities for the future and imaginative ways in which it may be shaped. As it happens, I have fairly recently become a grandparent: that is a traditional moment for reflections on futurity. Like Keynes at a less promising time, the beginning of the 1930s, I shall want to speculate in my conclusions on the social possibilities for my grandchildren, who will have no personal memory of the twentieth century but (I trust) every prospect of seeing their own new one evolve in better ways.

CHAPTER 1

Civil Society and Voluntary Action: Concepts and Issues

Every thing is what it is, and not another thing. (Joseph Butler, *Fifteen Sermons Preached at the Rolls Chapel* (1729), quoted by Henry Hardy, in Berlin, *The Roots of Romanticism*)

Basic strategy

In this book, I set out to assess the significance of the concepts of civil society and voluntary action, and their role in shaping events at local, national and global levels.

Developments now occurring under these two headings form part of a vast constellation of activities that are taking place in all societies and fall outside the boundaries of the state or the market. And, as I shall show, these boundaries are permeable, allowing interpenetration and exchanges to take place across them that exert a fundamental influence on the behaviour of organisations and individuals on either side of the border.

In particular, I hope to demonstrate that what is happening in and around the space characterised as 'civil society', much though not all of it propelled by voluntary action, is not merely relevant to the processes of change that are now occurring with such bewildering speed but central to them. To take only a few examples of the relevance of these questions to current debates:

- The presence of civil society has frequently been invoked as a key factor in redressing the oppressive weight of totalitarian

1

regimes – but what part can it play after these regimes have fallen? Can developments in civil society help to transform deformed societies and sustain a new set of social and economic relations and will it also be transformed itself, in the process?

- Partisans of a market economy have invoked voluntary action – usually in its guise as charity – to justify the consigning of the state to a marginal role in welfare. Can voluntary action cope with the resulting challenges? Should it even attempt to do so?
- Radical protest invokes new social movements to serve both as global capitalism's critics and as the instigators of domestic change. How can they hope to be effective, given the disparities in political power and financial resources between the critics and those they are criticising? And if they attempt to address that difficulty by resorting to direct action, how far are such tactics legitimate in a democratic polity?
- New technology offers the opportunity of evolving new modes for action. A critical mass of support for new interventions can now be assembled outside the traditional arenas for action by use of the Internet or mobile phones and pressure brought to bear in ways that evade the restrictions imposed by conventional legal and institutional systems – though those who use these tactics are not always on side of angels. Technology could also provide an occasion for reinventing philanthropy. How could any new model escape the weaknesses of the previous versions?

In all these and many other cases, voluntary organisations operating in civil society are active parties to the process of transformation, not passive subjects of change.

Tactics

I believe that the best way to approach the questions that I have set out to examine in this book is not through a focus tightly confined to voluntary action or 'third sector' bodies or drawn exclusively from the emerging literature about these organisations and their activities. There is a place for this approach, which is beginning to yield encouraging results: but not here. Examining the issues through the lens of civil society provides a wider perspective: despite the fact that, as we shall shortly see, the term itself is contested (or sometimes even rejected). By adopting such a perspective, which can either cross the boundaries of academic disciplines or evade them altogether, it is possible to connect with some of the debates now taking place both in the academic and what is usually called the 'real world'. Most of the work that I have found particularly stimulating and drawn upon here comes from those writers who have taken this broader perspective – their names emerge as I proceed.

I have also taken a broad approach in the geographical sense. Without attempting to be comprehensive, I have drawn on evidence from a number of different societies, in Europe and outside, principally the United States. I am personally familiar with some of them and have not hesitated to use personal experience where I think that would be helpful.

So I have tried to widen both the range of sources drawn upon and the type of material used. And I've also sought to present it in such a way as to make it accessible as possible. I dislike the promiscuous use of the Harvard method of referencing and echo David Donnison in his denunciation of the temptation it provides to us vain or lazy academics to exploit the system to show off our learning, without even having to prove that we have actually earned the right to do so by actually reading the sources cited. Nor, for much the same reasons, do I care for the all-inclusive bibliographies that are manufactured by accumulation from author to author, as the technology now makes it so childishly simple to do. (My late friend Kieron Walsh was the only academic I have ever known of whom I could confidently say that he had read all the books in his own bibliography). So I have used Harvard referencing sparingly, when I think it would genuinely assist readers. And I have provided, as an appendix, a short narrative account of those books that I have found helpful and the reasons why I believe others might find them useful.

In addition, I should make it plain that I have not set out to be prescriptive about the forms that voluntary action should take or ways in which its efficiency can be improved. In other words, this is not a management cook book or a guide to fund raising. But since I believe that the scope of voluntary action is bound to increase and the nature of the action taken by voluntary organisations and their capacity to undertake it effectively will become increasingly important I have also included references to sources on which readers can draw for information on these issues.

Readers will not find much, finally, by way of hard data in the body of the text, except where I've judged it essential to the line of argument I am developing. There are practical grounds for this: the inevitable delay in publication, the rapid decay of much factual material. Between hard covers, at least, nothing dates as quickly as the topical. But I have provided another appendix, which tells readers where they can secure the ready access to fresh data that the new technologies now allow.

What don't date are the underlying issues and key concepts. The topics that I am exploring require me to provide definitions of some of these key concepts, which may be unfamiliar to some readers and over-familiar to others. Some of the definitions are disputed; so when making my selection of preferred explanations – or devising my own – I will try to indicate where there are grounds for legitimate disagreement and what those are. Descriptions of the terms employed ('naming of parts') may therefore sometimes be conditional or even provisional.

Definitions

I shall be dealing in this book with a number of concepts, the two most important being *civil society* and *voluntary action*.

Civil society

This term is much debated and often defined, frequently in contradictory ways. Adam Seligman justly observes that: 'Right, Left and Center; North, South, East and West civil society is identified with everything from multi-party systems and the rights of citizenship to individual voluntarism and the spirit of community' (1997: 5).

Since we will need to start with a definition for working purposes, I propose to adopt that provided by the American historian Michael Walzer:

> The words 'civil society' name the space of uncoerced human association and also the set of relational networks – formed for the sake of family, faith, interest and ideology – that fill this space. (1995: 7)

What fills this space called civil society? What kind of activities take place there and what are the values that animate it?

Walzer's answer begins with the concept of identity, as defined through different forms of membership in society. Thus, what he terms a *republican* perspective defines membership through engagement by citizen action and rests on political activity, the badge of civic virtue. Membership is in the demos, the political community, sometimes restrictively identified by age, gender or ethnic origin. A *Marxist* paradigm defines membership through the class system, the arena of action as the economy and its form the class struggle. A *liberal* approach is similarly located in the marketplace but is individualistic, based on the freedom to associate autonomously through acceptance of the rules of the market, by contract rather than membership as such. Walzer's list ends with the *nationalist*, defined by verifiable membership of an ethnic or national grouping, usually conferring citizenship which defines both members and outsiders (1995). In some contexts this is associated with values that might best be labelled *conservative*, seeking to defend an inherited sense of membership based on nationality.

Walzer's catalogue could be extended in a number of other different directions. One, which has proved controversial in the past, is a *religious* definition of membership in society. Historically, this has been a powerful means of identification: choice of a set of beliefs (sometimes acquired by inheritance or even through coercion) conveying rights and obligations. Again, there are good grounds for identifying a distinctive *communitarian* perspective, deliberately pitched at the local level, concerned with obligations and duties arising out of proximity – neighbourliness and mutual aid, in the workplace, education and place of worship. But here, too, there are issues around coercion as against freely chosen behaviour.

Gender as well as ethnicity and class can provide an alternative focus for membership. By bridging the personal and the political, gender also provides an alternative basis for action; helping to build up networks that cross other boundaries, whose actions have become increasingly significant. This raises another controversial issue: can the intimate relations of the family be legitimately included within the definition of civil society, or do they stand apart: are they so different in character and outcome as to demand their exclusion? My answer, for reasons that will become apparent, is that they cannot be excluded – family linkages extend into the economy and the public arena and often help to influence events there.

Clearly these memberships are not all mutually exclusive; rather, they are plural and most individuals will have crosscutting loyalties, which operate with different strengths in different circumstances. Their significance may change: an identity, which once seemed marginal may become central, as it has recently done to lethal effect in former Yugoslavia.

Identity will be exemplified and reinforced by participation in the activities of organisations formed in the different arenas. Each paradigm will suggest a different emphasis: on political parties and pressure groups in the republican version, workers' organisations in the Marxist, charities in the liberal market and bodies like community groups, religious congregations or women's self-help groups in the others.

Some organisations will demand primacy in loyalty from their members: others are less exigent. An anarchist would argue that no organisations or form of membership that makes claims that we have to be coerced into accepting could be legitimate (and as I shall show, there are right-anarchists as well as left ones). Many lives in all kinds of society are led largely in private. In extreme cases people can exist as wholly isolated individuals or by focusing exclusively on narrower personal loyalties (family, neighbourhoods, *Landsmannschaft*). In former state socialist societies a common form of response to pressure to conform was voluntary 'internal exile', attempting by evasion to repudiate all claims that the state could make. There are also questions to be asked about how membership is acquired and how it may be lost, by sustained pressure of inequalities, discrimination or in extreme cases expulsion or even extermination.

Walzer presents the civil society project as 'anti-ideology'. He accepts the legitimacy of all the positions that he catalogues, in their own terms; but asserts that none of them have or should have irrefutable claims to primacy, in a mature society. All must leave room for the others; none can be uniquely privileged.

This view is not universally shared. Some prioritise one agenda over another. Some reject the legitimacy or relevance of particular values or activities. Some wish to distinguish different spheres of activity by separating the political and economic domains; others (Jürgen Habermas) designate a public sphere, distinct from the private and much influenced by the activities of the mass media. Some maintain that the term 'civil society' has already exhausted its explanatory value, except possibly in the crudest sense of designating an area apart from the market and the state. Others believe that it can be rescued by shifting the basis of the debate on to different ground, so that 'Instead of arguing about what is and is not included in civil society, we should be arguing about what is and is not included in the notion of the common public good'

(Knight and Hartnell, 2000: 18) – although the 'common good' itself can of course mean different things in different circumstances. Walzer himself is agnostic: he concludes that 'civil society is a project of projects; it requires many organising strategies' (1995: 27).

To rescue some degree of clarity, it may be helpful to concentrate on the idea of civil society as an *arena*, in which the various activities that take place are informed by the different values determined by the different perspectives Walzer describes. The various institutions that operate there will do so on the basis of different priorities, influenced by these perspectives. Individuals will do so on the basis of values inculcated through their background, education and experience. These priorities and values may well include a commitment to the 'common good' but are by no means certain to do so. As Stanley Katz suggests, 'civil society must be thought of as a process and a state of mind – a social process that generates trust and mutual understanding and mediates state and market pressures' (1999: 37). This process of mediation is dynamic and can take a variety of different forms.

By definition, transactions and relationships which are located in the civil society arena take place on terms not wholly dominated by the state in its various forms or by the values or procedures of the market. However, each perspective implies a different type of engagement – close or distant – with the state on one side and the market on the other. Republicans will want to employ the state to redress market failure, by regulation and control legitimated in the political arena. Liberals will seek to restrict the state's role to the minimum but invite the market in as guarantor of liberty and role model for efficient delivery of services. Marxists, at least in their current western form, will reject both, as Gramsci once did – seeing the state as no more than an 'executive committee', formed by the bourgeoisie to defend their class interests. Communitarians will assert the moral authority of the smallest possible unit, from the family upwards and attempt to populate civil society by empowering them to the maximum extent possible. Some religions welcome state and market into the arena occupied by civil society: others reject one or both. But from almost all these perspectives, the boundaries of the space in which civil society activities take place are permeable.

Where does this leave the individual? What choices do they have when confronted with these alternatives? Albert Hirschman's model of social action and the options open to individuals may be helpful here. It is derived from development economics and Hirschman's own observations of the workings of the Nigerian transport system. He divides the possible forms of response that individuals confronting a system can choose into three categories, which he labels Exit, Voice and Loyalty (Hirschman 1970). The strategy chosen will depend mainly on the individual's assessment of the likely outcomes of their choices.

We can relate these choices of individual strategies to the Walzer categories of different paradigms, slightly expanded, to produce a matrix as in Table 1.1.

A vital qualification has to be entered at this point. Despite increasingly frequent references to 'civil society organisations' all these different possible forms of activity in the arena of civil society are not fully captured by that term. For that, we need a different vocabulary.

Voluntary action

When discussing activity outside the state and the market I have preferred wherever possible to use terms that reflect motivation: action freely chosen by the participant. Hence I refer to *voluntary action* performed by *voluntary organisations* and use the term

Table 1.1   The approach to action

Perspective	Focus of action	Mode of action	Unit of action	Type of action
Marxist	Class	Solidarity, struggle	Organised labour	Loyalty, voice
Liberal	Market	Competition	Individual	Exit
Republican	Demos	Participation	Voters, parties	Voice, loyalty
Communitarian	Community	Through citizen rights and res- ponsibilities	Neighbour- hood	Loyalty, exit
Religious	Church (synagogue, mosque)	Transcendance	Congregation	Voice, exit
Conservative	Nation	Obedience	Subjects	Loyalty

Source: derived from Hirschman 1970 and Walzer 1995

voluntarism to describe a distinctive perspective on the totality of this activity.

In his exhaustive examination of these issues (1993), Barry Knight defined voluntary action as 'a form of energy, stemming from free will, having a moral purpose and undertaken in a spirit of independence' (xii) and proposed a number of criteria for identifying authentic voluntary bodies: independent beginnings, self-governing structures, independence from other agencies, independent funding, use of volunteers, distributing of surpluses but not for profit. This will normally suffice, for my purposes.

But readers must be warned that this terminology is not in universal use, either in the academic literature or the field. Scholars and activists in the United States and by extension areas that have fallen within their zone of influence prefer *non profit* as a description, which defines activity by a simple negative – action carried out by individuals or bodies not actively engaged in the market, trading for profit. Another alternative that has gained popularity among them is *third sector* – thus, for American scholars and their associates their professional organisation is the International Society of Third Sector Researchers (ISTR). This definition is also a negative: it assumes the primacy of the first and second sectors, the state and the market; it also assumes that each is a self-contained area with distinct boundaries and that the status of this third sector rests on not possessing any of the characteristics of the first two. Confusion is further compounded by another term, *independent sector*. Independent from what, or whom, one wonders. And by what tests?

In what was once called the Third World and now more often the 'South' another definition is dominant: organisations operating there in the civil society space are *non-governmental organisations* (NGOs) – another negative. In Continental Europe, by contrast, the term in general use has positive connotations: *association*. I would prefer to use this, in the sense of ventures taken for common advantage, were it not for cultural freight that this term carries, extending far further into the economic sphere and used to define a separate *économie sociale*.

The question of comparability has been addressed in the recent studies of the non-profit sector conducted from Johns Hopkins University in the United States. The discussion of these issues in these studies is important because it is based on extensive international comparative work. The main authors, Lester Salamon and Helmut Anheier, address what they call the 'terminological tangle' and pull out four different types of definition: the legal, the economic, the functional and finally what they call the 'structural-operational' definition. This emphasises not the purposes of the organisations or their sources of income but their basic structure and mode of operation. In this definition, the 'non-profit sector' is a collection of entities that are:

- organised
- private (institutionally separate from government)
- non-profit distributing
- self-governing; and
- voluntary (involving 'some meaningful degree of voluntary participation').

They conclude that this 'structural-operational' definition is the most satisfactory for purposes of international comparisons and I will follow them in using it where that is the main objective (1997: 33).

Other terms will appear and disappear depending on context – for example, *'new social movements'*, *'community groups'*, *'grass roots organisations'*. When they do, I will try to make it as clear as possible why I'm using which term and what their particular significance is at any time. Two other terms are of central relevance to my subsequent discussion – *democracy* and *citizenship*. I will provide brief definitions of both when embarking on that section of the argument.

Finally, there are two terms that are especially relevant to the discussion on England which require immediate clarification. These are *charity* and *philanthropy*. I shall define *charity* as either collective action or individual responses to the issue of poverty in general and to the poor as individuals. And I shall distinguish these responses as being expressions either of *philanthropy* or *mutual aid*. The first is action taken on behalf of the poor, in which the principal agent is the donor and recipients appear as passive subjects. The second is action taken as an exchange between two actors. This could be either to develop a mutually agreed approach to poverty or a situation in which the recipient acquires certain rights and duties as a result of transactions that may benefit both parties (Beveridge 1948). *Charity* in the English context also has a precise meaning in relation to legislation that defines charitable status and the benefits that go with it and subsequent interpretations of charity law that have modified its meaning.

A final point to stress is that none of these definitions are static. The terms have emerged in specific situations and are still evolving in response to changing circumstances. The discussion requires clarity but also has to take into account different cultural and historical contexts: a uniform usage would distort this variety. So readers will have to accept that in some circumstances I need to employ the vocabulary evolved in particular societies and at specific times and embedded in their culture and discourse. This may create some confusion. But as Isaiah Berlin comments in his discussion of romanticism, sometimes a certain lack of precision in definition confers 'a welcome license to roam' (Berlin 1999).

A key question

My choice of Michael Walzer's definition and the discussion that flows from it is based in part on the use he makes of it to ask a question that had real resonance: As the twenty-first century begins, what is meant by the good society?

This is not exactly an original question: many different individuals in different societies have attempted to answer it, in very different ways. These are the Grand Narratives of the past – political, ideological, ethical or religious. Disillusioned though we may be by the outcomes of many of these past enterprises, are there lessons that we can draw from accounts of their progress and failures that can be drawn upon in constructing more hopeful (presumably more modest) alternatives?

The idea of civil society as an essential element in that process has deep historical roots, but seemed to have faded from active use until recently. Those roots are now frequently dug up and re-examined; rival reviews of different uses of the term in their historical setting usually take us from civil society as the description of a condition in which violence had been contained and institutionalised through the state by the rule of law (a *Rechtstaat*, as the philosopher Hegel described it), to the alternative view of civil society as a 'commercial' society in which the arts of peace replace those of war and the market provides the arena for the free exercise of enterprise and choice, as the moral philosopher Adam Ferguson argued during the Scottish enlightenment. These definitions were important in their period: so was the less frequently mentioned New Liberal view developed in Edwardian England by political scientists and philosophers like Graham Wallas and J. H. Muirhead, that 'civic society' could be a means of constructing a model of citizenship not wholly dependent on the state – what might be called a premature 'third way'. Nonetheless, these earlier perspectives were until recently mainly of (literally) academic interest, chiefly to historians of ideas.

The concept of civil society only returned as a central idea in debates about the good society as a result of the manifest failure of the different projects that have dominated debate during much of the previous century (the twentieth) to create and sustain such a society. Their failures led to a growing recognition that the notion of civil society might have a substantial role to play in making good the deficiencies that had caused them to fail.

In the nineteenth century, the marriage of enlightenment ideas to the concept of the nation state had seemed to offer a logical means for achieving modernisation of institutions and material progress for citizens by the systematic application of human knowledge. Unfortunately, the nation state in its totalitarian variant has also proved capable of being employed for other purposes – territorial aggression, widespread spoliation of defeated rivals and slaughter of civilian populations. Events in the twentieth century have reflected the full impact of the destructive force of the nationalist agenda in this form.

The nation state can also show a more benevolent face, of course. In the period after the Second World War the western democracies appeared to have found the means of combining increased material prosperity and social stability by wider diffusion of the fruits of that prosperity and provision by the state of adequate support for those who might otherwise not be able to benefit directly from economic growth. For thirty years, before the instability of the system was exposed, the state possessed, in Ernest Gellner's rather crude formulation, a 'social bribery fund'. This was the so-called 'Keynesian Welfare State'. However, this combination of material prosperity and stability eluded other societies outside Western Europe and the United States and even in the West the Keynesian Welfare State's bribery fund eventually ran out – when cheap fuel did, at the beginning of the 1970s.

But its main rival, the Marxist project in the deformed version (sometimes called by its partisans, as long as it existed, 'actually existing socialism') that evolved in the Soviet Union, its satellite states in East and Central Europe and under rather different circumstances in much of the Far East also encountered difficulties that eventually proved insuperable, leading eventually to terminal loss of legitimacy as citizens withdrew their confidence from the system. Ignominious collapse followed, often in a highly dramatic and visible way.

All the various rival projects – totalitarianism of the right and left, liberal capitalism and social democracy in their different variants – which came into their full maturity during the course of the twentieth century can now be judged in terms of their effectiveness in reaching the objectives that they set for themselves – territorial aggrandisement and dominion, prosperity and the assertion of individual rights, social justice and equality, godly rule and responsibility and the pursuit of happiness and the common good.

Measured by these standards, the performance of all of them has been uneven at best, with some grossly impoverished outcomes: strikingly so in the case of forty years of experience of state socialism in East and Central Europe and the former Soviet Union; and of endemic poverty in the South. But there is also a manifest crisis of concern about the character and quality of life even in societies where material circumstances have patently improved almost out of all recognition over the course of the century.

Michael Ignatieff in his polemic *The Needs of Strangers* (1986) expresses this concern in a particularly urgent form. He argues that some of the solutions adopted within western democratic societies, which cast state welfare as the mid-twentieth-century solution to many of the issues posed by the attempt to create a good society, have created problems as well as resolved them, especially for those located outside the mainstream of conventional society: refugees, the elderly, the poorest. And, in addition, the institutions created to manage the welfare system have proved incapable of satisfying many of the most important claims of women, as presented by that most articulate of all modern social movements, feminism.

What are the alternatives? Increasingly, the answer has been seen to lie within the civil society space, through seeking out partners there who can provide services as efficiently or more cheaply, as a substitute for direct state provision or services purchased in the market and with greater sensitivity to the needs and human dignity of those receiving these services.

Civil society as the alternative arena

However, to judge from the behaviour of most governments, there is still no clear understanding of how the potential resource represented by activity outside the state and market, where it exists, can be brought into play and how the preconditions for effective action can be satisfied.

The Johns Hopkins studies offer one perspective: their summary of recent developments proposes that there is a 'global associational revolution' taking place; an exponential growth in the size and capacity of the 'non-profit' sector, common to all thirteen countries in the first wave of their comparative study (Salamon and Anheier 1997). Furthermore, they see this revolution not just as a result of a retreat by the state; it has been brought about, in their account, by the discovery (or rather rediscovery) of the 'reach' of voluntary action and its capacity to perform functions that neither the state nor the market can discharge. This capacity stems from the distinctive characteristics of voluntary organisations and the values that they embody and bring to action within the civil society sphere.

But it is arguable that the key distinctive characteristic of the world of voluntary association lies precisely in the unpredictable character of the form it takes and the diversity of the functions that it performs in different times and places. According to this view, a healthy civil society cannot be artificially created or imposed: it needs to grow spontaneously, over a considerable length of time and sometimes in ways not readily comprehensible to outsiders not familiar with the culture in which it has developed. (Compare the Victorian English gentleman's pity for foreigners who could not hear the secret harmonies of his country's unwritten constitution.) Moreover, this spontaneity means that it is difficult to use organisations from within civil society as a means to address agendas – like the provision of public goods – that were not set there. And some voluntary bodies have altogether different objectives of their own, which involve not implementing but resisting those agendas, in some cases to the point of civil disobedience or outright rebellion.

To explore these alternative views properly necessarily involves some attempt to come to terms with the history of voluntary activities of all kinds and the context in which they have taken place. It is questionable how far back in time the trail should lead. Evidence from the historical inheritance of individual societies may be necessary to the argument but is not sufficient in itself as an explanation. Comparisons across space are equally, if not more, important as those over time but these, too, are of variable explanatory value.

Different cultures assign different roles to the individual citizen and the activities she or he undertakes, in unison or by themselves.

These cultures develop different imperatives and different patterns of behaviour have emerged in different countries that vary by class, gender, region and language group. The structures that have emerged there have also taken a variety of different forms under the impact of a diverse range of influences.

Until the late twentieth century religion has consistently remained a factor of fundamental importance. Charity has its basic origins as a religious impulse, defined and enjoined in the sacred books of all religions, though different religions have shaped the form in which it is to be expressed in different ways. The Catholic Church has maintained its rival claim to authority in this field in the face of the state and has sought to retain responsibility for implementation of charitable works. Catholicism remains a powerful influence in shaping the texture of civil society, especially in southern Europe. Protestant individualism with its emphasis on justification by good works has exerted an equally strong influence, especially at the point of intersection between charity and business; Judaism (sometimes confusingly bundled together with rival Christian denominations as 'Judeo-Christian values') has also made a distinctive contribution to the evolution of philanthropy, in the context of migration.

Among the other major world religions, the capacity of Islam as a system of beliefs to adapt to modern circumstances has been strikingly demonstrated: religion has provided a legal and constitutional framework which is flexible enough to sustain a common setting which commands general adherence even where the state structure is fragile or dictatorial. But it is notable that until recently there was no significant sign of an organised civil society emerging, at least in the Arab world: only 'networks, quasi-tribes, kin-based alliances based in regional origins and common institutional experience' – usually in the armed forces (Gellner 1994: 27).

The interplay of diverse influences is especially striking in the case of the United States. Early experience in New England mandated godly living as the template for life in society, but left sufficient play for commerce to flourish – in contrast to the different experience of Islamic societies with their rigid restrictions on commercial practices like charging interest. This helps to explain some key differentiating features of the American situation, where society came before the state; democracy comes before bureaucracy; religious values infuse voluntary action and continue to do so and the market nourishes but also distorts philanthropy.

To each society, then, its own clusters of values and interplay of interests, notably those based on classes: expressed in the ways in which they have met the challenge of representative democracy and the evolution of citizenship, especially the emancipation of women. The significance of these developments and the interplay of different factors – including changes in the structure of the national economy and in applied technologies – is often best seen through individual case studies of developments over the last two centuries, which help to provide a context for exploration of the opening question about the foundations of a good society. It is therefore essential to bear in mind the distinctive cultural, legal, institutional and economic environment within which civil society has grown, developed, flourished or in some cases withered.

Changing contexts

In most societies, the space occupied by civil society has evolved as part of a dynamic process of adaptation and change and in the course of evolution has altered its character and composition. Gaps have opened up, new opportunities have appeared and voluntary bodies have taken up different roles and started to perform them in different ways, in part in response to shifts in the external environment. In particular, the institutions with which they interact have also been in a state of flux over the second half of the twentieth century.

The prime example is the state: after its apparently inexorable advance over the first half of the twentieth century, it has been rolled back over the second and its role modified in a number of crucial respects – sometimes portrayed as a shift 'from rowing to steering'. The basic rationale for state intervention in the public domain has usually been seen as its capacity to deliver what economists call public goods more equitably than the market and more efficiently (because more systematically) than the voluntary sector. The widespread perception common to politicians across the whole political spectrum that it has failed in that role has meant that this claim can no longer be sustained.

As a result, the once-mighty state, Thomas Hobbes's Leviathan, has been cloned: in place of one potentially oppressive monster the state is often now a shoal of smaller creatures, swimming in a sea of business values and subject to all sorts of market disciplines. These changes have taken different forms in different societies, of course – the process of rolling back has been more abrupt in some, barely perceptible in others. But as the Organisation for

Economic Co-operation and Development's (OECD) elaborate monitoring of this process has shown, there is a clear trend internationally: change of mode of operation as well as scale, strongly influenced by the example of the market. This has had a particular impact in the field of welfare, an area traditionally of great significance for voluntary organisations.

This is especially important at a point when liberal capitalism has escaped from the limitations imposed by the nation state and is having an impact on a global scale – the phenomenon usually known as 'globalisation'. One consequence is that the cultural distinctiveness of different societies has been progressively eroded. Markets have become international in their reach as a result of the rapid opening up of national economies which has taken place over the last two decades in consequence of free flows of goods and capital. As a result, the form in which goods and services are provided and the distribution of resources within societies have been fundamentally changed. This process has been facilitated by technical innovation (the information revolution) and the near universal adoption of the English language as the *lingua franca* of commerce.

So it will therefore be necessary to venture outside national boundaries, which for some purposes that I will be discussing are becoming less relevant – though this is not a uniform process and certain forms of nationalism have become more aggressively intrusive, in part as a response to these globalising trends. Protest, too, now has its international dimension and those participating in it are sometimes described, rather confusingly, as 'global civil society' – a term whose implications I will need to explore later.

At the same time, it is also important to penetrate below the level of the state, to the region, to cities and most of all to the locality. One of the recurrent features of debate is the rediscovery of the significance of the local – the village, the city block, the local school, and the corner store – in Edmund Burke's over-quoted phrase, the 'little platoon' to which our first loyalties are owed. But there are also intimate ties not based on locality – groups based on identities defined in other ways, by professional and occupational loyalties, by common experience, by gender and sexuality, through birth in a specific ethnic or language group, in the tribe or clan, the family – or the Mafia's *famiglia*.

Participation in these activities can provide the stage on which people are able to develop the skills that make small organisations of all kinds function – the 'gymnasium of democracy' in which 'active citizens' can develop their competences.

These smaller units also have the capacity to release and realise some of the most significant motive forces in human behaviour; love, friendship and affection, loyalty: the whole complex of emotions that animate mutual aid. But these intimate connections can also produce the opposite effects: love becomes hate; affection can turn to dislike; loyalty descends into vendetta; mutual aid slides into clientelism and corruption. Small, in short, is not always beautiful.

All these connections and activities, taken together, the virtuous with the less attractive, make up the basic sub-soil of civil society: a central concern must be the fertility of that soil and the nature of what grows in it and the implications, both positive and negative, for wider society and prospects for the 'common good'.

Mapping the territory

To capture all these different elements within the scope of one short account is clearly impossible: I will have to be selective. Some of my more detailed explorations will focus on individual societies but I will use them to illustrate specific clusters of issues. However, these issues cannot be confined within one case study: so I ask readers to think of my presentation as spokes in a wheel, radiating out in different directions from the hub which is civil society.

As a road map, Figure 1.1 represents the territory that I will set out to explore.

The terrain on which the bulk of the activity that I will be describing is contained in the centre, in the space labelled 'civil society' (as in Walzer's definition, given earlier). Much of what is usually classified as voluntary action takes place here and takes a variety of different forms and operates at different scales.

But the sum of this activity does not constitute a self-contained 'sector' – a term with which, for reasons I have already stated, I have become increasingly impatient. Rather, much of it tends to spill over into adjacent areas. Some of these border areas are familiar territory for voluntary action. The linkages between family, neighbourhood and voluntary activity at local level have already been stressed and need no further elaboration here. But although some of the 'borderlands' (a term borrowed from earlier debates in Britain) are territories long since colonised, other frontiers are still disputed. The interaction between the state and civil society is

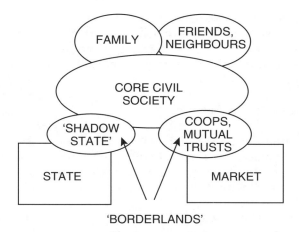

Figure 1.1 The Location of civil society

a particular case in point and it is this interaction which has produced organisations which may operate at the local as well as the national level that are sometimes described as the 'shadow state', combining characteristics from both.

The boundary with the market is perhaps less often stressed but is equally – if not by now more – important. The entry or invasion (as some would see it) into the civil society space by the market and business values is likely to be even more transforming and sharply contested over the next decades.

Changes in other areas – for example, in the role and composition of the family – are often excluded from discussion of these issues. But for a variety of reasons, not least the implications of these changes for the circumstances of women, I believe that they are fundamental for a rounded account of civil society.

Forces that occupy no specific space may exercise a pervasive influence – for example, the role of religion, whose potential significance is pervasive but fluctuates over time and varies between different localities: at different times and places, churches have enjoyed very close or rather distant relations with the state and voluntary associations. Another example is the media of communication and their influence on the public sphere, and the potentiality for further expansion as a result of the invention of the Internet and the creation of the World Wide Web.

So a further and final point to stress is that the situation that this approach seeks to capture is dynamic, not static; there are exchanges – sometimes skirmishes – taking place all the time in the borderlands, the outcome of which it is not yet possible to predict.

Structure of the discussion

Before setting out on substantive discussion of the issues identified in this preliminary sketch, I will set up some signposts for the readers, to enable them to see in which direction the argument will be proceeding and the main features of the landscape to be covered.

The next chapter, Chapter 2, focuses on a central concern in the history of voluntary action, the provision of welfare. This issue provides a test of the capacity of actions taken outside the state, in what has subsequently come to be known as civil society, to provide effectively against poverty. Most of this action was conducted under the rubric of charity. Here, I will explore the involvement of organised religion and impact of religious belief on individual motivation. Another key issue is the development of relations with the state and the institutional and financial links formed over time, how these have changed and their consequences for both partners to the encounter. The approach is historical; the focus on England. I will need to establish whether outcomes are the product of English exceptionalism – in other words, are the approaches adopted a product of differences in the Anglo-Saxon model of capitalism, of legal forms (English charitable law is famously idiosyncratic) or of culture – what is sometimes called 'English individualism'. Among the substantive issues that I will have to resolve are the validity over the longer term of philanthropy both as an approach to the presenting question and more generally for the future.

In Chapter 3, I will be testing the claims of an alternative approach, essentially one based on mutual aid through collective actions taken at the level of the community and their capacity to deliver solutions on a 'bottom up' basis. Here, the focus is on the borderland between the personal domain and wider civil society. As I will show, the communitarian approach represents the revival of a traditional perspective, but in a new context – the evident failures of the state (and perhaps the market) and the emergence of new social movements, notably feminism. For some communitarians, these developments march with a decline in standards of morality and civility. The approach this time is sociological, the range of evidence I shall call up will be wider, at least in the geographical sense. Among the questions to resolve will be the significance of the concept of social capital, as a resource that can perhaps be drawn upon to address re-emerging problems and revitalise volunteering as an activity.

Chapter 4 explores questions arising from the longstanding debate about the respective merits of civic virtue as demonstrated in the political sphere – the main claim made by republicanism – and the looser liberal concept of association. What should the role of the citizen body be and how is it best expressed? Does individual action suffice or is there a collective interest that can only be expressed collectively? If so, must it be through active participation in the political process or can it flow through other channels and networks?

Alexis de Tocqueville's account of American democracy presents free association on the basis of equality of status and mutual respect as the means of developing democratic customs (*moeurs*) and practice. In the late twentieth century, despite its survival in the face of the challenge of the dictatorships there has been increasing anxiety about the vitality of western democracy. There is concern about the defection of the elites (to 'gated communities') and the disillusionment of the masses – participation in elections and political action generally diminishing and hence the dissipation of social capital. Does this stem from the weakening of associational life, the reluctance to engage in voluntary activity? Have there been changes in the campaigning role of third-sector organisations – witness the critique of 'mere dues paying' bodies. Latterly, there have been other concerns about the increasingly dominant role of the market, and the media, especially television and (for outsiders) the cultural hegemony of the Anglo-Saxons. The approach here is broadly through political science and much of the evidence comes from the United States, posing issues about distinctive American circumstances (for example, the role of religion) but also some general ones, like the potential for sustaining active citizenship.

In Chapter 5, the relevance of the concept of civil society will be explored in a different context. It is often argued that the previous existence of the institutions of a free society – the rule of law, democracy, a free press and the market – is an indispensable condition for the existence of a viable civil society. In Hungary, the location of this chapter's case study, none of these preconditions applied before 1989.

The first issue to explore is therefore whether a civil society in any meaningful sense existed before the sudden transformation. What remained possible, in the dissident communities that formed in all the countries of East and Central Europe, was to 'live in truth' in the private sphere: a value best expressed for some of its advocates as an attempt to create a civil society. Did this provide a genuine alternative, overcoming the chosen isolation of individuals who would not accept the regime's values or participate in its structures?

Events after the transition throw up important questions about the continuing viability of civil society conceived in that form and the experience of those who tried to carry the values of dissidence through into a new environment. This leads to another crucial issue: what has the rapid transformation achieved in terms of creating and sustaining a democratic polity and a free market economy and what implications does the interaction between the two have for the future viability of both and the health of civil society?

If democracy is indeed securely implanted what of the role of the state and attitudes towards it? And have voluntary organisations made good use of opportunities with which they have been presented in service provision? Trust is a central issue here: does the shadow of past experience still diminish it? Has this enhanced or inhibited the role of the third sector in its oppositional capacity? A fundamental question here is about liberty – how can it be secured and best maintained.

In Chapter 6 the debate is further extended to a broader set of issues by opening up the question of civil society in a global context in which the market is increasingly a dominant factor. The discussion here involves exploring the role of voluntary organisations, here styled NGOs, as players: both in their opposition to established authority and as alternative sources of provision of aid in goods and services to the South. This is a controversial area: values and approaches imported there and into 'transition' countries have caused increasing resentment, especially where the interventions of western NGOs cannot be shown to be especially effective. How can these issues best be addressed? The approach from some state funding agencies has been to look for indigenous civil society organisations and promote alternative low-cost approaches.

In Chapter 7, this discussion will be developed in the context of globalisation – the development of the global market and activities of international finance capital. This reflects the new circumstances at the end of the century, with the Liberal paradigm in full possession of the field, in its newly triumphalist mode. The architecture of the public institutions that operate at the global level in the context of the new, post-cold war, world order will be described: of particular relevance is the growing interest of international agencies like the IMF and the World Bank in civil society, which has sometimes been seen as the potential guarantor of credit worthiness of any given society. A central question to resolve here is whether there is such a thing as 'global civil society' and if so how can it act effectively to challenge some of these developments?

Next, in Chapter 8, I explore the possibility of using the concept of Utopia as a tool to review various different shapes that civil society might take, providing a description of alternative forms and the obstacles that might be encountered on the way. The views of critics and advocates of Utopian approaches will be examined, both those of the optimists who believe in the perfectibility of humanity and pessimists convinced of the inevitability of original sin. Most of these Utopias are fictional; but I will also explore some actual Utopian experiments in the United States – different models of cooperation, communitarianism and indeed communism. Other routes to Utopia have been identified: science and technology producing abundance – communitarian critics of that approach prefer to call these dystopias. More modestly, there are models of rationality and planning to consider and the perennial problem of how the platonic guardians of these processes are to be selected, perhaps as a meritocracy? There are also some alternative images of a shrunken state: anarchic utopias and the market version – Utopia, Ltd. These, too have their critics as well as advocates. A final issue here: is civil society itself a Utopian project?

In the final chapter, having travelled a long distance through time and space, I conclude by offering a set of final reflections on the different forms that voluntary activity now takes and the contribution that civil society in its various forms has made and could make in future. This will involve reassessing the value of philanthropy and exploring some possibilities for the future, in the light of the social, economic and technical developments that have taken place over the past century.

CHAPTER 2

Civil Society, Charity and Welfare

Charity is the most mischievous sort of pruriency ... Those who minister to poverty and disease are accomplices in the two worst of all crimes. (George Bernard Shaw, *The Revolutionist's Handbook*)

Introduction

In this chapter, I will begin the exploration of the different activities that occur within the civil society space and along its borders with an examination of the connections between charity and welfare. The litmus test of charity in action is poverty: the fundamental practical and moral problem in both medieval and early modern societies and one to which all the great world religions enjoin both individual and collective response. That is the lens that I propose to employ in scrutinising charity in action.

I define *charity* as I did in the opening chapter, distinguishing *philanthropy*, the main focus of this chapter, from *mutual aid*. In addition, I shall use the term *voluntarism* to describe the form of philanthropic action taken from choice, in a situation which the participant has not been coerced into acting. Strictly speaking, this is anachronistic, since the term cannot be traced further back than the beginning of the twentieth century (though there are earlier appearances as *voluntaryism*). This is to distinguish such action from that taken by the state through legislation or in the market, in pursuit of profit. Finally, I shall refer to forms of collective action in pursuit of mutual aid and assistance as *association* – ventures taken for common advantage. I will be examining these in greater detail in Chapter 3, but I need to refer to them here, since they form a vital constituent part of the history of charity in England.

I have chosen England as the location for this exercise because, apart from the obvious pragmatic reason that it is the country that I know best, there are a number of distinctive features that make it particularly apt. First, England (in the strict sense) has a history of three hundred years of stability within existing national boundaries. It was also the first industrial nation and experienced the resulting economic and social upheavals before any of its subsequent rivals. Once the main religious conflicts had been resolved, the English nation was until the mid-twentieth century culturally homogeneous, in the literal sense of having no linguistic minorities or significant ethnic differences. That has now changed. But despite these changes English society is still characterised by a deeply-rooted system of class differentiation, constructed in fine gradations and by entrenched attitudes about the status of women. If, as is often suggested, the English have a cultural predisposition to voluntarism which impels them to start voluntary organisations to address every imaginable need or cause, this impulse has at all stages been strongly marked by both class and gender differences.

These distinctive characteristics are helpful in attempting to address the main theme of this chapter: the functions charity performs, how its role has changed over time, how it acquired sufficient flexibility to adapt to new circumstances and where and why any significant continuities have persisted.

Why should we need history to understand charity? Because the way in which structures, attitudes and relationships have developed can only be understood in the context of the situations in which they have evolved, over time. There is also an issue about where any review of the relationship between charity and welfare should begin – exactly how much history we need. Until recently, it would probably not have been thought necessary to start earlier than the nineteenth century, perhaps with the New Poor Law of 1834. The standard histories of welfare carried with them the unspoken assumption of a smooth progression from charity and philanthropy to state provision, reaching its perfect form in the mid-twentieth-century welfare state. This is a kind of history whose driving force is what is sometimes called the welfare state escalator, a smooth upward progression through successive periods divided into 'before the welfare state', the 'coming of the welfare state' and its seamless completion. That was always a misleading approach. As an aspiration, it was highly contestable; and as a description, it is now wholly untenable. The state did not

arrive on the scene from nowhere: nor did voluntarism subsequently desert it. Both the market and the informal world of family
and neighbourhood have had crucial roles to play throughout.
Activities have spilt over from the civil society space in different
directions, into the 'borderlands', involving collaborations (and
conflicts) with agencies and individuals based in those other
spheres occupied by the state and market.

The history of these collaborations and conflicts and their outcomes have left a deep mark on the various forms that charity has
taken. They have helped to determine the potentiality for adaptation
and change and define those factors that have remained constant
and also to shape attitudes towards charity in action. What is important, I shall argue, is not so much the location of these activities –
where they take place, in 'sectoral' terms – but their content:
what's actually done, how and on what terms.

Charity under the four Georges

The starting point I have chosen for my narrative is the revolution
of 1689: 'glorious' to its partisans to the point of being attributed
to divine intervention but, seen in retrospect, an event owing quite
as much to worldly calculations. The eventual accession in 1714 of
the Hanoverian monarchs confirmed the Anglican religious settlement, confined the power of the Crown and entrenched the rule of
law and the Whig aristocracy. The revolution ushered in the political establishment of the 'Protestant Nation' over a period during
which England absorbed Scotland and survived two Jacobite ris-
ings and a series of conflicts with other competing European powers. Domestically, social and economic changes were stimulated by
new technologies – promoting the processes of industrialisation,
developed through its attendant institutions, banks, joint stock
companies and the emergence of an entrepreneurial middle class.

Essentially, the institutions of early eighteenth-century charity
were still those first set in place after the sixteenth-century
Reformation. The structures established then and the functions
they performed were based on locality; and inherited from the
medieval parish system. These were secularised at the end of
Elizabeth's reign: the Statute of Charitable Uses of 1601 'set the
course for the evolution of philanthropy as a voluntary partnership
between the citizen and the state to fund and achieve social objectives' (Bromley and Bromley 2000: 16). The poor law structures

also set in place by Elizabethan legislation contained a strong dose of state intervention in the form of parish overseers and the system rested on tax based funding (the poor rate). Poverty being accepted as a natural accompaniment of rural life, assisting the poor was not always a matter of financial support. Studies of parish relief show a varied pattern of assistance (Daunton 1996); but essentially problems were addressed and usually resolved locally. A broadly similar pattern existed in most towns, based on established charities funded by donations and managed by municipal corporations. During the course of the eighteenth century, however, that pattern changed.

Hogarth's profile

The key invention of this period is the charitable association. This form of enterprise was based partly on the model of the joint stock company, evolved to secure the capital for new commercial undertakings. It provided a vehicle through which the philanthropic impulse could express itself, in the spirit of the age. This 'associative philanthropy' was located in the public domain, supported by subscription, and its advocates frequently lobbied for legal changes. It also developed strong links with religious dissent, which helped to provide the organisational model and much of the intellectual driving force.

One distinctive outcome of this activity was the creation of new charitable organisations. The characteristic institution of medieval charity had been the hospital (in the broadest sense of that term) established to provide residential care for the sick and elderly. The impetus to set up new foundations had ceased at the Reformation but was now revived in the eighteenth century. A striking example was the Foundling Hospital created by Thomas Coram. The genesis of William Hogarth's remarkable portrait of Coram is analysed in Jenny Uglow's biography as an example of innovation by both artist and sitter. As she puts it, 'Coram had adapted mechanisms of law, of aristocratic ends, of company organisation to new charitable ends: in painting him Hogarth too adapted conventions and filled them with new substance' (1997: 333). Coram's creation of the Hospital was made possible by enlisting support through the existing social system (though, interestingly, not the established church); but perhaps surprisingly, the regime there was strictly practical, and free of the moralistic overtones of later philanthropy.

A key characteristic of enlightenment philanthropy was optimism about the process of reform and the capacity of individuals for self-improvement. A variety of means and agencies were designated to release this and achieve a rational solution to social problems. Early political economists provided justification for belief in human progress and an explanation of how the charitable impulse and the pursuit of profit could be reconciled (compare Adam Smith's *Theory of Moral Sentiments*). Viewed in European terms, Joanna Innes sees this as the moment when an active civil society first comes into being, as: 'the flowering, against the background of varying and fluctuating degrees of government tolerance and approval of what contemporaries termed "the associative spirit" (1998: 19). 'The English state', Innes adds 'was precocious in the ability it displayed to summon into being reasonably efficient systems of public provision' (23–4). In essence, this was what in a later period came to be called a 'mixed economy of welfare', distinguished from its European neighbours by the comparatively modest part played by the church and the more active role of the state. But this pattern of division of labour was less significant than the term 'mixed economy' might imply to a twenty-first-century reader, to whom statism and voluntarism are necessarily distinct concepts.

As Cunningham and Innes put it,

> The terms 'charity' and 'philanthropy', like the modern term 'welfare' designated broad areas of concern, rather than particular modes of addressing those concerns. The polarity of charity and philanthropy on the one hand and state action on the other was unknown for the former could include the latter'. (1998: 2)

The same was true of the relation between charity and business; John Lansley quotes the founding charter of the Philanthropic Society (1788), which sought 'to unite the spirit of society with the principles of trade, and to erect a temple to philanthropy on the foundations of virtuous industry' (cited in Lansley 2000).

Philanthropic action could also serve a wider political function; in an important sense charity was 'patriotic' (as Thomas Coram had emphasised in appealing for support for his enterprise). But the Georgian welfare settlement was not stable. A number of factors conspired to undermine it: urbanisation, which put a system linked with locality under great stress, especially in larger cities; and demographic growth, which did same for rural areas as well. By the 1770s, as Michael Roberts puts it: 'it was clear that the era of "manageable" population growth and "bearable" poor-rate burdens was at an end' (in Cunningham and Innes 1998: 69). Discontent provoked the nascent urban working class to political association, perceived as subversive and addressed as such in repressive legislation. Charity could provide a resource for authority: 'both at civic and national level' say Cunningham and Innes 'charity lent or was meant to lend legitimacy to what were, in a revolutionary age, often fragile structures of power' (1998: 10). Religion also helped to promote a form of stability. The religious revival at all levels of society, which begins with Methodism in the late eighteenth century, eventually helped to facilitate the process of constructing a new welfare settlement.

The Georgian legacy could be summarised (quasi-telegraphically) as being:

- General acceptance of need to address poverty by a variety of means and through cooperation between state and charitable and philanthropic action.
- The devising of forms which would serve the functions of stabilisation and solidarity in society (de Swaan 1988) – the development of 'associative charity' on commercial models.
- State formation having reached the point at which effective social policies could be developed and implemented, though still principally at local level.
- A social philosophy, not of conventional religious origins, capable of reconciling accumulation of wealth with virtue expressed through charitable action, alongside.
- Economic success of members of dissenting sects, especially Quakers, excluded from direct involvement in the political arena and the learned professions. This eventually leads to direct provision for the welfare of employees by charitable employers.
- The beginning of a distinctive role for women in philanthropic enterprises.

Victorian philanthropy

In discussing the Victorian legacy, it is difficult to escape the imprint of previous interpretations: those in which the 'welfare state escalator' first starts to move (jerkily) upward; or the converse: those who see a golden age of voluntarism eventually perverted by state interference. Neither seems to me to capture the essence of this complex period and the mindset of those whose motives and actions we too easily dismiss with the label, 'Victorian values'.

The first crucial event actually falls slightly before the Victorian period, strictly defined – the passage of the New Poor Law (1834). This was driven partly by economic change and the resulting growth in rural pauperism that had undermined the parochial charitable system and also by political concerns: fear of the sturdy beggar in the cap of liberty and the implications of the beginnings of working-class organisation.

There was also discontent with the morality and efficiency of the existing poor law, under the impact of the rapid growth of population and the expansion of industry. The system of waged employment this had created required labour to be both disciplined and mobile in response to market demand. The new political economists like David Ricardo stressed individual responsibility and the importance of the 'spur of poverty' in motivating workers. The Checklands comment:

> in individualist thinking, the provision of poor relief for the able-bodied would have the further effect of placing a premium upon idleness and thus promote a deterioration of standards and of personality which would spread until a large part of the labour force was debauched. Malthus and Ricardo shared this view and propagated it. (1973: 22)

In this view, relief of poverty by outdoor relief in the form of financial doles (as practised by overseers in rural parishes) ran the risk of undermining the motivation of workers. The remedy was to make relief contingent upon admission to the workhouse where 'less eligible' circumstances would act as an effective deterrent. A new administrative apparatus of poor law guardians was created locally and a Commission set up in London to run it.

This attempt to impose a new system from the centre was in the event a failure: possibly in its own terms a heroic one. Despite titanic efforts, the Commissioners were unable to impose their will universally. The reaction in many localities was to temper and adapt the system to meet local circumstances and the downswings of the trade cycle; neither those who were operating the system locally nor those towards whom it was directed were ever fully reconciled to the system. But it left a highly visible legacy in the form of the new workhouses: the Bastille, hated symbol of centralised authority.

A more humane alternative was the facilitating of self-help. This prescription makes an early appearance in the experiments of the Scottish divine Thomas Chalmers, whose experimental system in central Glasgow disconnected the poor altogether from the poor law system, in favour of promoting mutual aid in the working class and active voluntary participation by the middle class, acting through the church to administer parochial aid (Checklands 1973: 28).

In this view of poverty, the remedy lay largely in the hands of the poor themselves. Powerful reinforcement for this approach was provided by the radical journalist and polemicist Samuel Smiles, whose book *Self Help*, often cited but seldom read, is periodically put back into print in support of an individualist agenda. In fact, *Self Help* is by no means pure individualism (Smiles was a former sympathiser with the Chartists). Working-class self-help, he asserted, could be collective as well as individual. But in essence the message conveyed through brief exemplary biographies, in his immensely popular book, was that character, formed by thrift and duty (also titles of subsequent books by Smiles) could open up opportunities to the energetic and enterprising individual from all ranks of society.

Mutual aid could and did take different forms. From the beginning of the century, formal structures for collaboration were being established by the working class themselves. This first took the form of friendly societies, devices for sharing risk and providing some form of insurance against (truly Dickensian) hard times. The earliest of these fell foul of authority's paranoia about secret societies – they were normally oath bound, like the Freemasons and there was an element of deliberate mystification in terms and titles used – and the hostility of the political economists, by whom they were seen as restraint of trade. This explains the continued illegality of the other child of those times, the trades unions. By mid-century, a variety of other working-class organisations had put in an appearance and were providing a supporting structure under direct control of the workers themselves which gave the skilled worker and his family some measure of practical assistance and a means of saving, to provide security against the contingencies of life and death (including sickness, old age and burial). These developed beyond their local bases by affiliation and evolved democratic structures modelled in part on nonconformist organisational forms.

Religion and scientific charity

Religion also supplied the other main motive force in shaping mid-Victorian charity through the evangelical revival. In this form,

7-4212

religious belief represented the ultimate individualism, salvation secured only through personal covenant with the Almighty. The one and only religious census of 1851 had revealed an astonishing degree of ignorance of religion in the new urban working class. The churches, of all denominations, set out to remedy this. Through their missions, located in all major cities, they aimed to provide instruction in Christianity and moral support for those struggling to come to terms with the chronic instability of a Victorian labourer's life.

Prominent among those who participated actively in the missions to their less fortunate fellow beings were middle-class women (Prochaska 1980). Both at the time and subsequently there have been uncharitable comments about the mixture of motivations involved in the tasks they performed and the ways in which they performed them. Women, themselves not fully emancipated, were able to offer only limited material assistance but could provide advice, befriending, and access to the comforts of organised religion. The lady visitor, brutally caricatured by Charles Dickens, became one of the stock images of Victorian philanthropy, with infinite patronage implied in that role.

Behind the lady visitor lay organised charities, some descended from the associative charities of the eighteenth century, others newly established to deal with an increasing range of social issues identified as suitable cases for action. These in turn were supported by a vast engine of fund raising involving a whole range of increasingly sophisticated marketing devices – collecting, canvassing, bazaars, charity shops, flag days – that eventually produced a situation in which English charities had an independent income from charitable donations greater than the gross domestic product of a number of substantial European countries (Prochaska, 1988).

For political economists, this rapid growth in charitable support for the poor, sick, orphans and widows posed problems. What in the mid-Victorian vocabulary was categorised as 'eleemosynary' (that is, alms-giving) action ran the risk of undermining independence and encouraging that most dreaded of all possible consequences, charity mongering – systematic abuse of the goodwill of the charitable by the idle poor. Like their lineal descendants the welfare scroungers, the charity mongers existed as much in the imagination of the public and press as in reality, but had a powerful influence in shaping the response of the middle classes. This concern

also reinforced the developing tendency towards institutional remedies for the social problems identified as worthy topics for action.

The chosen means of addressing this issue was to be 'scientific'
charity and the instrument for delivering it, charity organisation.
The Charity Organisation Society (usually 'COS': strictly, the
Society for Organising Charitable Relief and Suppression of
Mendicity) dates from mid-century (1869) and marks of the emergence of a more developed system. The science was still supplied
by classical political economy; but by now this was being supplemented by early sociology, which began very early to focus on the
identification of poverty and soon started to offer alternative
explanations of its causes and different proposals for remedying it.

Another such indicator of change was the Royal Commission
on Friendly Societies (1874) which offered symbolic state recognition for key working-class institutions – some of the witnesses
appearing before it would have gone further still and added state
financial support. The approaches were in some senses comple-
mentary: re-moralisation of the working class through visiting, voluntary support managed through a scientifically devised system
with a strong emphasis on fostering individual self-improvement
and the encouragement of mutual support in those enterprises
that were organised and run in a manner that encouraged thrift and
sobriety – though this was not necessarily the original intention of
those that founded them.

As for the state, George Goschen's minute of 1870, issued by the
central Poor Law Board, attempted to lay down a basis for cooperation between state and voluntarism in addressing what he saw as
a rise in pauperism. This involved a division of labour between
them, with the hard cases allocated to the state and its institutions
as the providers of last resort and the deserving poor at risk of
falling into destitution allocated to philanthropy. Like the creation
of the Charity Commission in 1853, the Goschen minute was one
reflection of the mid-Victorian administrative style – the impulse
towards tidying up its inherited legacy of diversity of provision
and variety of sources of support. Both were designed to ensure
that a clear division was made between the public and the private:
the state's role now clearly one of regulation and inspection but
narrowing provision down to strict application of new poor law
principles to those remaining cases that could not be catered for
by private and voluntary effort, in the form of institutional care.
Or so the theory went.

The woman who opens the door

The charitable encounter in mid-Victorian England characteristically involved women. Women on the doorstep, with their cargo of tracts or small offerings of food or children's clothes (often knitted in the all-women 'Dorcas circle' set up in emulation of scriptural accounts of clothing the poor) and women in the building, answering the knock because the man couldn't or wouldn't respond to it. The process that the knock initiated often developed into a relationship. But the form this took was not necessarily a one-sided transaction with an active giver and passive recipient (in which it was more blessed to give than receive?) but more as a species of negotiation, even a performance.

By the mid-century, the wife and mother would be likelier to be found at home: the family in which all the members were wage earners, including the children (even if wages were often pitifully small) was being replaced by one in which only the man was likely to be in regular employment. Mothers were taking over responsibility for the domestic economy and the task of conjuring up sufficient resources from a variety of sources to supplement whatever the man was able to earn; and if he left the household, through death or desertion, to cope with the consequences.

Even a short stroll through a municipal cemetery in an English industrial city will show how frequently nineteenth-century families were disrupted by death. It is not only the deaths of children, so painful to twenty-first-century sensibility, that the gravestones commemorate, but numerous adults in what would now be regarded as the prime of life. When the death was that of a man, the consequences for his surviving family were potentially disastrous. But women, even as widows, were not without the capacity to confront these problems. They could manoeuvre to maximise the amount of money that could be raised from a whole range of possible sources, Charitable donation was one obvious resort, supplemented where absolutely necessary by resort to institutional care for individual members of the family (a sick child, an elderly mother).

However, women's rights were still very restricted, and the presumption of their dependent status narrowed the space in which they had to operate still further. So risk management conducted on an individual basis was always going to be a tricky business; but charity provided one route through which problems could be at least temporarily contained. Success required dexterity in juggling possibilities and plausibility in the approaches made (hence the inherent theatricality of some exchanges, with both parties playing to a script and performing in pre-cast characters). Truculence could have disastrous consequences. But as for shame, the stigma that the recipient of charity was supposed to sense and the resulting deterrence that was intended to discourage return, recent scholarship has tended to confirm Rudolf Klein's dismissal of the whole notion as the equivalent of the natural scientists' mythical substance, phlogiston (Mandler 1990).

Risk could also be diminished by collective action. This is where the gathering strength of the organisations of mutual aid was of increasing importance as they extended their coverage downwards from the skilled working class. The range of activity widens with the arrival of the permanent building society; and the legal status of trades unions was now put beyond doubt. The cooperative movement was by now well launched on the journey that had begun in Rochdale to become the vast edifice that so impressed the young Beatrice Webb when she set out on her first social investigation.

Octavia Hill and social control

This expansion of organisations designed by the working class ran in parallel with those designed for it, most notably in the housing field – the model dwellings and buildings initiated by Prince Albert at the Great Exhibition of 1851. Sanitary reform designed to prevent epidemic disease was one of the main planks of Victorian social action: it is not essential to see cynicism in this aspect of reform but very possible to see patronage – what the historian David Roberts prefers to call 'paternalism'. Debates about housing and the appalling conditions which the urban working class were forced to endure dwelt not just on disease but morality and the remedies were held to be as much about reinforcing character as about teaching the arts of domestic management (or helping tenants to afford to pay the rent).

Octavia Hill, now the darling of the late twentieth-century neoliberals, was very strong on morality and also on profitability. Here we have, in the 'five per cent philanthropy' of the purpose-built model dwellings whose management she helped to pioneer, the paradigm case of the market, in the form of profit-seeking investment, being brought to bear on the problems of the poor. Octavia Hill was clear in her assertion that it was the tenants, rather than the buildings that most needed improvement: that in the disagreeable image then current, the pig made the pigsty, not the pigsty the pig. [This, by the way, is a gross libel on pigs.] The notion that the working classes might want to have their say in the ways in which they would prefer to live their lives also seems remote from her world, though this may simply be failure of understanding. Late-Victorians often used metaphors from tropical exploration to describe their encounters with their fellow Londoners (as in the title of William Booth's *In Darkest England*) and many of their descriptions have the wide-eyed quality of the man in the solar topee first encountering the tribal elders.

All these initiatives can be made to fit a theory of social control, in which the self-interest of the middle class backed by the authority of the state and the churches and aided by the passivity of the skilled working class (the 'labour aristocracy') combine to deflect and frustrate the authentic ambitions of the working class for radical change without satisfying their real needs. George Bernard Shaw's brilliant satire in his play *Major Barbara* showed how even in its most radical form (the Salvation Army) the religious impulse was also open to cooption of this kind.

In this interpretation, the 'chocolate charity' of philanthropic employers like the Frys, the Rowntrees and Cadburys becomes another means of manipulating the workforce into increasing the owners' opportunities for profit. But it is impossible to deny the sincerity of the religious impulse that motivated many philanthropists, especially women – or the self-sacrifice of some reformers, tiresome though they could often appear to those that did not share their obsessions, like the Earl of Shaftesbury, the bull in the china shop of early Victorian philanthropy.

The participation of the provincial middle class in charitable work had its special flavour; Belcham and Hardy comment of Liverpool that:

> Philanthropy was an important credential for a member of the plutocracy, while indiscriminate charity, including cash handouts by individuals, on the street or at the house, was frowned upon. This latter – the 'national error of Englishmen' – was mischievous and ostentatious. Ahead of London urban gentry, Liverpool's gentlemanly capitalists appreciated the need for 'scientific charity': (in Kidd and Nicholls 1998: 62)

These were the attitudes that helped to sustain the funding of charity at an unprecedented level and produced the tangible memorials to Victorian philanthropy in the institutional buildings that still stand in many large towns, inscribed with the customary proud assertion: 'supported entirely by voluntary contribution'. (These days the survivors have become 'themed' restaurants, night clubs or flybynight commercial storage units). This was what Geoffrey Finlayson has termed a 'citizenship of contribution' (1994: 101).

The challenge of collectivism: a 'scramble for socialism'?

The economic difficulties of the 1880s once again destabilised what had appeared to be a situation in balance. It produced a marked advance in working-class political activity and the appearance of what came to be a regular series of calls for the state to play a more active role in confronting poverty. The Congregationalist minister Andrew Mearns' widely publicised *Bitter Cry of Outcast London* (1883) was a case in point. His claims that the machinery of relief had completely broken down may have been exaggerated: but the full extent of urban poverty in the metropolis was soon to be firmly established by the investigations of Charles Booth, shortly to be followed by similar investigations in other cities (most famously, Seebohm Rowntree in York). Social science was about to make its most important contribution to public debate and to provide Sidney and Beatrice Webb with the basis for their life's work.

The question was not so much whether to act, but what to do and above all who should take responsibility for doing it – pushing out the boundaries of collective responsibility. The notion that some responsibility must ultimately rest on the state emerged from a surprisingly wide range of sources, from the more obvious quarters, the infant Fabian Society (whose first pamphlet was *Why are the many poor?*) and the Labour movement's first generation of political leaders, through to the pioneers of the University settlements now appearing in poorer districts of London and large provincial cities. It extended to those Fellows at Oxford colleges now hard at work educating and forming the attitudes of the next generation of young reformers by offering them an alternative and positive concept of state action to meet common interests.

This kind of approach did not imply an appetite for a wholesale taking over of responsibility by the state: that would have been to succumb to the kind of Prussian centralising that ran against the grain of all previous approaches. But the perceptible shift in attitudes was picked up and lamented by what were becoming old-fashioned liberals like the social philosopher Herbert Spencer in his polemic *Man versus the State* and the constitutional lawyer A. V. Dicey.

There was also a marked tendency to frame the desire for intervention in the form of an invocation of the desirability of socialism. The Warden of Toynbee Hall, the best-known of the University settlements, Samuel Barnett and his formidable wife Henrietta entitled their manifesto *Practicable Socialism* (1894). The Liberal politician Sir William Harcourt's 'we are all socialists now' may have been almost literally exact if 'all' is taken to cover social reformers as a body. Stephen Yeo rather cynically describes this process as a 'scramble for socialism,' on the lines of the contemporaneous scramble for Africa.

A prototype of the confused state of values and profusion of proposed remedies was B. Kirkman Gray, whose posthumous *Philanthropy and the State* (1908) is briskly (and misleadingly) despatched as mere polemic by Robert Whelan in his polemical *The Corruption of Charity* (1996). Gray did not dismiss philanthropy as such: rather the opposite. His admittedly sometimes fragmentary argument (he died before completing the text) represented an attempt to identify various roles into which philanthropic action might fit and by which its relationships with the state could be shaped. He comments that the state has developed a repertoire of different forms of action which he categorises as: 'Annexation, Cooperation, Supervision, Coordination and Delegation', in all of which the state has 'taken cognisance' of philanthropy (1908: 220). The role which philanthropy should now perform would be best expressed at the level of the city and better executed through the municipality, 'a new and capable instrument of socio-political action' (71). The direction of reform – the content of the new 'social politics' – will be determined by the findings of social science reinforced by information gathered by the state in its inspectoral role. He concludes, in a striking pre-echo of William Beveridge:

> There is no fact of human life without social implications. Wherever knowledge penetrates intervention comes. Philanthropy has striven to deal with the misfortunes of individuals and is pressed on by the force of its own unconscious principle until the State itself shall become what J. S. Mill spoke of as a 'National Benefit Society'. (Gray 1908: 40)

Standing apart from this move towards collectivism were the COS on one side of the debate and a large part of the working-class mutual aid movement on the other. Both mistrusted the state, both for its intentions and the likely consequences of its interventions, though they framed their objections in very different terms. The COS principally feared what they saw as the likely corruption of character but what they meant by independence was not what friendly society and Cooperative leadership had in mind. One was concerned with the individual, the other the collective interest, sharpened in the latter case by suspicion of the motives of middle-class socialists urging the necessity of empowering the state to take over responsibilities which the workers were succeeding in addressing on their own account. (Finlayson 1994, Yeo 1979). The half-way house of 'Cooperation without Annexation' (to use Kirkman Gray's terminology) was represented by the Guilds of Help that emerged in several industrial cities during this period, operating under local control without the moralistic agenda of the COS (Leybourne 1997).

Conflicts and crosscurrents can be seen in full flood in several episodes around the turn of the century, most notably in the famous debates over the reform of the Poor Law as expressed in the Majority and Minority reports of the Royal Commission that considered this topic. But in some ways the contradictions emerge more clearly on a smaller scale, in cases like the debate about the introduction of state support for school meals. This was singled out by Dicey as one of the most damaging of the state's intrusions into the private and family sphere. In her subtle essay, 'Hungry Children: Housewives and London Charity 1870–1918' (in Mandler 1990), Ellen Ross shows how working-class housewives, their circumstances memorably captured for posterity in the sophisticated reportage of the Fabian Women's Group study *Round About a Pound a Week*, struggled to reshape the gifts of phil-anthropists into a form that they could use for their families' best advantage.

> Classes and interests came into contact and opposition over the meals, and it was the wives at the doorstep or in the committee room rather than the husband. For the student of charity as a social issue the school meals provide a striking case study in the gift relationship. (175)

The COS as an organisation always opposed free feeding from any source, as liable to 'weaken parental responsibility and

discourage effort'. But faced with self-evident need of many
children, individual COS members could not refrain from helping
to provide them. For the Left, school meals were a foot in the door,
opening to leading to the acceptance of universal provision without stigma, as entitlement . In practice, the grudging acceptance of
the principle of free meals was hedged around with investigations
and tests. And then there was the issue of the quality of the meals
provided (some things don't change). But all the power did not lie
on one side: as Ross comments, the charity workers, excited by the
'sacramental' quality of the gift they were providing, also had
needs, for children and young people to join the settlement clubs,
or adults to attend the church services which the poor found so
unattractive.

Sidney and Beatrice Webb breakfast with the
Chancellor of the Exchequer

The event which according to escalator theory is the one which
started the process of movement towards state based welfare in
earnest, was the then Chancellor David Lloyd George's national
insurance legislation of 1911. We are fortunate in having an inside
account of this process from one of the key participants, the
Treasury civil servant W. J. Braithwaite. His account described in
considerable detail how the traditional friendly societies were
enticed into the scheme which eventually produced a system of
health insurance to which the beneficiary contributed that
extended to five sixths of the country's inhabitants and imposed
new duties on employers, officials, doctors and the insured themselves.

Braithwaite himself had socialist sympathies and a friendly
society background and his intention was to see an insurance system constructed on mutual, local, autonomous, and self-governing
lines. He wanted membership arrangements to be a precondition
of societies' participation and scrutiny by democratically elected
local management committees. But he and the traditional societies
were outsmarted by the industrial insurance industry organised
around collection of subscriptions door to door, of which the prototype was the Prudential and their 'man from the Pru', a familiar
presence on the working-class doorstep. These larger commercial
organizations formed a cartel known as the 'Combine' to oppose
the legislation in its original form and recruited as allies the British

Medical Association, the medical profession being as usual not backward in coming forward to defend its own interests.

The outcome was a clear victory for the Combine, to the intense frustration and lasting bitterness of Braithwaite and those who thought like him. As the historian of the episode, Bentley Gilbert, summarises the implications:

> The measure had contemplated a simple extension of the fraternal Friendly Society principle to those elements of the population hitherto not covered. It became instead a form of national compulsory savings, administered awkwardly and expensively by private insurance firms. Most of them saw the programme only as an avenue for the extension of their private business. The result was to destroy the fraternal aspects of even the strongest friendly societies and to turn them into semi-official agencies whose only reason for existence was the administration of health insurance. (Gilbert 1966: 428)

But the distortion of the original objectives of the traditional, membership-based friendly societies was not the only ground of criticism. Those already formidable campaigners, Sidney and Beatrice Webb, were also grossly dissatisfied. During the passage of the Bill they had called on the Chancellor to give him the benefit of their views. Braithwaite, who described the whole event in his diary, comments that 'the breakfast was Homeric and deserves to be historic'. Let us oblige him. Braithwaite's record of events runs as follows:

> Chancellor duly tempted on, begins to unfold a little bit here and there. Before he can speak, Mr. and Mrs. Webb singly and in pairs leap down his throat 'That's absurd', 'that will never do', 'you should adopt our plan', 'sickness should be prevented, not cured'; 'friendly societies are quite incapable of dealing with the question', 'it's criminal to take poor people's money and use it to insure them; if you take it you should give it to the Public Health authority to prevent them being ill again'. [His note concludes] LG and Sidney Webb were such an utter contrast, Webb so precise, LG feeling his way, Webb knowing already all about everything. And then the outburst! (1957: 116)

What the Webbs knew, precisely, was the state provided the logical alternative and that the professional approach to the solution of social problems involved bringing the power of the state to bear and using the technical expertise of trained experts in the service, not the power of profit or the confraternities but of the citizen body as a whole. This argument, in its various forms, was the one that they had employed in their minority report on the Poor Law and was the one they would use in its various forms for the next twenty years, to be developed and eventually applied by their then disciple, the 'boy Beveridge'.

As for voluntarism, their analysis saw it as moving on from what they call the 'cowcatcher' principle of deterrence in which the destitute paupers are simply swept aside and the 'parallel bars' approach (their summary of the Goschen principle of division of labour between state and voluntarism) to what they called the 'extension ladder'. In this model, voluntarism supplements and extends the reach of the state. As they put it:

> We suggest that this 'extension ladder' theory of the relationship between state action and voluntary agencies and the organic connection which it establishes between the specialised municipal departments and the similarly specialised voluntary workers and philanthropic institutions affords, for the first time, a most promising avenue for that real organisation of charity which is so badly required.... Far from degrading the volunteer and the voluntary agency to be nothing but a servant and a subordinate to the public authority, this 'extension ladder' theory of their mutual relationship gives, in reality, to the voluntary agency the highest duty and the most important function. It is in serving that it will rule. The public authority must always be dealing, in the main, on normal and regular lines, with the ordinary and common case, or with the universal requirements. Its social danger is the apathy and dullness and rigidity of official machinery and routine. The volunteer workers in each specialised municipal department and the managing committees of the voluntary associations associated with it, are, of all people, the best qualified and the most competent to supply criticism and suggestiveness, to furnish new ideas and invent fresh administrative devices. (1911: 257–9)

This is precise, where Kirkman Gray was misty. But it had its critics even among those who were thinking along broadly similar lines, like the idealist philosopher J. H. Muirhead, who observed in his critique of the minority report that:

> The reformer himself should be the last to desire to restrict the free development of voluntary effort, seeing that it is just out of the knowledge and conviction that actual personal experience gives, that the driving power and the intelligent direction of reform must come. (1909)

For the meanwhile, the Webbs had to be content with the half-loaf of the Lloyd George and Churchill reforms. Together these made up what could be called a 'mixed polity of welfare', in which voluntarism played an active role alongside the state and private profit (acting as Jane Lewis (1995) puts it, as 'mediating organisations'). Why was this mix not stable? Something not entirely unlike this combination of voluntarism and implementation by private agencies based on the insurance principle, under the direction and supervision of the state provided the model for the delivery of welfare in other European countries for most of the twentieth century. The escalator did not have to move on in the way that it eventually did. Statism was not culturally preordained. By now, the principle of association had deep roots.

One answer would be that citizenship was only half evolved and that the pressure to extend its reach from a citizenship of contribution to one of entitlement (to use Geoffrey Finlayson's terms) was growing all the time. This was a claim that the 'New Liberals' of Edwardian England, in and on the fringes of political power, had come to recognise as irresistible, both in relation to the political citizenship of the suffrage (women's claim to which had still not been conceded) and the social citizenship of access to welfare. The question of how these were to be secured still remained unresolved: but the state was the obvious candidate to be the guarantor and perhaps provider, as well.

Charity after the war

One obvious reason why the Edwardian welfare settlement proved to be unstable was the impact of the Great War (to give it the contemporary title) which broke out in 1914. Charity was directly affected by the challenge of wartime conditions. Domestically, it created emergencies to respond to – family welfare with so many men absent from home first in the trenches, then killed. New charities like the British Legion were created, together with new causes for collecting charities and new objects for philanthropy (for example, the war wounded and orphans).

Perhaps even more significantly, in the longer term, voluntarism was directly affected by massive social changes brought about by the war, especially in the status and circumstances of women. Their contribution to the war effort, in replacing absent men at the factory and in the service sector, was symbolically rewarded by concession of the franchise. Equally important, women had assumed an active role in the professions, as the citadels of male exclusiveness – medicine, business, law, the academy – were all successively stormed and in government, locally and at Westminster. The exhortation to younger feminists to 'go in for government' found an ample response in the crop of able women MPs entering parliament in the 1920s. Talent that once flowed into voluntary effort had another channel to enter now, where policies could be directly addressed rather than merely indirectly influenced.

The post-war scene was strongly marked by a sense of 'never again' – witness the creation of the National Council of Social Service (NCSS), founded on the basis of a scrap of paper left by a young officer killed in the trenches. Voluntary service, in the shape of the Save the Children Fund, also promoted involvement in international activities designed to build bridges between former enemies – an activity which I will revisit in Chapter 7.

The war also brought about, indirectly, the destruction of the old party political system, after the fall of the Lloyd George coalition in 1922; and the rise of Labour, which formed its first government in 1924. Labour brought to government rather different attitudes towards welfare, as the working class had encountered it. Urban local government had already begun to pass under Labour control: from being the tool of the class enemy, the state had become an instrument capable of being employed. The definition of working relationships with charities at local level was becoming a key issue, as the Webbs had forecast. Clement Attlee, an East London Mayor at the beginning of his political career, set out crisply his view (1920) of the limits of voluntary action – of which he was, however, never an outright opponent:

> The true antidote to the harmful sort of charity is the better provision for all the needs of life and the prevention of the causes of poverty. Where actual poverty exists owing to low wages, sickness, unemployment or old age, it is impossible to condemn those who, though in an unfortunate manner, endeavour to relieve suffering, without more strongly condemning the indifference that does nothing at all. (55)

Another significant influence on the evolution of charity was reform of local government. The 1929 Local Government Act involved gathering in of powers and functions into the state sector: consolidation in the name of efficiency. However, as Stephen

Yeo suggests, the reform deprived the working class of possible alternative power bases in special purpose authorities – even the Poor Law Boards of Guardians, as effective action by the Labour guardians in the London Borough of Poplar protesting at levels of poor relief had shown. This gathering in of power accelerated the rise of professionalism in many of the state-run social services and intensified the pressure on charities as alternative providers.

A new philanthropy?

Voluntarism, though far from defunct, was now operating in a changing environment and looking for new roles. Some of the leading participants in the nineteenth-century expansion were under particular pressure. As already indicated, approved friendly societies were losing their mutual character in the new system. On the individualist wing, the COS still struggled to defend their purist position; but overall, voluntary action was being increasingly drawn into cooperation with the state along the lines the Webbs had sketched out, a development reflected in the increased proportion of funding of voluntary action coming from the government (Braithwaite 1957).

An obvious test case arose during the inter-war period. Economic depression brought poverty back to the centre of the picture, especially after 1931 when unemployment rose to three million. In such circumstances, what was the appropriate role for voluntarism? In a speech in 1932, the Prince of Wales described high unemployment as 'a national opportunity for voluntary social service': A major charitable foundation, the Pilgrim Trust, pursued the same theme; as a subsequent annual report rather insensitively put it, work with the unemployed presented 'an unparalleled opportunity' (Finlayson 1994: 241).

But there were hazards attached to over-close involvement in unemployment schemes. The trades unions had harboured suspicion of the intervention of volunteers ever since the role they had performed in maintaining public services during the general strike of 1926. The relationship, however indirect, with national government policies on employment and relief also posed the risk of contamination by association. The NCSS's schemes in South Wales came into conflict with the agendas pursued by very different organisations, like the Communist Party's 'disciplined' political approach to involving middle-class volunteers – essentially, as described by one of them, Jennifer Hart, in her autobiography, recruiting them into the party through the close personal attention of selected cadre.

No room at the Bauhaus?

A fundamental issue was whether charity, still in many respects firmly attached to its nineteenth-century roots, was compatible with the new Modernism: the post-war reaction against traditional ways of doing things. Central to this new approach was the gospel of planning: a systematic approach, based on the best available modern scientific evidence, tidied and streamlined to promote maximum progress. This 'bauhaus social policy' involved planning a rational allocation of resources, in an environment reconstructed to the highest architectural standards, employing the new technology which had made the tower block a feasible proposition. The Peckham Pioneer Health Centre in South London was a typical case in point – a purpose-built structure providing services that would not merely respond to medical emergencies but promote healthy living. Progressive local authorities were eager to buy into this agenda, notably the London County Council, which came under Labour control after 1934 and was led by Herbert Morrison, also an enthusiastic advocate of closer collaboration with voluntarism, if the terms were right for the local authority.

How could voluntarism relate to a changing public sphere of that sort? Only with difficulty, its critics suggested. T. S. Simey in his pioneering text, *Principles of Social Administration* (1937) argued strongly that voluntary organisations couldn't contribute to 'mass production services' because their resources were too limited and they remained over-reliant on volunteers – he also greatly disliked what he saw as the class bias of voluntary action. Successive reports by Political and Economic Planning, the independent research organisation and epitome of the planning movement, on social services and health indicted the voluntary organisations on a variety of grounds: untidiness, inability to plan, presenting impossible problems of coordination. If there was to be a 'New Philanthropy' (the title of an influential contemporary text by Elizabeth Macadam, 1934) there needed to be a formula for collaboration:

One approach was to use voluntarism as the terrain of experiment. Education was a potentially attractive area: the progressive agenda could be pursued experimentally in a limited number of privately funded schools and the benefits of the experience gained there passed on for use in the state sector. Another potential locus of experiment was mental health – using innovations in psychotherapy mainly developed by émigré psychiatrists: for example, Anna Freud and her innovative work with children.

But a new philanthropy must also be one that would use these 'modern' skills. As social work professionalised and moved away from its original association with charity and volunteering, so new techniques were adopted (or adapted) that would authenticate the professionalism of those that employed them. The social psychologists moved in on casework; but it was still the case, as Eileen Younghusband put it, that 'social workers, like cats, are traditionally feminine' (1947: 5).

Finlayson observes of this period that: 'if the frontiers of the state moved, those of voluntarism moved with it' (1994: 262). But the frontier may be the wrong image here – or if it is, increasingly large numbers of participants possessed a laissez-passer. The areas in which these innovations were taking place are better seen as border zones, across which those with professional skills could readily move; and ideas exchanged in a process of cross fertilisation that affected outcomes on both sides. The Webbs' extension ladder was not merely being pushed further out but extended in new directions.

Citizenship under threat

Without hyperbole, the emergency of 1940 – the imminent risk of invasion by German forces after the fall of France – can be described as the most extreme danger faced by Britain in three hundred years. The response was a conscription of national resources on an unparalleled scale: but patches of voluntarism survived and even *in extremis* the state still looked for partnerships.

The Women's Voluntary Service (WVS) had been set up by the Home Office in 1938 in order to provide a means of coordinating women's work in the anticipated national emergency: bombing of the civilian population was now seen as inevitable after the experience of the Spanish Civil War. The WVS was a hybrid organisation; the Director was appointed by the Home Secretary but the prime movers were women volunteers like the formidable Lady Reading. It was also an effective one, not just in the dramas of the Blitz but in the less dramatic but equally significant work involved in the evacuation of the civilian population from large cities. Most of those concerned in these activities were volunteers, a process extending throughout society down to the children.

Civil society survived in a militarised world but on that world's terms. In wartime society to 'volunteer' was customarily used in the drill corporal's sense, as a synonym for compulsion. Some took to it with gusto – Air Raid Wardens who patrolled their localities, keen to punish abuses of the blackout – some with resignation (ritual fire watching on office buildings during air raids). Nevertheless, wartime propaganda was punctuated with reminders that we were 'citizens at war' (Stephen Spender's title for his account of the auxiliary fire service). Persistent use was made of the term 'volunteers' – admittedly historically hallowed terminology in military circles – to distinguish professional soldiers and sailors from temporary members of the armed forces. But the experience of the ordinary citizen in wartime was full of reminders of the arbitrary powers taken by the state: rationing of goods and 'requisitioning' of private property, compulsory evacuation, severe restrictions on civil rights, the carrying of identity cards and above all conscription (after 1942, of both genders).

Cultural resistance to dictatorship was also a much publicised feature of the wartime scene. Artists contributed their services to the maintenance of morale; Myra Hess and her fellow musicians dispensed high culture in the National Gallery concerts. Yehudi Menuhin crossed the Atlantic in an American bomber to play Bach and Brahms for the BBC. Variety and music hall artists did their bit; there was ENSA for the troops (meaning 'every night something awful', said the cynics in uniform).

Does this ('the culture we're fighting to defend') provide an index of the continued health of civil society under extreme stress? But the dictatorships had their culture too. Furtwängler and the Berlin Philharmonic were recorded for posterity, in a famous image, defending German values by playing Beethoven's Ninth in the last winter of the Third Reich; Shostakovich's Leningrad Symphony commemorated a heroic defence, but one conducted on behalf of an equally tyrannical regime, of which the composer himself had been a victim.

Reconstruction and Beveridge

The social scientists were also mobilised in their own struggle; the planning of post-war reconstruction. The case they made for reform incorporated voluntarism (as in the Nuffield Social Reconstruction study) but as a resource to be factored in within the grand project of replanning the physical, social and institutional environment. Citizenship and its attendant rights became an increasingly important guiding concept, invoked to legitimise policies of all kinds. For example, social rights were now taken to include the right to work (in the Coalition Government White Paper on Unemployment): who could credibly guarantee that rights like these could be exercised?

The state eventually came out on top by virtue of having had 'a good war': previously neutral observers saw lessons in the technical efficiency of wartime planning of resources. In an image drawn from the era of air raids, the war period had been an opportunity – a 'planners' moon'. War also exposed the weaknesses of the existing system (neither health nor housing provision passed the audit of evacuation). The question was whether the lessons of wartime mobilisation of resources could be applied to peace, when the unresolved problems of the pre-war period would be waiting to be addressed.

Beveridge the 'reluctant collectivist' provided one set of answers. His 1942 report presented social insurance as an expression of common citizenship, a universe in which all would contribute equally and benefit modestly, 'as of right and without means test' and the state performed the tasks of collection and distribution, this being the most efficient means of doing so. The rest would be up to the individual: 'the state in organising security should not stifle incentive, opportunity, responsibility ... it should leave room and encouragement for voluntary action by each individual' (1942, para. 9).

But if the five giants that Beveridge portrayed as standing in the way of progress were to be slain, it wouldn't be by voluntary action. Want was now beyond the capacity of mutual aid. Other techniques could deliver an end to Idleness – the approach seen in his later Keynes-and-water unemployment report and Ignorance – a more efficient education system. Disease (a national failure especially singled out in the report) required national planning; Squalor could be left to municipal enterprise and workers' flats designed on good Bauhaus lines.

Richard Titmuss's subsequent account of social policy at war reckoned up charity's accounts, and gave them his approval, as having provided a useful supplement to state action. But it was already clear that the new world that would succeed the wartime emergency would be based on a citizenship of entitlement, not charity.

Rolling back frontiers?

The reform of welfare that began in the war years was completed by 1948. The new architecture of the system was mainly dominated by institutional structures funded and managed by the state. This situation was frequently presented as a 'crisis' of voluntary action, but in practice, the alarm expressed was not justified. Many of the larger charities continued undisturbed on their way and voluntarism was not 'crowded out' so much as moved on to new territory. It helped that the leadership of the Labour Government (Clem Attlee, Herbert Morrison) was generally friendly to voluntarism, if with an element of patronage in their approval. Subsequent analysis suggesting doctrinaire hostility is largely based on one speech given much later by Richard Crossman, who did not serve in that government.

The senior Minister whose actions had most drastic consequences for charities was Aneurin Bevan: one of the most significant changes was his nationalisation of the hospital sector, which removed one of the remaining areas of voluntary sector activity in mainstream provision. Bevan rationalised his dislike of voluntary provision by dismissing it as 'unplanned'; but he was not hostile to the voluntary sector's general record. Nevertheless, the National Health Service (NHS) was explicitly introduced to the public in explanatory leaflets as being 'not charity', with stress on universal access of right, with provision free at the point of delivery.

The message to the voluntary sector was that it should specialise, concentrate on the vanguard pioneering role and filling the gaps by experiments which could then be incorporated into state provision, once their success had been satisfactorily demonstrated. For example, the process of professionalising social work had by now been almost completed; but this was still seen as compatible with voluntarism in its pioneering role. One example was the work done with 'problem' families by the Family Service Units. Founded as the Pacifist Service Units in the Second World War, the units were located in deprived neighbourhoods and evolved a style of intensive casework with families as a complete entity, mixed with action research and a decentralised mode of organisation. They soon acquired a reputation for innovative techniques and local authorities made extensive use of their services, for which they provided financial support. Yet they remained outside the state sector by choice and continued to raise funds in order to do so (Philp 1963). The model of innovation being test flown outside the state and then structurally transferred into it did not apply here.

In 1948 Beveridge revisited the scene in his third report, *Voluntary Action*. His brief was from and for the friendly societies, who had fallen victims to the Labour reforms of social security, although Beveridge himself had supplied much of the ammunition for their supplanting. Beveridge sets out his ideal image of the division of labour between voluntary organisations and the state in what is essentially a Webb image – a partnership, with voluntary bodies as junior partner in the welfare firm but with a distinctive role in fields like the supply of impartial information and advice. A stress on the importance of continued independence underlies his approach to a modified form of philanthropic action: but his real commitment is to mutual aid. His final image of mankind as the universal friendly society recalls Kirkman Gray half a century earlier. The report received a polite but muted reception: the government used the opportunity to stress their continuing commitment to sustaining independent voluntary action.

So classic philanthropy continued and adapted to these changed circumstances; but after a period of consolidation under the Conservatives, a second wave of modernisation which began at the start of the 1960s presented new challenges.

Strategic planning and voluntarism

This phase in social and economic policy was based on a revival of the notion of strategic planning (which reached its apogee in George Brown's ill-fated National Plan) to be implemented by new public institutions. This meant among other things reform of local government by substituting larger and fewer units and a massive public housing programme. But it also meant new measures of a different kind to address the rediscovered question of poverty: first, the Urban Programme and then the Community Development Programme (CDP) and a 'bottom up' view of how action to address poverty should be mounted. That allowed substantial play for voluntary action in the role of innovator. Volunteers had once again come into favour (Aves 1969).

But after 1970 the rational planning approach hit the buffers. The manifest failures of economic management under successive administrations of both parties were matched by the evident inability of state housing and social services to cope with increased levels of need and by perennial crisis in the health service.

The grass roots rebelled: a new voluntary sector drawing lessons from the civil rights movement in the United States and from second wave feminism set out to challenge the state on its own turf, locally and nationally. This new voluntarism offered one set of alternatives: local authorities faced the challenge of community action (to which CDP contributed) in direct opposition to their policies and practices. Adopting market-based policies would provide the other.

Faced with these challenges, the National Council for Voluntary Organisations (NCVO, successor to NCSS) on behalf of the voluntary sector set out to define a new role for itself (Wolfenden 1978), conceived as coordination with, not annexation by the public sector (to use Kirkman Gray's categories) and underlining the importance of 'umbrella groups' within the sector as a device for obtaining maximum benefit from local voluntary activity.

In the following year, Francis Gladstone, analysing prospects for the future for the NCVO could cite a general assumption that the state had failed in welfare as the centrepiece for his argument for a new declaration of independence for voluntarism. And in a practical sense, the process of rolling back the frontiers of the state that began that year with the election of Margaret Thatcher's Conservative Government necessarily involved bringing back voluntarism in some form to fill the spaces that would open up as the state withdrew from providing (but not from funding) services. But which organisations? And on what terms?

Markets and morality

There developed a triangle of forces, balancing an increased role for voluntary bodies against tighter control of the additional funding offered to support that role and an enhanced role for the market and market-based devices. From Margaret Thatcher's speech to the WRVS (1981) onwards, the Conservative Government courted the voluntary sector but on its own agenda. As in the 1930s, this meant principally schemes that would assist the government's

Manpower Services Commission with the attempt to cope with problems around unemployment, also once again at three million. This time, too, the experience of voluntary organisations repeated that of the NCVO in the 1930s: suspicion of their involvement, shading into hostility, among the unions and the unemployed themselves and little concern on the part of government, when the impact of involvement in official schemes proved problematic for the organisations themselves and for volunteers and paid workers in them (Addy and Scott 1987).

From then on, the pressure was to find models for delivery of services through voluntary action in the market, not in among the grassroots. The route to greater responsiveness and efficiency in delivery was to be empowerment of individuals using services as consumers, not participants. The quality of these services was to be secured by customer pressure and extending the use of contracts as substitutes for grants. The Conservatives also pressed on with attempts at the revival of volunteering, the promotion of individual action in the form of 'active citizenship' and the conscription in order to do so of the 'little platoons' of the neighbourhood, to employ the image from Edmund Burke to which Conservative politicians had become obsessively addicted.

At the same time, greater emphasis was being placed on the role of the family and the 'remoralisation' of individual relations, as a third pole. This was the message that Margaret Thatcher took with her in her address to the Church of Scotland (the so-called 'Sermon on the Mound'), where it received a less than enthusiastic response. This was symptomatic of the resistance of the established churches to the government's agenda also expressed in the Church of England's critique in their report *Faith in the City*.

A succession of formal policy reviews began in 1990 with an Efficiency Scrutiny of central government's relations with voluntary organisations conducted by the Home Office and continued with another, *Voluntary Action* (Knight 1993) funded from the same source but reaching conclusions that were far from reflecting official dogma. Knight's praise for the authenticity of community groups as against the bureaucracy of larger organisations from which he wished to strip away the privileges associated with charitable status earned him instant condemnation from almost every quarter. This was not the fate of the third and perhaps more diplomatic effort, in a further inquiry set up by the NCVO. Their proposal for a formal compact between state and voluntary organisations opens a new stage in the relationship – and subsequently led to significant progress towards a new settlement, after the election in 1997 of a new Labour Government, already committed to change while in opposition.

The partial withdrawal of the state from certain activities was an important factor in promoting the 'unparalleled growth and change' that had taken place among voluntary bodies over the 1990s, captured in the series of studies undertaken by the team based at Johns Hopkins which we have already encountered in Chapter 1. Their analysis of the changes provides a helpful benchmark of progress over this period.

They pointed to rapid growth in paid work in the voluntary sector – by 1995, this accounted for 6.3 per cent of employment in the economy as a whole – and a fundamental change in its resource base, with public sector funding now a primary source of income for the sector, as government departments and local authorities have moved towards contracting out a wide range of responsibilities. Such developments were taking place across the whole range of voluntary sector activity (Kendall and Almond 1998). Reviewing the field five years later for the *UK Voluntary Sector Almanac 2000*, Passey and his colleagues found a pattern of continued if less rapid growth but one very dependent on the size of organisations. There were by that date 136 000 active charities with 485 000 paid employees and more than three million volunteers, making a contribution to national GDP of at least £4.8 bn. But 'the economic weight of the sector', they concluded, 'is concentrated in a relatively small number of large organisations – 90 per cent of gross income is accounted for by fewer than 10 per cent of organisations' (Passey, Hems and Jas 2000: 4). Individual giving had been in decline for most of the decade of the 1990s; and this shortfall was not being made good by funding from official sources. These were issues attracting considerable attention from government and independent commentators as the century closed, alongside concern about the implications of a closer relationship with the state (embodied in formal compacts between government at different levels and the voluntary sector) and emerging evidence of a degree of public scepticism about the future role of charity.

Conclusion

Although welfare has been always a key focus for voluntary action there are aspects of the story that has just been told that are distinctively English. Charity does take a particular form in England, where relationships with the state developed earlier and have remained especially significant – locally, it was present from the beginning of the period I have described, not as an intruder but as a potential partner. But the rules of engagement between the two have evolved as the nature of the tasks performed by the partners has changed. So has the role of business, at some stages providing a model for action, at others a vital source of funding, at others still remaining marginal, especially at local level. In these as in other respects, the English experience has diverged from that in much of the rest of Europe and to some extent the United States as well. And although modes of religious activity in the two countries matched each other closely over the nineteenth century, with organisational models created on one side of the Atlantic taking root on the other, in the twentieth century the role of religion in England, unlike the United States, has sharply diminished.

The account just given shows how the charitable approach to welfare mutates and adapts, survives doomsayers in doing so, flows into the spaces left by other actors, makes coalitions and forms new alliances. In this way, it retains a place across and within the whole range of different spheres, public, market, civil society and the private domain. But as a result, the coherence of charity, as a concept, has been fractured – it is notable how far public perception and legal definition of that term have now drifted apart.

Even the alternative idea of locating all the activities described in a separate 'voluntary sector' presented as a self-contained area of activity is misleading, because much voluntary action takes place on the terrain of the state (especially the local state) and some within the sphere of the market. So when operating in the market sphere voluntary organisations may play by market rules and try to simulate a 'bottom line' of profit and loss; once in state quadrant they must observe the regulations governing spending of public money and rules of bureaucratic accountability. In the process, their character and capacities may change or possibly even be corrupted, as the neo-liberals at the Institute of Economic Affairs argue (Whelan 1996) – although the market, as much as the state, may be the guilty party.

It is also impossible to tell the whole story of voluntary action simply in relation to provision of welfare. Voluntarism has a much wider field of action, as the new social movements of the 1960s once again demonstrated. This encompasses advocacy as well as provision; opposition, even confrontation and outright rebellion as well as cooperation. So there is a need to look more widely at a range of other activities, if voluntary action is to be properly understood and put in context.

We need to probe the extent to which civil society space is an ungoverned area, a *terrain vague*, a seedbed, or zone of altruism or of tensions, and try to establish what is special about the activities that take place in that area, especially those undertaken by smaller bodies, at the local level. What are the consequences of voluntary actions of this kind: are they subversive or conservative? What is the significance of community for voluntary action? And what is this substance called 'social capital' which communities apparently have a hand in developing? It is time to leave the national level, cease concentrating on the Anglo-Saxon scene and look 'below the radar', at what has been happening in a number of different localities.

CHAPTER 3

Civil Society and Community

There can be no community, nor a stable society, without a shared moral culture. (Amitai Etzioni, 'Banding Together', *Times Literary Supplement* 14 July 2000)

Introduction

The previous chapter ended with the unresolved debate about the provision of welfare and the respective roles of state, market and charitable or voluntary organisations as providers of goods and services. In this chapter the focus is not on action *for* others but on action *by* groups and individuals undertaken in their own interests: mutual aid as opposed to philanthropy. This is the basic distinction drawn by William Beveridge in *Voluntary Action*, where he describes mutual aid as 'a sense of one's own need for security against misfortune, and the realisation that, since all one's fellows have the same need, by undertaking to help one another all may help themselves' (1948: 9).

The emphasis here will be primarily on individuals and communities, and small groups and associations within them, not on the larger formal organisations with which we were concerned in Chapter 2. Here, I will be examining informal and smaller scale activity located in the 'civil society space' and along the borderline with family and neighbourhood.

Motivation, as Beveridge suggests, is one way of sorting out which actions come within the definition of voluntarism. But unlike in the previous chapter, where the focus was on organising to secure change on a substantial – sometimes even heroic – scale, here it will be on acts performed, as William Blake once urged the virtuous to do, 'in minute particulars'. Sometimes it will be on activity undertaken in defence of a collective interest. The cumulative effect of actions at the small scale may be to create a kind of moral climate, which sets standards of behaviour and helps to produce a shared culture. But we will also have to accept that action of this kind is not necessarily always benevolent either in intention or outcome: defence of one group's set of interests can do damage to those of others and therefore cannot be said to contribute to the common good. And some informal action, self-help in the literal sense, falls outside the scope of any definition of voluntary action – it is pure reflex, unplanned acts for individual self-satisfaction or self-defence. But other forms of activity, especially those organised informally around enthusiasms, arguably do fall within our range of interests.

The line is hard to draw with any precision. To assemble the evidence that will help me to do so, the journey this time will be not through time but through space and we will need to leave the broad highway and explore the back streets and side alleys. Although many of these will once again be found in England, I also propose to draw on some examples from the rest of Europe and the United States.

Membership and belonging

A key issue to explore, in terms of action, will be the capacity of individuals and communities (of whatever kind) for mutual aid. So we need to explore the context within which we join together as 'members one of another' (as the Anglican Book of Common Prayer has it) and the terms on which we do so. In a developed society, what are our memberships, how do we acquire them and what do they mean to us? To whom do we owe *duties* and from whom can we claim *rights*?

What are the principles on which we choose to associate with one another – or not to do so? What form do the resulting associations take and what purposes can they perform, potentially or actually – and what are their limits? And where can we best look for authenticity of emotion and the unselfish engagement of affections, outside the family circle? How attentive are we to the needs of strangers: does satisfying them strain altruism beyond our willingness – or our capacity – to deliver?

There are two concepts that may help at this point to define membership and locate the sense of belonging. One is informal, one formal; the first notoriously imprecise; the other apparently capable of rigorous legal definition – though they have more in common than these contrasts might at first suggest. They are *community* and *citizenship*.

Community

Complaints about the vagueness of the term 'community' are legion, though, as Amitai Etzioni comments, 'community can be defined at least with the same amount of precision as other widely used but often contested concepts, such as class, power and even rationality' (2000b: 9). Peter Willmott has helpfully distinguished a number of different definitions of community, including those based on kinship and geographical neighbourhoods ('territorial communities'), those based on common occupations, religions or skills ('communities of interest') and those formed round other attachments – what he calls 'community without propinquity' (1989: 3).

Starting with the first, any established community which is more than a primitive settlement or encampment will contain a variety of different levels of memberships and intensity of commitment arising from them. First and for most people still the most fundamental, is the family: a membership not chosen (except perhaps in the case of adoptions), sometimes repudiated but always likely to command a loyalty of the most basic instinctive kind. 'Favouritism' (Michael Walzer remarks) 'begins in the family – and is only then extended into politics and religion, in schools, markets and workplaces' (1983: 229)

The next link in the chain is the extended kin group: here there is substantial variation in the level of loyalty and commitment that these connections can command. This shades into the clan, often through cousinage (the relationship so enthusiastically claimed by Walter Scott's Highlanders in *Rob Roy*) and the tribe. As a crude generalisation, modernisation tends to weaken or even dissolve these connections; but there are significant variations in tenacity between different ethnic, religious and language groups. Many 'ethnic' communities tend to spread membership more widely and retain stronger linkages across time and space, especially when displaced – the wider the dispersal, the tighter the links sometimes become. The different diasporas produced by mass emigrations in the nineteenth and twentieth centuries – the Overseas Chinese, Indians and Irish – are a case in point. They are frequent recipients of appeals for support based upon ethnic loyalties and periodic attempts, as with the Jewish diaspora, at a gathering in of the dispersed. Often the wider – or more brutal – the dispersal, the tighter the bonds.

The next tier of loyalties has an explicitly geographical point of reference and reinforces the importance of the issue of scale. In an urban setting, the upward sequence runs from neighbourhood to city and perhaps region or province; the rural equivalent from village through town and county. At each level, there are institutions to which loyalties can attach themselves through participation and use: schools and colleges, churches, temples, mosques and synagogues and their congregations, workplaces (factories, offices, farms) and less formally stores, cafes and clubs (in the early, not the late twentieth-century sense). Friendships made in all these locations, from the playgroup or 'little red schoolhouse' onwards, are formed in a locality but may survive geographical separation.

Roger Lohmann has popularised a revival of the concept of the commons, an image drawn from the village pastures of late medieval and early modern England, the common ground to which all local inhabitants enjoy equal rights of access and use. The way in which these commons were used and maintained without damaging exploitation by 'free riders' is perplexing for orthodox economistic analysts, just as the loss of these common spaces by enclosure is a powerful metaphor for what modernisation did to human relations at the local level. The revival of this notion offers, Lohmann (1992) suggests, an alternative model in which rights are shared and duties pooled through spontaneous cooperation, governed by collective notions of fairness and just desert, not regulation or rules imposed by authority. However, the stability of this type of arrangement depends crucially on individual interests not diverging too widely and a strong collective sense of a common good.

Communitarian theory offers an image of the existing world reformed in a less sweeping form by nesting all existing individual loyalties and memberships inside each other – the image of the Chinese boxes is often employed to explain this concept. As Amitai Etzioni, the principal exponent of this position, puts it: 'Communities nestled within more encompassing commons with layered loyalties are the wave of the future and the heart of the communitarian agenda' (1995: xii).

Citizenship

Derek Heater in his comprehensive review of the history and practice of citizenship grounds it in identity and civic virtue; and distinguishes three specific facets: legal, political and social (1990: 331). He shows how diversity of allegiances, to languages, religions, customs and practices (for example, in marriage and child rearing) may reinforce loyalties generated within the community. A plurality of possible sources of loyalty and obligation is inescapable with multiple memberships – and creates a dense web of connections and possible obligations.

We operate in the civil society space as adults with many of these memberships already an accomplished fact. We acquire some of them at birth, either by inheritance from our parents or by the fact of the physical location at which we enter the world. Others are gained over our life span, either automatically, on reaching a certain age or through negotiation or competition. But the ultimate anchorage point is likely to be membership as a citizen of state or nation (although there are nations without states and states, like the United Kingdom, with several nations). It is from the state that rights can be claimed and to which duties are owed, like taxation and conscription. In the fully developed concept of citizenship rights, duties, entitlements and responsibilities should all march together. This can then provide the framework within which uncoerced charitable action to promote common interests can take place.

In practice, things are by no means as simple as that. As T. H. Marshall's classic account of the development of the concept of citizenship in Britain demonstrated, the progress towards the completion of a structure of rights of all kinds (civil, social and political) to which all citizens can have unfettered access is still incomplete in many respects, of which gender and race are only the most conspicuous examples.

Moreover, some of the plural memberships to which communitarians refer don't reinforce each other but compete for loyalty and generate conflicts of interest for individuals with competing attachments and within and between groups – for example, members of ethnic, linguistic and religious minorities, adherents to customs and practices that divide and groups with definitions of membership that some people cannot satisfy. Some choose to define membership negatively, by identification of these outsiders – 'there ain't no Black in the Union Jack' – and mandate their exclusion as a threat to the homogeneity of the 'real' community.

To enjoy the full benefits of citizenship, we need to have access to what Michael Walzer calls 'candidate rights' (1983: 148), which we can exercise as we qualify for them. But some of those who live alongside us will not. They will be those who are called, in the bureaucratic not the science fiction sense, 'aliens' – people whose rights are constrained by their status as migrants without citizenship of the society which they have entered. Sometimes citizen rights and duties are imposed, not chosen, by events over which individuals have no control. For instance, in Alsace, people born in 1868 and living there for eighty years would have found their citizenship changed four times as an outcome of successive Franco-German conflicts and their children and grandchildren conscripted to fight on one or other side in those countries' rival armies. Sometimes rights have been lost by political action – the deprivation by legislation of the civil rights of Jews in Nazi Germany, which began the process of dehumanising and which ended for some of them in the death camps. Others fled; but flight may also cost refugees their rights and turn them into stateless beings, with no formal recourse for protection: the ultimate strangers at the gate without even candidate claims on the societies in which they have found refuge.

Citizenship is still often withheld from those who reside as immigrants within a state, even when they have children born there (Turks in Germany) or is granted in provisional or partial terms to those already established on the territory but not perceived by the majority as full members of the community (Roma, Arab Israelis). As Walzer suggests, the principle of mutual aid cannot generally override these differences of status (1983: 51).

In addition – and this is important for the present theme – some loyalties and memberships are not directly related to nationality, geography or kinship. These are what Peter Willmott in his review of the concept of community calls 'interest communities', which are linked by class, occupation (not necessarily the same) gender, or age; or else what he calls 'attachment communities', which confer a sense of identity without being linked to birth, residence or circumstances but are based on common beliefs, secular or religious, or shared personal or professional interests. Some of these will be examples of Willmott's 'communities without propinquity', their existence and development facilitated by new information technology and the exponential growth of activity on the World Wide Web.

Finally, the nation state as a site of activity and resources and source of rights and duties for its citizens is in danger of being subverted by these and other changes – the evolution of a global market over which national governments can exercise little or no control. It is also threatened by the slow, uneven but progressive encroachment on its prerogatives being brought about by the growth of supra-national institutions like the European Union. The modern pluralistic and secular state is also challenged from the opposite direction by some extreme reactions to what are seen as threats to national identity. These often take the outward and highly visible form of frantic exhibition of the badges of belonging – flags and symbols deployed aggressively to accentuate distinct and separate identities. The extreme case here is soccer hooligans, currently one of England's major visible exports.

Changes and challenges

As a result of these changes, which have gathered pace over the second half of the twentieth century, the traditional values and structures of mutual aid have come under increasing pressure. In this section, I will identify some of the main challenges to community and mutual aid and some of the responses to them – first, the impact of capitalism.

It is often suggested that atomised individualism is the likely form of the future in the 'turbo-capitalist' global economy and that consequently community – at least in the first two of Willmott's definitions, kinship and territorial ties – is not likely to remain a significant factor in modern urban society. However, many liberals, in the classical sense of that term, see virtues in these changes. They have traditionally seen the market as enabling, not constraining and individual choice exercised in that space as liberating, allowing full scope for entrepreneurial talent. The city air breathed by the enterprising releases energies repressed by stagnant traditional communities.

The acerbic debate between advocates of this form of liberalism and critics who see the ultimate outcome of market liberalism as a society with no fixed moral values, destructive of the cohesion of traditional communities, has intensified as the pressure generated by the progress of globalisation has brought the issues into sharper focus. Christopher Lasch, in his last book *The Revolt of the Elites and the Betrayal of Democracy*, (1995) portrays liberalism as torn between the state and the market but unable to recognise that the market:

> notoriously tends to universalise itself. It does not easily coexist with institutions that operate according to principles antithetical to itself: schools and universities, newspapers and magazines, charities, families. Sooner or later the market tends to absorb them all. It puts almost irresistible pressure on every activity to justify itself in the only terms it recognises: to become a business proposition, to pay its own way, to show black ink on the bottom line...Inexorably, it remodels every institution in its own image. (97–8)

Stephen Holmes in his critique of communitarianism retaliates by suggesting that critics of liberalism 'obscure the possibility of private virtue. They also suggest that individualism is necessarily antisocial, whereas individualism can involve a heightened concern *for others* as individuals rather than as members of ascriptive groups. The greatest threat to social cohesion, moreover, arises not from individualism but from collective passions, ideological conflicts, and inherited rivalries between belligerent factions. In factional settings, solidarity is a problem, not a solution' (1993: 180).

Optimists and pessimists

Should the dominant social form in the twenty-first century prove to be hyper-individualism the prospects for mutual aid as a basis for voluntary action – either in spontaneous or organised form – must be problematic. In the welter of commentary on the future prospects for community-based voluntary action, it is possible to detect a spectrum of opinion running from extreme pessimism to guarded optimism.

Those who are moderately pessimistic about the current situation (like Amitai Etzioni) assert that the individualising trends in the global economy and changes in work patterns and the priority given to career imperatives by both men and women will be reinforced by social change. Etzioni points to what he sees as the decline in the traditional family form in advanced western societies and the impact this is having on socialisation of children – the increasing neglect by parents of their obligations to contribute to the moral upbringing of their offspring. The parent–child relationship, so crucial to the internalisation of proper values, needs to be constantly reinforced by the development of character in school, support for which should be supplied by institutions in the neighbourhood.

The immediate consequences of the failure to deliver in these respects that more extreme pessimists like, for example, Norman Dennis or Charles Murray detect range from a loss of 'civility' (meaning tolerance and courtesy in discourse between strangers) and, in more extreme cases, an overall catastrophic decline in morality, attributed mainly to the collapse of the traditional family form reflected in rapidly rising rates of 'illegitimacy'.

As Etzioni puts it: the record shows, even after only a cursory examination of our world, that from drug abuse to corporate crime, illegal and immoral behaviors have broken through (the) important line of voluntary self-restraint. *Large segments of the population do not voluntarily do what they are supposed to do'* (1995: 30, my italics).

But among these disobedient people, feminist critics have often suggested, are women, with their increasing reluctance to continue to behave inside and outside the home in ways defined for them by men. These critics argue that the legitimacy of different conceptions of rights and duties and the place of personal choices has only belatedly been accepted by most men.

Concern over these developments is linked with other anxieties about changes that have affected the late twentieth-century city, especially the loss through demolition of the geographical bases that sustained neighbourhood-based associations and the dispersal of their members to new locations and the destruction in the process of networks, both formal and informal, that had taken generations to develop.

This has become a standard theme of critiques of urban planning, most eloquently stated by Jane Jacobs (1961) in her influential polemic *Death and Life of Great American Cities*. More recently, this theme has been taken up and developed by Robert Putnam, who criticised in his earlier writings those government programmes 'such as urban renewal and public housing projects' that 'have heedlessly ravaged existing social networks' (1993b).

However, it is possible to take a more optimistic view of all these developments. Even on the critics' own terms it is not clear that all the signs point to continued decline in civility and morality. Crime rates, frequently cited (by Charles Murray in particular) as a dire warning are an uncertain guide at best: but what they now suggest is that many of the trends that caused such alarm in

Britain and the United States in the last decade have gone into reverse.

Family forms are certainly changing but not necessarily for the worse, in the sense of threatening social stability. The most important development that has taken place in developed countries has been the widespread incorporation of women into the labour force and the consequences for patterns of child rearing. Working parents have to contend with mounting pressures at a time when flexible job markets make employment increasingly insecure; and it would be foolish to maintain that these do not sometimes cause major stresses which impact on children and adversely affect their experience of family life. This redefinition of family and its meaning that began (feminists like Judith Stacey argue) in the working class under such pressures has been reinterpreted and extended by women at all levels to begin evolving a multi-earner, joint carer model of the family unit. Some optimists refer to the gradual emergence of this alternative model as a precursor to fundamental and positive changes in social relations.

Optimists also point to the vitality still shown by villages in the city, especially the 'Fourth World' enclaves of migrants from developing countries and new centres of creativity, sometimes associated with other sorts of minority – 'gay communities' – sometimes with new technology (silicon gulches, valleys and glens), sometimes the early twenty-first-century equivalent of the early twentieth-century artists' *quartier*, wherever that perennial mirage 'swinging London' has most recently been sighted.

There are other factors working in favour of continued association. Willmott cites the better health and greater vitality of older people in the 'third age' and much evidence of continued activity at level of family, and locality, though not all of it necessarily benevolent and in many instances restricted in commitment to communal objectives – what he calls 'community of limited liability' (1989: 18). Certainly, communal life still flourishes in the 'burbs, supported by the energies of the indefatigable 'soccer moms' and local studies on both sides of the Atlantic show continued density of associational life. Etzioni himself professes to observe a 'welcome return to small town life of sorts' in modern America, not just in geographical locations but in professional groups (he cites law firms, apparently without irony, as an example of a communitarian milieu). Informal association among the young, organised semi-spontaneously, has become a powerful influence on behaviour and patterns of consumption, in its own right.

How strong, in sum, is the communitarian case, in either its pessimistic analysis or in optimistic prescriptions? Among the moderate pessimists is the Chief Rabbi of the Commonwealth, Jonathan Sacks. His *Politics of Hope* (1997) is a passionate plea for a new approach: but he joins the sceptics in doubting whether the restoration of a traditional sense of community is sufficient in itself to achieve that objective. He comments that:

> The 'quest for community' which can seem so desirable in the atom-ised world of British and American cities, can look quite different from the perspective of Northern Ireland or Bosnia or Lebanon or India or a dozen other places where communitarian values look more like an ancient tribalism of a particularly bloody kind.

Hence, he continues: ...

> my argument has not been for a politics of community alone. Instead, it has been for a restoration of balance in the body politics. Without a state there is anarchy. Without a respect for individuals as individuals there is tyranny. But without morality and the civil institutions within which it lives, breathes and has its being, there is too little to prevent the pen-dulum swinging between tyranny and anarchy (Sacks 1997: 229–30).

Amitai Etzioni calls in *The New Golden Rule* (1998) for a restora-tion of moral responsibility through reinforcement of conscience. For him, the core concept is the provision of 'shared foundations of the good' and community is a means to that end, not a goal in itself. Lack of precision in the definition of community 'matters little on the stump', where he himself is frequently to be found, provided that a moral culture can be created and sustained. But the dynamic of change driven by 'turbo-capitalism' still poses problems to address, for communities of all kinds. Might one con-sequence of the transformations now taking place be to compro-mise opportunities for free association outside the state and the potential of mutual aid for positive action? If so, how can the bal-ance be redressed?

Some alternative perspectives

Over the years since the ending of the post-war period of prosperity – roughly, 1945–73 – a sense has developed of failure first by the state and increasingly of late the market to provide solutions on a human scale with humane content. This has prompted a series of different reactions, some simply lashing out against change (for example, by trashing your neighbourhood McDonalds); others through systematic attempts to address these themes from a range of different perspectives which have in turn helped to create new organisational approaches and forms.

Among the most significant of these responses have been feminism and 'new social movements' – explicitly, those directed towards marking out a space away from both state and market. Both of these embody utopian aspirations (which I will revisit systematically in Chapter 8) and explicitly attempt to reconnect personal aspirations with broader political goals.

One of the the the principal contributions of late twentieth-century *feminism* has been the constant pressure feminists have exerted to elide the boundaries between the personal sphere and the political, or even collapse the two into one another. 'Second wave' feminism vigorously assailed old top-down 'vanguardist' left politics. Where old male worker-dominated politics had seen social policy and objectives as marginal or at best secondary to securing economic change, feminists have insisted on their primacy. Tactically, feminists have placed a premium on non-hierarchical organisation, egalitarian objectives and direct action to achieve them. The form of organisations, the composition of leadership groups and nature and objectives of campaigns undertaken through voluntary action have all been permanently affected by the imprint of feminism.

Among those most directly influenced have been the *new social movements*, addressing a broader range of issues but from a similarly critical perspective. These have taken a wide range of different forms and their impact in the diverse fields in which they have operated has often been highly significant. Robert Putnam provides some examples of the American experience: from the civil rights movement through the free speech movement in Berkeley, California through the Vietnam war protests, to the Stonewall Inn uprising for gay rights to environmental protest and campaigns for and against abortion. He comments that:

> Standing at the close of the century, it is virtually impossible to overstate the impact of these social movements on the lives of most American communities and individuals and most American citizens. In our most private moments, as in our most public ones, our behavior and our values bear the imprint of those movements. (2000: 152)

Their common characteristics, in their English manifestations, have been brilliantly anatomised (and satirised) from the inside in *What a Way to Run a Railroad* (Landry et al. 1985). This account charts the trajectory – in most cases a brief rise and rapid fall – of a number of radical community-based projects that helped to make up the 'counter-culture' of the period. 'Too often', the authors comment 'these organisations have focused exclusively on their internal relations. Instead of developing strategies for winning more space in popular markets (which would presumably reek too much of commercialism) they have concentrated on building a self-contained alternative world, somehow parallel to and preferably insulated from, the world of commerce. This can only be a recipe for introversion, exclusivity and decay'. And they add, in a telling touch: 'Many collectives have concentrated on sharing out the swabbing of the Titanic's decks but forgotten to post a lookout for icebergs' (1985: 31–2).

On the margin of credibility, some of these projects have carried rejection of existing institutions to extreme lengths – living in elected poverty, in communes rejecting conventional family forms. Others have made various compromises with conventional working procedures and attempted to evolve their own internal systems with a premium on participation and internal democracy, practising collective leadership and decision-taking. However, as the authors of *What a Way ...* point out, one paradoxical outcome of the ultra-democratic style is that it breeds a perverse form of elitism. Moreover, the attempt to impose collectivism creates a universe where individual personalities become all-important and in which 'you can't criticise anyone's performance of a particular task without it being seen as a total attack on the person. It thus becomes impossible to distinguish "doing a bad job" from "being a bad person"' (Landry et al. 1985: 44).

These developments, in turn, have had a growing impact on the world of community organisation and politics eventually spreading outwards into the 'voluntary sector' with both the pluses and minuses of this style. In many cases, this meant learning to be – as the title of one tract for those times had it – both 'in and against' the state.

This approach, neither state- nor market-centred, also connected with the revival of a half-spent impulse, more conventionally but of fundamental significance, the community action and organisation movement. In Britain, this began in the late 1940s, was exported to the British colonies, and expanded after their independence through the volunteering programme, VSO (Voluntary Service Overseas), part-modelled on the American Peace Corps. This approach then returned to the metropolitan country in the 1960s as Community Service Volunteers, bringing young people to work on community projects in inner city areas and as social development workers in new towns and then remained largely dormant for another thirty years.

In the United States, the initial thrust of Saul Alinsky's remarkable work in Chicago in a deprived white working-class neighbourhood, Back-of-the-Yards, described in his tract *Reveille for Radicals*, also fell initially into this category but built on another, older tradition of working-class mutual aid based on solidarity (for which see Chapter 2). It also made connections with the dramatic new force for social change that had emerged in the course of the 1960s, the civil rights movement. Lessons from that movement, vividly reflected in television coverage of peaceful protest in the South and expressed through the (literally) charismatic personality of Martin Luther King, crossed the Atlantic and influenced the style and content of protest movements in Britain.

Another avenue of response has been explicitly through religion. There have been new attempts to reconstruct the Puritans' 'City on a Hill' in the United States: and in Britain and Western Europe the steady decline of mainstream Christian religion has been partly balanced by a countervailing rise in informal and Pentecostal churches; and the consolidation of the foothold in Europe by migration of other world religions (for example, Islam and Sikhism). Religious congregations have come to form one of the key resources that deprived inner city groups can call upon to confront their new circumstances through collective action. In the United States, they are perhaps the only significant institutions remaining in inner city areas with the capacity to provide practical assistance and leadership.

Communitarianism as a broad church contains both a right as well as a left tendency but in the United States, at least, both have a strong tincture of religious sentiment. The 're-moralisation' approach characteristic of this line of argument places its stress on religious membership (usually characterised as 'Judeo-Christian') as laying down a sound foundation of moral values, inculcated in the family sphere, and never mind the theological details. But this approach also represents an attempt to reconcile voluntary action and market values, within a religiose frame of reference (a theme I revisit in Chapter 6).

One way of conceptualising this whole debate is as a search for 'glue' – if society is a vertical mosaic, what holds the individual pieces in place? How much 'glue' is needed, where is it to be found and how is it applied: can the separate pieces be held together without any other intermediate connections? Or, less fancifully put, what are the best ways of ensuring that successful association in civil society can be sustained under the pressures of globalisation?

Social capital and trust

The notion of *social capital* has been employed as a means of explaining how an environment of mutual trust, once created, helps to build up a bank of resources that can be used to support a whole variety of organisations and initiatives and serve a succession of different functions. As Robert Putnam defines it, social capital 'refers to connections among individuals – social networks and the norms of reciprocity and trustworthiness that arise from them' (2000: 19).

The first substantial attempt to use the idea of social capital in the public policy debate is Jane Jacobs' analysis, in the context of community action and planning in post-war American cities and the loss of community networks as a result of insensitive urban redevelopment schemes. The concept was later developed by the American sociologist James Coleman: in his approach, it forms the basis for collective action, made possible by the accumulation of human capital. The next stage (so far) in the evolution of the debate is Robert Putnam's discussion of social capital as a foundation for civic engagement. Putnam draws an important distinction between social capital that bonds communities and capital that bridges. An illustration of the two different uses of social capital would be some African-American churches in the United States, which bond their membership together but help them to bridge across class and so obtain access to wider society and its resources. (Putnam 2000: 68–9; more on this in Chapter 4).

Social capital can perhaps best be seen as a 'public good', an outcome of the active presence of three separate but linked elements, all of which, in Putnam's phrase, help to generate 'stocks' of social capital, which 'tend to be self-reinforcing and cumulative' (1993a: 37). One of these is trust; the other two norms and networks. However, all three raise issues that are potentially problematic.

The presence or absence of *trust* between individuals and organ-isations is frequently raised as an issue in the debate about the future of association in the context of global capitalism. This has led to exploration of the circumstances in which trust can be cre-ated and consolidated, the functions that it can perform and how it can be deployed in situations of diversity and plurality of interests (Seligman 1997). But trust itself as a factor can be highly controver-sial. It is easy enough to demonstrate how trust can function posi-tively among well established communities and serve not just social but economic functions. In some models, it is seen as the basis for development of different patterns of economic association – infor-mal trust-based organisations (the standard example is of diamond brokers trading objects of immense value, without any formalities) leading to fully-fledged western capitalism, in which 'trusts' fea-ture prominently – and sometimes deceptively. The rise and now the decline of Lloyds of London as a centre of the insurance indus-try illustrates how trust can serve a function at a certain stage of economic development which then becomes redundant – or worse – in a modernised economy. But trust can also serve as the basis for 'black' or at least grey economic transactions.

Outside the economic sphere, trust can serve as the basis for social action or political collaborations. Under this heading, it is important to take account of informal customs and practices and the ways in which they are internalised and influence patterns of behaviour, some of which will fall into the 'old Spanish customs' category – traditional ways of doing jobs that allow for informal profit-taking by participants. However, this takes us into the prob-lematic area of anti-social trust: codes of conduct that impose secrecy and permit clientelism and corruption (or worse) to flour-ish. The Mafia is the obvious example here, in its capacity as both an economic and as a criminal organisation: the resources of loy-alty and resulting expectations of behaviour *(omertà)* on which it draws can be seen as a form of 'anti-social capital' (whose political aspects are explored later).

Networks are probably best seen as connections, of an informal or semi-formal kind, customarily extending horizontally, within the extended family, or through neighbourhoods; but also taking the form of linkages to institutions, locally or centrally and vertical connections arising from these linkages. But what is the relative importance of these two different levels? What does inclusion confer and how does exclusion deprive? Many large cities in Britain con-tain minority ethnic communities with strong horizontal linkages but whose leaders lack the political skills to make vertical connections that American black churches have learned to put in place. Networks when restricted or selective can also be disabling as well as empowering, segmenting as well as uniting.

Norms (and values) are best seen as common sets of beliefs and cues for behaviour developed in close association. For some economists, these are a potent source of support for willingness to take advantage of market opportunities – entrepreneurship is often seen as a culturally predetermined activity. David Landes after commenting that 'culture makes all the difference' adds the rider that 'culture, in the sense of the inner values and attitudes that guide a population, frightens scholars. It has a sulfuric odor of race and inheritance, an air of immutability. In thoughtful moments, economists and social scientists recognize that this is not true and indeed salute examples of cultural change for the better while deploring changes for the worse' (1998: 516). Sceptics should perhaps have remembered Max Weber and R. H. Tawney's demonstration of the importance of religious belief and its cultural expressions, as the key influence in determining the location and form taken by early capitalism.

Given these qualifications, can we say that social capital is an actually existing resource that can be measured and compared? And if it exists in a finite, existing quantity, can it be mobilised as a public good for public policy purposes – or indeed for others, like the welfare of families or individuals?

Robert Putnam (2000) has succeeded in constructing an analysis based on demographic and opinion data which enables him to plot the distribution of social capital, in his definition, across regions of the United States and through time. Taken in these terms, his data show a decline on all the indicators of communal activity that he has devised. One example he gives of this decay is the decline of sociable sporting activities symbolised in the image that has now become famous and which gives his book its title: the solitary bowler, *Bowling Alone*. Among the benefits that the presence of social capital can provide and which in Putnam's analysis are at risk are the sustaining of civic order (or civility), promoting social inclusion and facilitating civic education – skills that enable individuals and groups to function successfully. However, all these three potential assets may also contain latent liabilities

In the first place, it is misleading to see the formation of a civic community as inevitable – a cumulative process, founded on a virtuous circle of steadily increasing social capital formation and increased density of relationships on which individuals can come to rely. It is also possible to observe cases of a vicious circle in which the value of social capital is exhausted and individuals face agonising dilemmas in isolation, when the rules of civilised conduct have been abrogated. Victor Klemperer's diaries of the experiences of a Jew in Nazi Germany immediately before the Second World War provide a unique record of the gradual erosion of civil rights and the deliberately imposed increases in social isolation that were linked to this process.

On the value of social capital for addressing issues of social exclusion, there is the basic problem that supplies of social capital, seen as the result of the accumulation of contacts and networking skills, are distributed differentially by class and gender and indeed location as well (Jane Jacobs' original point). And on civic education, there is an issue of whether the skills and experience are transferable, between different situations and individuals or groups. For example, 'committee skills' learned by participation in activities managed by public bureaucracies are relevant to some situations and completely useless or worse in others, where they serve to mystify and repel those not familiar with the vocabulary and rules. (This might be called the 'through you, madam chair' syndrome, after one particularly obscure piece of committee jargon).

One means of addressing these issues is through promotion of volunteering. In the United Kingdom during the 1980s, there was a revival of interest in promoting what became known as 'active citizenship', by exhortation and by education – a Speaker's Committee on Citizenship was convened at the end of the decade. However, the evidence from these and more recent campaigns designed to promote volunteering (*'Make a Difference'*, *'Millennium Volunteers'*) suggests that even with the resources of modern advertising techniques it is difficult to capture, still less sustain interest and involvement on a large scale.

There are a variety of possible explanations. Volunteering has always been differentially distributed by class and age in the United Kingdom: competition for available time in the peak age group (30–45) has increased as the working week lengthens. Among the young, the vocabulary and ethos of traditional volunteering has proved to be a major obstacle, especially at a period when traditional 'uniformed' youth groups are in a phase of rapid decline. 'Good causes' are perceived as catered for by the casual purchase of National Lottery tickets, not through extended commitment of time. The uneven distribution of social skills by class may mean that there is less chance of mobilising groups (the socially isolated, many of the unemployed) for whom volunteering might provide practical benefits on a quasi-exchange basis. (There is also a special situation in many ethnic minority groups, among whom informal assistance rather than formal volunteering provides the crucial element of help when in difficulties.)

When considering the uses to which social capital can be put, the issue of *scale* becomes crucial. It is clearly possible to conceive of social and political, even economic action at the small scale being facilitated by networks that are 'socially embedded': but how can this be translated into effective responses to larger issues? Etzioni's assumption is that moral responsibility to deliver attaches to the community itself. Accordingly, he asserts, on 'any of the well-known host of social problems that beset us the first social responsibility lies with those who share a community' (1995: 146); though this seems to me to mistake the wish for the deed. How is it possible to move upwards and outwards beyond the point where the strength of relationships rests on their being made and sustained face-to-face? What about conflicts between communities over resource allocation or policy priorities? There is also a 'club goods' problem when the benefits of actions are confined to an inner circle of members only, a problem that Etzioni recognises but to which he has no solution to propose beyond admonishing communities to behave wherever possible in an inclusive style. Finally, these small-scale interactions – the preservation of the commons, in Lohmann's terms – are not proof against the impact of change: increased mobility, changes in family structure, the consequences of the introduction of new technology. How far are they needed, even, in postmodern circumstances? Some examples may help to clarify these issues.

Some cases of community under scrutiny

Robert Putnam's earlier case study, *Making Democracy Work* (1993a) is perhaps the best known recent example of a review of the social and economic implications of the presence or absence of strong communities. This study compares northern and southern Italy and the ways in which networks, norms and trust reinforce one another, or fail to do so. The context is the creation of regional government in Italy in 1970 and the evident successes or failures of different regional public administrations in promoting social and economic growth. Putnam's conclusion is that the success of some regions in the North can be traced to the existence of social networks that are organised horizontally, not hierarchically. Such networks can be formed in all sorts of ways – Putman cites cooperatives, mutual aid societies, neighbourhood associations and choral societies as examples – and have had significant consequences for society and polity as well as economy, in underpinning solidarity, civic participation and integrity. These networks, he argues, have deep historical roots. Norms and values and levels of civic engagement differ fundamentally in the South and with them the level of trust and the lack of success of regional government (though in the South the *omertà* that sustains the Mafia is certainly a form of trust, as we saw earlier). Critics of Putnam (for example, Maloney, Smith and Stoker 1997) point to his neglect of vertical networks and the positive role that the state can perform in this way, in providing the right context for developments of all kinds. Putnam also rather surprisingly omits any reference to the impact of totalitarian rule – the consequences of twenty years of a full-blown fascist system of government imposed on both north and south alike – and there is a certain *naïveté* about his account of the then (1980s) existing Italian political system. Even then, surely, the 'Italy that works' was not regional government?

Another case is Richard Rose's examination of circumstances in Russia after the collapse of Communism and the ways in which individual Russians meet their requirements for welfare in a situation of scarcity: how basic needs for income, food and health can be satisfied. When questioned, most Russians say that they are not members of any formal network; but have connections that can be mobilised to meet specific needs ('better a thousand friends than a thousand roubles', the saying goes). Trust is differentially distributed among these connections; but there is no question of institutions (either those of the state or the market) being trusted after experience of the widespread non-payment of pensions and the wiping out of savings by bank failures. In these conditions survival depends on developing a 'portfolio approach' to solving immediate and pressing problems not encountered in normal circumstances in most developed societies and use of techniques not now familiar in the West *(blat or barter)*. The 'cultural' explanation of the failure, so far, of Russia to develop a stable economy or polity is that it will take a generation, or more, to accustom the population to the notion of legitimate trust, either in institutions or individuals, after the ingrained cynicism of 'former times'. But the sharpening of effective survival skills suggests that developed capacities exist which must be relevant, but are highly individualised. (I will return to some of these issues in Chapter 5.)

A third example would be the East Asian case – a group of modernising economies, illustrating how the family can also serve as the basic building block, where networks exist (like those of the Overseas Chinese), together with universal norms of commitment – a work ethic whose focus is on achieving collective rather than individual goals. The resulting high growth economies, based on 'high product for low wages' – the 'little tigers' of the Pacific rim – achieved for a while at least miraculous status. But economic setbacks in the late 1990s exposed a failure of 'reach' of trust up to government level and endemic problems of corruption and the superficiality of commitment to democratic values and institutions (Landes 1998: 471–5).

These cases show the variety of ways in which collaborative ventures for mutual advantage can be addressed at community level and below in different societies, with different priority given to family, neighbourhood or other informal associations. There are also aspects of the British scene which provide an especially vivid picture of the distinctive way in which mutual aid can find expression outside formal organisational frameworks (but within the civil society space) and the ways in which trust can be formed and retained at community level.

The 'invisible organisation'

This distinctiveness is clearly brought out in Bishop and Hoggett's *Organizing Around Enthusiasms*, an account of cultural and leisure activities in Britain in the 1980s, based in extensive fieldwork. Theirs is one of a very few studies to have penetrated the world of informal association in any depth, describing a self-sustaining system, organised and managed from self-generated resources. This is a world in which the adjective 'voluntary' is not accepted as self-description, 'sector' is not seen as appropriate to describe the collectivity – and the term 'hobby' is never employed.

The participants in this system are productive but consume their own product; relations between the organisers and organised are characterised by reciprocity, as individuals move from one role to the other. Organisations operate often with minimal rules and constitutions but within very clearly understood conventions. One example given by Bishop and Hoggett is the rules on jam and cakes at horticultural shows. (While both cake and jam when exhibited separately must each be homemade, there is no restriction on what sort of jam should go into homemade cakes as filling.) The essence is informal social exchange, sustained by common enthusiasm. The form the activity takes can be either collaborative or competitive – the latter more likely in the case of sports, but covering a wide range of activities and involving judges that can be 'part scientist and part shaman' (1986: 58). Individuals are free to join and to leave as their interests and skills develop in different directions. Conflict does occur; but normally resolves itself by the departure of those who cannot persuade their fellow-members to accept their preferences. In Albert Hirschman's terms, exit is readily available to those who do not wish to persist in loyalty and whose voices have not proved effective.

These sorts of sports and leisure activities don't function to meet need, since the activity itself isn't defined in those terms except by those outside the informal world, in the formally organised and funded services. They do not feature in the 'grant economy'. Yet the scale of the activities being undertaken may be quite extensive, and involvement intensive, even obsessional.

Rather, this type of informal leisure activity begins beyond need. 'The self-interest underlying forms of communal leisure is therefore not based on neediness but upon enthusiasm, pleasure and enjoyment' (Bishop and Hoggett 1986: 128). It is impossible to imagine activities of this kind being captured in the concept of volunteering or the desires they express and fulfil being filtered through a system of appraisal which calculates need by appraisal and awards support on the basis of an assumed deficit from an officially set standard of provision.

The point is further brought home in Ruth Finnegan's *The Hidden Musicians* (1989). She discovered a vast range of musical activity in a wide range of different idioms taking place in one city (Milton Keynes), but outside the scope of formal organisation, often passing through a life cycle, when enthusiasm for a particular activity and the skills of those participating increased and then fell away to be succeeded by new ones. This was not 'community arts' in a cosy, enclosed, *Gemeinschaft* communal sense but widespread participation based on a multiplicity of opportunities open to all. Finnegan summarises what she has described as being based upon:

> the invisible organisation – fragile, changing, but continuing, embued both with every day practicality and transcendant overtones – which

in late twentieth-century Britain is maintained by, and depends upon, people's active engagement along their local pathways.' (1989: 339)

Both these cases illustrate Peter Willmott's point about the potential strengths of communities of attachment. Some similar outcomes, flowing from membership of a variety of formally constituted religious congregations, are described by Margaret Harris in a series of case studies (1998). These also exhibit the same signs that Bishop and Hoggett and Finnegan have noted, of cycles of activity and splits within groups trying to impose their own sense of direction on reluctant fellow-members. Some of the benefits of participation will be similar to those obtained by participants in a secular organisation, some will be transcendental: spiritual experiences impossible to assess by the same criteria.

But in all these cases, membership provides all sorts of non-material rewards whose primary purpose is not promoting the public good though (Robert Putnam would argue) this may, in certain circumstances, be an indirect outcome of these activities.

In the worlds described by Bishop and Hoggett and Finnegan, there is a culture of altruism: such commercial activity as takes place is subsidiary and to do with securing wider public access to the product, not profit. Free exchange is the founding principle. There is an expectation of mutual aid in its most practical form (for example, passing on sports equipment, tools, musical instruments or music) from which a stranger or new entrant to these worlds can also expect to benefit, regardless of their financial means.

However, for some participants the market would be a welcome arrival. Some of Ruth Finnegan's hidden musicians would dearly like to be discovered, with all the monetary consequences that flow from discovery in a world of conspicuous consumption. Not for nothing is their product known as 'popular' music and not only success but quality is judged by the extent of its popularity. The youth culture switches easily from self-consumption to marketing and making profits. Most people in that world know the rules of this game and many of them will want to play it, while at the same time seeking to retain control, to allow them to continue to experiment and innovate on their own terms. That knowledge may not be enough to prevent them from being exploited.

Some problems with this type of small-scale activity have been identified by Paul Hoggett in his analysis for Demos (1994). One is exclusiveness, although this may be the reverse side of a coin that provides substantial rewards for informal organisations. Hoggett himself in his earlier work comments further on the alleged 'sectionalism' of this activity that it is 'a crucial element of the strength of organisations, both as an expression of the immediacy and concreteness of whatever theme brings members together and as a form of defence against homogenising external pressures'(128). The same holds true of solidarity in a form that explicitly excludes – the 'working man's club' syndrome, once a strength, now a means of shoring up communities under threat at the cost of excluding others with different claims. Another issue is lack of transparency: some forms of association wish to be seen as private and informal but in fact have objectives that relate to public issues. These flourish in a climate of secrecy, from Freemasons downwards through Fascist cagoule and racist Ku Klux Klan to neo-Nazi groupuscules. Some forms of informal association may be anti-democratic or worse – ethnic associations formed to block off the claims of rival groups, vigilante posses aggressively imposing majority values, even looters and lynch mobs.

Finally, in the informal world, there is often an expectation and imposition of majority values – for example, in some social and sporting bodies, like the golf club which perpetuates particular norms of behaviour by maintaining one-class, one-gender or even one-race situations.

Implications of promoting local mutual aid

Many commentators, from William Beveridge onwards, would want to argue that mutual aid at the local level is the most authentic form of voluntary action, which has value not just in its own right but as a symbol of the virtues of spontaneity and active citizenship. But before concluding that all these informal activities should be automatically favoured, it is worth drawing attention to some recent research findings (Burns and Taylor 1998).

These suggest that (for example) the product of some forms of associational activity may be low quality, even compared with mass produced goods (like organic vegetables, which in my own experience are always costly and often contain an excessive ratio of soil to product). Communal services (community care; or local financial services, like credit unions) may for a variety of reasons – cost factors, scale of operation, calibre of staff – not be first-class services. Or they may be 'club goods' which may not be generally accessible except by entering into membership arrangements that may restrict members' rights. Some forms of activity may be transitional (for example, those using fundraising techniques based on financial procedures being superseded by new technologies like electronic data processing).

There are also potential problems of transferability: systems or methods of organisation that work in one sector of life or service area may not be transferable sideways or upwards. They may be fragile, with limits on their capacity to sustain activity. Burns and Taylor suggest that 'dense' local ties and networks may be less effective in this way than looser 'modern' ones.

There may be an increasing 'privatisation problem'; market invasion of sectors of associational life may lead to decline of trusteeship and stewardship as values (witness the decay of many organisations based on the principle of mutual aid, like building societies and insurance companies. And, finally, the absence of local associational activity may not be sinister; it may reflect satisfaction or sufficient prosperity; and hence no pressing internal need for creating new organisations or survival networks.

Conclusion

In this chapter, I have reviewed some of the evidence about action taken at local level, in the context of community (however defined) and intended to promote mutual aid. Some like Amitai Etzioni, see this type of activity as having a moral dimension and action taken in this segment of the civil society space as forming the crucial building blocks in the construction of an edifice of moral virtue. Community is a term that carries a variety of meanings and associations, not all of them favourable to the exercise of citizenship, another contested term, which sets the framework for action conducted at a variety of different levels, by defining rights and responsibilities.

The impact of accelerating social and economic change has posed a daunting set of challenges: I have described some of these and sketched a variety of responses that have emerged over the past half-century in different places. One resource that has the potential, it is suggested, to be called upon in this context is social capital. Robert Putnam's account of the distribution of stocks of social capital and what he sees as their depletion illustrates some of the ways in which the vitality of local connections can affect the quality of community life – though some of his critics are less impressed by the conclusions he draws from this evidence. And meanwhile, 'below the radar', informal activities continue along local 'pathways' which are difficult to characterise in terms of formal organisational logic but which often provide intense satisfaction to those that participate in them.

Does most of this activity belong in the private domain, beyond the reach of public policy and public law and regulation? There are strong arguments for allowing a form of 'creative chaos' to flourish, to avoid formality in organisation and keep charity regulation at a long arm's length. Perhaps more controversially, should community be best viewed as functioning naturally 'without politics', as David Green argues in his pamphlet for the Institute of Economic Affairs? But mutual aid can be a flag of convenience for both individuals and communities, a prelude to shutting themselves away – or fencing themselves off, raising the drawbridge that separates the 'gated communities' of the prosperous from the rest of society. It can also serve as a pretext for abandoning groups that are perceived, whether accurately or not, as possessing sufficient resources to cope with their own problems without the need for outside assistance. (What could be called the 'Asian elder' syndrome, by reference to a community with a particularly strong tradition of communal support for the elderly).

Does the sub-soil of informal activity have its own value, regardless of the plants that grow in it? The past experience of dictatorships attempting to take over organisations and informal activities even at this level, to which I shall be referring in later chapters, is evidence of a negative kind of the importance of organisations that ostensibly have no policy significance.

A key question here is who has the responsibility of representing the common good in such situations and how can it be identified and legitimated? Citizenship's limits may have been reached when diversity arrives at the point of eliminating any solidarity; common membership at the level of the central state may then cease to have any unifying value. The resulting fragmentation can be creative or destructive – a decline into the world of war of all against all described by Thomas Hobbes. On the other side, the oxygen of liberty may be needed as a precaution against the stifling effects of imposed communal values. This raises the question of how best, in Albert Hirschman's terms (introduced in Chapter 1) to balance loyalty and the rights of voice and exit.

The communitarian response is to argue for a collectively established conception of what will make the community better or worse off. This necessitates not just a set of common values but also the existence of machinery that will allow disagreements to be resolved without placing illegitimate constraints on the rights of minorities. For that, some form of established and accepted political process will be necessary – the theme of the next chapter.

CHAPTER 4

Civil Society and Democracy

Not only does democracy make every man forget his ancestors; but it hides his descendants and separates his contemporaries from him; it throws him back for ever upon himself alone and threatens in the end to confine him entirely within the solitudes of his own heart. (Alexis de Tocqueville, *Democracy in America*)

Introduction: in search of civic virtue

In the previous chapter, I explored some of the ramifications of the debate around the communitarian view of associations, their functions and the principles on which they operate and the consequences of their activities for the future of civil society. This discussion exposed a contrast between liberal assertions that healthy communal associations are essential elements in the workings of a good society and those who hold that small-scale community-based activities serve no particular social function beyond the pleasure that they give participants.

Some of those who maintain that the good health of civil society depends on a wide diversity of activities of all kinds, at a range of different levels, nevertheless argue that the benefits that these confer are best seen as operating outside the political arena, and 'without politics' (Green 1993). This view is challenged by those (John Keane, Paul Hirst) who argue for the central importance of maintaining an active political sphere. A key condition for achieving this goal, they suggest, is the presence of civic virtue among citizens – a willingness to participate actively in the political arena in pursuit of the common good. These civic 'republicans' (as they are termed in Michael

84

Walzer's analysis, already referred to in Chapter 1) attach special importance to the institutions that provide a framework for legitimate political activity (legislative assemblies, agencies of central and local government, political parties) and to forms of participation that directly engage with those institutions and help to determine the outcomes of their activities. The mode of political organisation that best reflects these priorities is of course democracy.

This approach raises a number of key issues about the role of citizens in a modern democracy. Are their interests best articulated through individual acts (like voting) or is there a common interest that can only be expressed by collective political action, through party political organisations or by campaigning or demonstrating? If there is, can this only find effective expression in the political arena through organisations like political parties, trades unions or policy coalitions, or can it flow through other channels and networks, like those described in Chapter 3, and nonetheless have an impact on events there?

Additionally, can civic engagement take place effectively at the local level ('bottom-up'), where it may gain value – 'authenticity' – through closeness to those involved? Or does the nature and location of political power mean that action can only be really effective if undertaken top-down, through capturing what used to be called the 'commanding heights' of the economy and polity? Furthermore, is activity of any kind a rational form of behaviour or is the possibility of securing significant change through political action too remote to justify the investment of an individual's energies, time or indeed money?

Finally, how far are the terms on which voluntary associations engage with the state at every level affected, for either participant, by the use of democratic means or attempts to secure democracy as an end? And since coherent debate depends on clarity on this score, what exactly does democracy mean, in theory and in practice? As Anthony Arblaster puts it:

> At the root of all definitions of democracy, however refined and complex, lies the idea of popular power, of a situation in which power, and perhaps authority, rests with the people. That power or authority is usually thought of as being political, and it often therefore takes the form of an idea of popular sovereignty – the people as the ultimate political authority. But it need not be exclusively political. Democracy is not always taken to signify only a form of government, or of choosing a government: it may be a term applied to a whole society. (Arblaster 1994: 9)

Alexis in America

These questions, of course, are not new. Alexis de Tocqueville's famous investigation of nineteenth-century American democracy has become the almost inevitable starting point for such a discussion. Tocqueville's expedition, which took place in 1831–2 and was undertaken ostensibly to study the prison system in the United States, had its origins in circumstances in his own country. A recent commentator has put it in its starkest form: in *Democracy in America* (1835) 'Tocqueville attempted something extraordinary, the overturn of the established European idea of the state' (Siedentop 1994: 41). The reasons why he should have wished to do this are intimately connected with his own personal experience of an especially turbulent period of French history.

His own background was in the provincial minor aristocracy and his family had suffered severely in the course of the Revolution – grandparents, aunts and cousins had all been guillotined in 1794, during the Reign of Terror. As a young man with some political ambitions Tocqueville had himself experienced the impact of the repressive regime installed after the Bourbon restoration following the final defeat of Napoleon in 1815, with its harsh restrictions on civil and political rights. His concern with the exercise (and misuse) of state power, as experienced in France was therefore far from theoretical. He had observed at close quarters the consequences of both the excesses of maximalist democracy under the Revolution and the subsequent centralisation of repressive power by the royalist ultras, resting on the unchecked exercise of authority by the aristocracy and the Catholic Church. Tocqueville's experiences and his liberal instincts made him profoundly distrustful of both these political systems.

However, the alternative model of the English method of government that attracted many of his French contemporaries and which Edmund Burke had advocated in his commentary on the French Revolution did not appeal to him either. Tocqueville admired the active role of the English state which, he observed 'had the compact vigour of one man, and its will puts immense masses in motion' (1998: 41). But he saw weaknesses as well. The state's power needed to be counterbalanced; decentralisation was an essential corrective to ward off the abuses of absolutism. In England, the local gentry supplied that counterweight by their involvement in local institutions; but the capacity to achieve this did not yet exist in France. This led Tocqueville to ask a different question: could the United States, a new society that had adopted new solutions to the perennial problems of power and authority, provide a viable alternative approach that could be introduced into the debate in Europe?

Tocqueville's expedition was therefore essentially an exercise in seeking American answers to traditional European questions. The analysis that he provided when he returned and published in two successive volumes, suggested that the exercise of popular power could be checked by the strength of intermediate bodies ('associations'), operating within the rule of law, even without the guidance or direction of a hereditary governing class. State power could be contained by the separation of functions between different branches of government and by the decentralisation of authority to the local level. But there were still (for him) some unresolved questions. For example, the individualism which was one of the main features of American society also posed problems. As Tocqueville observed:

> Individualism is a mature and calm feeling, which disposes each member of the community to sever himself from the mass of his fellows and to draw apart with his family and his friends, so that after he has thus formed a little circle of his own, he willingly leaves society at large to itself ... individualism, at first, only saps the virtues of public life; but in the long run it attacks and destroys all others and is at length absorbed in downright selfishness. (1898: 205)

This danger was likely to be exacerbated by the 'terrible restlessness' that individual ambition generated. There was also a perennial risk in 'democratic' systems (meaning ones in which all male adults had the vote) of the tyranny of the majority over minorities of all kinds.

The question was therefore whether all these effects could be tempered to achieve a sense of the common good and if so how. A linked question was about how far social equality can go without compromising the integrity of society by 'making common indifference a sort of public virtue'.

The answer lay in the development of common patterns of behaviour – '*moeurs*' in Tocqueville's terminology – which were values common to society as a whole that would find expression in the habit of association. Local autonomy, by providing all citizens with the opportunity to take part in public affairs, enables them to address issues by helping one another voluntarily, rather than through compulsion by a governing class. The key issue then becomes how these *moeurs* can be inculcated – or transplanted.

It was not clear when Tocqueville wrote *Democracy in America* whether the lessons he had drawn from his American experience had general application or whether they were a product of the particular circumstances of the time in the United States. It was also uncertain whether Tocqueville had actually got it right – his fieldwork had been selective (to put it kindly) and his assessment of the role of associations, which was central to his analysis, was mostly obtained at second hand and distinctly optimistic. There is no warrant for his assessment of their importance in the founding texts of the American republic (like *The Federalist Papers*) and some scepticism to be found there about the possible implications of some of the activities of associations as likely to promote 'mischiefs of faction' (Putnam 2000: 337).

As the century advanced, it seemed increasingly evident that in some important respects the American experience was exceptional, being the result of factors like:

- the fact that civil society, as initially established in New England, predated the appearance of the state in any developed form;
- the implications of the constitutional separation of church and state at the revolution;
- the dispersal of power to states and below within the federal system;
- the rise of mass political parties operating on what eventually became a universal (free male) franchise;
- the constitutional entrenchment of rights like freedom of speech.

None of these factors applied in Europe at the time at which Tocqueville was writing. At the same time, it's important not to overstress the differences: there are common Anglo-Saxon traditions in law and social philosophy (as we have already seen in Chapter 2) and much transatlantic transfer of experience, as for example about philanthropic enterprises conducted on a religious base. These connections remained close after the revolution and in some respects became closer towards the end of the nineteenth century.

Meanwhile, within the United States itself, there was a rapid growth in the density of associational life as the country came to terms with the vast territorial and economic growth of the second half of the nineteenth century and addressed the social and political challenges posed by the excesses of the robber baron capitalism of the 'Gilded Age' (Putnam 2000: 384–5).

Democracy in Europe

In Britain, the heyday of associations in the mid-nineteenth century (as described in Chapter 2) was not that of democracy, except in an exceptionally narrow definition of the term. An Englishman's cherished – and much celebrated – liberties were in practice tightly circumscribed. Indeed, the whole concept was suspect: democracy was not generally accepted as a legitimate form of government. Although the demands of the Chartists in the 1840s contained important elements that would subsequently be seen as democratic, even political radicals were careful to distance themselves from the advocacy of democracy as such. As the radical liberal John Bright once put it: 'I do not pretend myself to be a democrat. I never accepted that title and I believe those who knew me and spoke honestly of me never applied it to me' (quoted in Arblaster 1994: 46).

'Paternalism' remained a better description of a regime in which the bulk of the working class and all women were excluded from all political participation. John Stuart Mill, a great admirer of Tocqueville, is typical in his careful balancing of the arguments about representative democracy, though untypical in his advocacy of women's rights. His emphasis was on the need for checks and balances that would ensure that the general principle of democracy should be reconciled with the retention of power by an elite of the enlightened, since 'the best government (need it be said?) must be the government of the wisest and these must always be a few' (quoted in Arblaster 1994: 46).

The mid-Victorian political class liked to present England as the 'peaceable kingdom', by comparison both with its own past and the tumult of the revolutionary year of 1848 in Europe. This meant a society in which foreign influences, especially centralisation, are kept at bay and responsible citizens – so defined by their birth and ownership of property – play their traditional active role in local governance, especially the criminal justice system. A mid-century denunciation of these subversive trends is worth quoting, as typical:

> a foreign principle called the principle of centralisation is creeping in amongst us ... as if France and Prussia were fit examples for the imitation of Britain ... there are two vices inherent in the centralisation principle

which are quite sufficient to render it odious to all true Englishmen. In the first place, it must necessarily create a tribe of subordinate traders in government. [and second] it is by the principles alone of self-government by small communities that a nation can be brought to enjoy a vigorous moral health and its consequences – real prosperity. It is by the same principle alone that social feelings can be duly called into action, and that men, taken in the mass, can be noble, generous, intelligent and free. (Knight 1854)

The administrative reforms of the mid-Victorian period (to which Knight's polemic takes such vigorous objection) did indeed strengthen the power of the national state. But this was balanced by the gradual expansion of the franchise over the course of the century, which took place after anxious debate but largely by consent (women's suffrage being the partial exception) and the growth of a whole series of intermediate institutions standing between the central state and the citizen. Some of these were based on the churches, some were secular organisations created and run by the bourgeoisie (increasingly women); others were based in the skilled working class, evidence of their desire to manage their own affairs and their ability to do so (see Chapter 2).

Similar debates about the distribution and exercise of power were conducted within the boundaries of the different nation states, now entering the period of their maximum importance. Different patterns emerged across Europe and were modified over time. In France, for example, the end of monarchy with the fall of Louis Philippe doesn't spell an end of centralisation – the Jacobins of the brief Second Republic, like their predecessors, were equally centralisers, thereby demonstrating that belief in centralism was not necessarily incompatible with democratic principles. The Second Republic was succeeded in turn by the plebiscitary dictatorship of the Second Empire of Napoleon III (which marked the end of Tocqueville's own political career), showing that elections on a wider suffrage did not necessarily promote and sustain democratic institutions. The Third Republic that followed also displayed inherited republican suspicions about associations as intermediate bodies standing between state and citizen – legislation that conferred the right to associate on the French had to wait until the beginning of the twentieth century.

The rise of socialism

One common factor over the second half of the century was that all the various different regimes, in all developed industrial societies with the solitary exception of the United States (Lipset 1984) found themselves confronted by the socialist challenge. This eventually took the form of mass movements of the industrial working class, based on solidarity based on institutions formed in the workplace, promoted by class-based parties. These movements were divided between those who wished to overthrow the capitalist system and the state that supported it and substitute an entirely new system and those who envisaged capturing state power and using existing structures but for different ends (Sassoon 1996). Marx's influence predominates among the first group but was significant throughout European socialist parties (even in the milk and water version found in Britain), all of whom accept his theories of power and social relations being founded in ownership of the means of production (see Keane 1998b: 58).

Socialism in all its protean forms was internationalist, at least in conception and also recruited outside the working class. But one particular source of its growing strength that is especially relevant for present purpose lay in the alternative social institutions created around the party and reinforcing working-class solidarity. There had always been an element of utopianism about the socialist movement: we will be visiting some of the examples of this tendency, so brutally castigated by Marx, to invent ideal communities founded on principles of justice and peace and free from the conflicts of industrial society, in Chapter 7. However, on a more limited basis all the significant European socialist parties began to construct their own associational worlds within worlds. The most extreme case was the Social Democrats (SPD) in Germany with a whole series of newspapers, discussion groups, sporting and social organisations for both genders and all age groups; but the development was common to all European socialist parties – clarion cyclists and socialist Sunday schools in England, the *casa del popolo* in Italy. In the development of these institutions and the provision of services to fellow-socialists through mutual aid were the roots of the 'associational socialism' to which Stephen Yeo refers (see Chapter 2).

However, the main objective of these organisations was political education, of an overtly propagandist kind: they were founded not just in mutual trust, but also in mistrust of the existing institutions and values of the wider society. As Skocpol and Fiorina point out, democracy grew out of struggles between authority, in the shape of the state and their subjects and in that sense 'first liberal-democratic regimes and then democracies were a product of organised conflict and *distrust*. The energy to forge liberal and democratic regimes came when people crystallised their misgivings about concentrated or arbitrary political power. What is more, middling and subordinate groups had to organise, amass resources and assert themselves' (1998: 18).

In this process, John Keane argues, state and civil society were both engaged on a similar process of democratising themselves and organisations in the civil society space were developing their role as 'thorns in the side of the state' (1998: 15).

Twentieth-century rivals to democracy

The First World War shattered fondly felt illusions about a whole range of beliefs, in the inevitability of progress, in the possibility of international cooperation to resolve disputes between nations, in the unity of the working class across national boundaries. It also raised questions about democracy and the capacity of democratic regimes to cope with the extreme stresses generated by total war under conditions created by modern technology.

The legitimacy of mass parties as expressions of the popular will had also come under close scrutiny as a result of developments in electoral politics in the United States at city and national level and the growing success of socialist parties in Europe at the ballot box. A major theme of the new and largely Anglo-Saxon discipline of political science (Walter Lippman, Graham Wallas), was concern about the implications for these developments for government and society. Critics postulated the inevitability of distortion of democratic processes by manipulative elites – the 'iron law of oligarchy' detected by Robert Michels – the distorting effects of class interests and the eventual intrusion of corruption. Or as George Bernard Shaw put it in 1903:

we have yet to see the man who, having any practical experience of Proletarian democracy, has any belief in its capacity for solving great political problems, or even for doing ordinary parochial work intelligently and economically. Only under despotisms and oligarchies has the radical faith in 'universal suffrage' as a political panacea arisen. It withers the moment it is exposed to practical trial, because Democracy cannot rise above the level of the human material of which its voters are made. (Shaw 1948: 242)

During the decade after the First World War, the United States turned its back on Europe; and a succession of major European countries, starting with Russia and Italy, passed under different forms of totalitarian rule. In some, though not all of these cases, the precipitating factor was defeat; but as Mark Mazower comments 'democracy's shallow roots in Europe's political tradition helped to explain why anti-liberal regimes were installed with such ease and so little protest' (1999: 25). Although ideologically poles apart, the resulting regimes had a number of important characteristics in common: a stress on mechanical efficiency as an objective, achieved by centralisation of power in the state; the use of ruling (and sole) parties as vehicles to deliver the objectives laid down by the leadership at the centre and their use as a buttressing device for exercise of state power at all levels. Alongside this extreme version of centralisation, there was a corresponding emphasis on the cooption or destruction of all alternative forms of organisation extending well into the private sphere. As Lenin curtly put it: 'private life has been abolished' (cited in Shapiro 1972: 34). And in the new workers' state, the independent institutions of the working class had become redundant or mere husks; all passed under the control of the party.

The rationale for the introduction of these regimes rested in part on a form of bastard modernism, presenting the totalitarian state as the appropriate mechanism for managing complex modern societies with new technologies (compare Lenin's formula: 'socialism + electrification = Soviet power' and Mussolini's comment on the restoration of the Spanish republic: 'this is like reverting to gas lamps in an age of electricity'). This presumed efficiency was contrasted – and not just by its protagonists – with the ineffectiveness and potential (or actual) corruption of democracy.

The whole totalitarian edifice was reinforced by the cult of the leader, vastly amplified by use of the new media of mass communications (cinema, radio) as well as the press and more traditional mass meetings – the Nazis' Nuremberg rallies being the epitome of this approach. In this way, citizen and leader could be brought into a direct relationship: there was no need for intermediaries or interpreters. The resulting forms of organisation were consistent with market-type economic arrangements, but not with the possession of individual civil and political rights. Plebiscites under strictly controlled conditions were the only form of participation permitted, inevitably returning the ritual assent, usually by implausibly huge margins, although there is evidence that Hitler's popularity among Germans was genuine – and perhaps Stalin's in the USSR as large as well. Despite this superficial appearance of consent, these were subject, not citizen societies. The socialisation of the young, a prime objective of all such regimes, was specifically geared to securing their willing acceptance of that status.

The impact on local life and associations of the imposition of totalitarian regimes has been the focus of a number of studies; one of the best known is still William Sheridan Allen's account of the Nazi seizure of power in a small German town. This was followed by the incorporation of organisations of all kinds into a uniform National Socialist culture, making up a civil society of a kind, but not one that could be confidently taken as an expression of the wishes and preferences of the members of those organisations (Allen 1976). The process of takeover was guided by the principle that all organs of society at all levels and of every kind must reflect in their values and composition the domination of National Socialism ('*Gleichschaltung*'). As a result, the title, officers and committee members of all forms of organisation had to carry the imprimatur of the state, even including choral societies and bowling clubs (compare Putnam on team bowling as a resource for democracy). This led to the elimination of any potential focus for alternative views or activities, not as has sometimes been asserted by abolition, but by absorption. This was especially significant in the town in question which had previously had a strong social democratic tradition, nurtured at community level by a network of working-class welfare and recreational associations. These centres for class-based loyalty were replaced by developing an ostentatiously 'classless' culture and by creating new organisations specifically geared to indoctrination – most notoriously, the Hitler Youth.

The same pattern was repeated at national level, although some existing organisations survived, to be assimilated into the new National Socialist approach to social policy. This 'promoted the health of the national community at the same time as suppressing its international biological enemies' (Mazower 1999: 99). The history of the Red Cross – which continued to function as a mass organisation in Nazi Germany and whose leaders were complicit in the Final Solution – was a vivid illustration of the consequences of incorporation for values, even where standards were ostensibly set internationally (Moorehead 1999: 414ff).

The assize of democracy

What was the democratic response to the rapid growth of totalitarianism during the inter-war period? After the debacle of the great depression precipitated by the 1929 Wall Street crash, it was distinctly muted. Liberal capitalism appeared to have failed the basic tests of efficient delivery of increased wealth and effective exercise of responsibility to its citizens. In the demoralisation of the depression years of the early 1930s, many of the ideas that appealed were those associated with dictatorships (Stalin's Five Year Plans, subsequently imitated by the Nazis, are a case in point): one of the much-debated questions was whether these could be given a democratic gloss without impairing their effectiveness. Another was whether plural- ism and dispersal of power was consistent with effective means of dealing, first with economic problems (in particular mass unemploy- ment) and then with the imminent prospect of armed conflict with the dictatorships. A significant number of the intelligentsia on both sides of the Atlantic were prepared to toy, at least, with the notion that a disinterested elite, Mill's 'wisest people', under whatever title – a disciplined vanguard group, samurai, guardians, technocrats or slightly less ambitiously, an Economic General Staff – was required to deal with exceptional circumstances. (Much of this was utopian in form or aspiration and will be treated as such in Chapter 8).

The eventual recovery of the American economy under Roosevelt's New Deal suggested that a democracy could provide legitimate answers to the first question; the performance of the Anglo-American Allies in the Second World War when it eventu- ally broke out ultimately provided what could be presented as a response to the second. But although these outcomes provided what appear to be positive lessons for the argument about the effi- ciency of democracy there were questions that remained unresolved about the internal structure and balance of power within democratic societies. This would involve developing tools for managing the economy and polity, which were open and accountable, not techni- cal and closed; and creating systems that would involve associations outside the state in the public sphere, but without incorporating them. As Mazower puts it:

> The Second World War became a struggle to define the relationship between the community as a whole, the individual citizen and social policy, paving the way for the very different forms of welfare state that would emerge after 1945. (1999: 79)

War and resistance

Total war also set another test: how far could democratic forms and procedures survive in situations of extreme stress and what role could free associations play in that process? The history of resistance in German-occupied Europe during the Second World War provides some striking illustrations, once the accumulated overlay of myths and legends is discarded.

Occupation stripped off the carapace of civilisation. Although the German occupiers left some of the institutions of civil society in place, circumstances in most occupied countries in Europe accurately reproduced the Hobbesian situation of the individual confronted by an all-powerful Leviathan. The reaction of the vast majority of those who were able to do so was to retreat into the private world of the family and trusted immediate neighbours, unless or until they were forced out of it by abnormal events, like bombing, military action or hostage-taking. The issue for those not prepared to assent, even passively, to the New Order that German National Socialism sought to impose across Europe became one of weighing up private obligations against what could be conceived as wider citizen responsibilities or patriotic duty.

The dilemma for individuals could be particularly acute in those situations where the indigenous authorities collaborating with the occupiers represented a legitimate form of state power and citizen action had to take place not just outside but in opposition to the state. Here, the French example is especially interesting.

The military defeat of France was followed in 1940 by a change of regime. The German occupiers exercised direct control over a large part of northern France, including Paris; but a quasi-independent French government, the *État Français* (the so-called 'Vichy' state) ruled the rest of the country and retained some nominal authority outside this non-occupied 'Southern Zone'. Contrary to subsequent rhetorical claims, this regime was legitimate; power was properly ceded by its predecessor, the Third Republic and so exercised. Ambassadors were accredited to Vichy by (among others) the United States. However, in 1942 the remaining territory of metropolitan France was also occupied by the Germans and *de facto* though not *de jure* French civil authority ceased to function except in certain limited respects directly related to the maintenance of law and order (for which read the suppression of dissent and the increasingly significant resistance movement). Although recognised as a 'co-belligerent' by the Allies, de Gaulle's rival 'Free France' was not like other European governments that had gone into exile in Britain and still possessed the status of elected bodies. Its limited legitimacy rested on de Gaulle's own personality (and his brief tenure as a junior minister in 1940) and its civilian adherents in France caught in the field were treated as rebels against established authority and were at risk of being peremptorily shot.

A choice of loyalties in these circumstances carried drastic consequences. The civil society space had been drastically depopulated: peaceful passive resistance was no longer an option. Throughout Occupied Europe, any attempts at strikes or demonstrations were suppressed by the occupiers with exemplary force. Despite much subsequent myth-making, those who chose the alternative path of active clandestine resistance were always a small minority, although their numbers grew dramatically as the likely outcome of the war became clearer after 1943. The networks (in France, *réseaux*) that were established were small groupings with widely divergent ideologies and objectives, heavily dependent logistically on support provided from outside France by various organisations in England, often with competing objectives. Recruitment and maintenance of these groups was a hazardous business; they were frequently penetrated and their members betrayed to the Vichy authorities or the Gestapo, with fatal consequences. In the last phase after the Allied invasion of metropolitan France in 1944 both parties, the collaborationist French authorities through their militia (the *milice*) acting in collusion with but independently from the German occupying forces, and the resistance in its various rival forms, engaged in a series of high profile murders mainly designed to warn the civilian population of the consequences of adherence to the other side. The intended lesson was that to emerge from the private world and engage in these activities was to risk not just your own lives but those of your family and members of your community.

'The Occupation' says its historian Ian Ousby 'dispersed society, divided it, set it so profoundly at odds with itself as to endanger the very notion of society. It created both the circumstances and the need for people to fall back on, to build their loyalties at the microcosmic levels. So France became a country of factions split into smaller factions and splintered again into tiny fragments, each passionate in its solidarity with itself, passionate in its warfare with the rest' (1999: 258).

There were broadly similar events at the same time in northern Italy, where the Germans had installed a puppet fascist regime, the Republic of Salo, vividly described by Italo Calvino in his early novel *The Path to the Nest of Spiders.*

The nature of the experience of resistance also has important implications for debates about trust and the way in which relationships develop and extend in semi-clandestine circumstances through different forms of organisation. Most accounts of resistance stress heroism exemplified in specific episodes: sabotage, assassination, or passing fugitives along the escape lines which brought back many allied airmen from occupied Europe – what has been called 'silk-and-cyanide' resistance: parachuting in with the suicide pill as a last resort to avoid capture. This has almost always been expressed in what H. R. Kedward (1999) calls 'the discourse of personality', anecdotes that focus on the heroic male agent with the blazing sten gun, although there are signs that this is changing, as the essential role played day to day by women secures greater recognition. Accounts dwell less often on the more mundane side of organising a life lived in secrecy – which means of necessity *not* living in what a later generation of those resisting totalitarian government called 'truth'.

An exception is the account of the Norwegian underground provided by a sociologist who was himself an active participant, Vilheim Aubert. His description of the culture of resistance, with its own values, hierarchies and structures and cultivation of particular skills is especially valuable in stressing the extent to which some of the normal rules (*moeurs*) of a developed society had to be inverted in order to cope with exceptional circumstances. Deception becomes a virtue, not a vice: suspicion a life-saving not a demeaning quality; ordinary social networks a potential threat, not a reinforcement or resource. In particular, his account shows how parsimoniously trust had to be extended, given the extreme penalty attached to errors of judgement, and the forms in which trust was eventually expressed (Rumpelstiltskin-like, revealing one's real name becomes the final badge of confidence). The extreme test of such trust came after capture and imprisonment: in all the European resistance movements there are well-authenticated stories both of great bravery (fortitude under torture to the point of death) and of gross betrayal. The solidarity of small groups formed under conditions of extreme danger was reflected in attitudes towards outsiders, who were seen as incapable of understanding or adequately recognising the stresses under which resistance workers operated. These attitudes lingered long after the war. After liberation, active participants in the Norwegian underground refused all state decorations.

Because the Allies won the war, much of this activity was sanctified in retrospect (and sanitised too). Certainly, behaviour under the extreme stresses encountered in these circumstances tells us a good deal about courage and something about our theme of civic virtue as acceptance of collective responsibility. But the cloak of resistance also covered deviant behaviour, sometimes ideologically fuelled, sometimes simply undertaken for its own sake. Armed resistance was almost always associated with nationalist objectives expressed in terms of patriotic rhetoric, though there were some exceptions among the Communists, who came late to resistance but were almost everywhere among its most effective and ruthless members.

There was also a great deal of self-dramatisation: reckless behaviour by self-appointed leaders, young men careless of the consequences of their actions for the rest of the civilian population. (As de Gaulle commented ironically, confronted by a group of these self-confident youths, adorned with self-awarded military titles: *'tant de colonels!'* – 'what a lot of colonels'.) The claims asserted by active resisters operating outside the scope of the rule of law to act purely on the basis of their own judgement of what was necessary in exceptional circumstances were and are open to abuse. For these issues continue to resonate, as for example in the more recent activities of the Irish Republican Army, a fraction from which once collaborated with the Nazis (Coogan 1995), who have also justified their acts of terror against the civilian population by rejecting the legitimacy of the state they confront. (They also use the term 'volunteer' to describe the active participants in their war.) Nelson Mandela, too, has provided a vivid description of his period 'underground', before his long imprisonment, when he eventually decided to abandon passive resistance and take part in an armed struggle against the apartheid state – a struggle which also produced casualties among the civilian population for which the African National Congress eventually had to account before the post-apartheid Truth and Reconciliation Commission.

Reconnecting the citizen and the state

The western victor nations attached immense symbolic significance to democracy as a distinguishing principle in their struggle (glossing over the inconvenient question of the internal arrangements in the Soviet Union) and displayed this in practical form in commitment to promoting the notion of civil engagement. This led to an emphasis on the legitimacy of organisation outside the state as one cardinal principle; and the extension of citizen rights from the classic civil and political forms, now belatedly achieved in France by the extension of the franchise at the end of the war to women, to social rights. As Mazower comments: 'Hitler's defeat would allow democracy to root itself once more in European life, through a new sense of social solidarity and national cohesion' (1999: 79). All this was reflected in the principles laid down in a variety of international protocols and conventions drawn up after the war and the practices of the Allied regimes in occupied Germany – the differences that rapidly opened up between the Soviet-occupied East zone and Anglo-Franco-American West zone (described in Annan 1995).

The installation throughout Western Europe in broadly similar forms of the Keynesian Welfare State had major implications for civil society, as the state took on the main responsibility for discharging a wider range of functions, in pursuit of 'third generation' social rights to employment and social provision. This had apparently resolved the pre-war conundrum of combining efficiency and democratic accountability. The post-war settlement had critics to the left, who argued that the mixed economy provided insufficient guarantee of equitable delivery of goods and services, the state being seen as the only competent guarantor – and provider. On the right the Hayekian view held that any form of state intervention through redistributive planning of resources was *ipso facto* tyrannical. But by the early fifties the debate was apparently resolved in favour of the mixed economy and state-led welfare systems, in which social democratic governments played a leading role. Associations were accepted as participants in the system but in a subordinate capacity, operating within the framework of state direction – explicitly, in the German and Southern European case by subsidiarity – the allocation downwards to third-sector bodies of responsibility for service delivery. Meanwhile, in East and Central Europe, a different type of regime had been forcibly installed which had no place for independent associations and to which a large part of the local population eventually responded by retreating into private life (see Chapter 5; Mazower 1999).

The terrain as it had emerged from the post-war settlement was surveyed by Almond and Verba in their massive comparative study, *The Civic Culture* (1965). The sharp distinction they drew between totalitarian and democratic regimes hinges on the extent of civic participation. The particular form that participation takes, they suggest, depends on the 'civic culture' of a society. Such a culture, in their definition, 'is a political culture in which attitudes favourable to participation play a major role...but so do such nonpolitical attitudes as trust in other people and social participation in general' (1965: 30).

The comparisons Almond and Verba draw between Anglo-Saxon and other democracies stress the close overlap in the former of social and political activity, a lack of partisan fragmentation, and what they call the 'capillary structure' of advanced democracies (1965: 105). They see a sharp contrast with the culture in Italy (characterised by chronic mistrust) and West Germany (where individuals still appeared to be inhibited from full participation). They describe the development of civic culture over time and space as a dynamic process, from 'parochial' societies to 'subject' and then to fully participant ones. These different clusters of attitudes and behaviour can still coexist within a single society; however, they do not attempt to break down the detailed patterns they are describing below national level (so no direct comparison is possible with Robert Putnam, whose analysis depends on contrasts within a single nation state).

Finally, they refer to 'latent political functions' performed by voluntary associations which are necessary for a 'balanced' political culture. These functions include providing the opportunity for their members to acquire a practical competence. As the authors summarise the position:

> In all nations, on both levels of education (*high and low*) those who are members of a nonpolitical organisation are more likely to feel subjectively competent than those who belong to no organisation. This, then, appears to confirm the fact that latent political functions are performed by voluntary associations, whether these organisations are explicitly political or not. (1965: 254–5)

The argument is further developed by Jürgen Habermas on his discussion of the nature of the public sphere. Habermas's account of how values and norms (*moeurs*) are sustained in the arena in which political strategies are developed and policies derived lays particular emphasis on the role of the media, in forming and transmitting public opinion and helping to provide the fora in which democratic political judgements can be reached and then conveyed. In this way, the public sphere generates communicative power, which in a modern democracy can be seen as parallel to administrative and economic power.

This can be clearly demonstrated in relation to other forms of major crisis – civilian emergencies produced by earthquake, flood or famine and the different forms of response they evoke. Often, the spontaneous response of local communities is most effective in addressing immediate needs: but the extent of involvement of various official agencies and of large charities is often determined by the extent of publicity the episode has generated. This shows the impact of television, in particular, in the late twentieth century in communicating images of disaster and promoting active responses – but not necessarily always in the most helpful form.

Tocqueville revisited: the associative alternative

By the early 1970s, the Keynesian Welfare State, which had functioned efficiently for almost thirty years by guaranteeing full employment and providing acceptable minimum levels of social security, had begun to lose credibility and increasingly came to be seen as what right-wing critics called 'the future that doesn't work'. Especially after the impact of OPEC's decision to quadruple the oil price, full employment could no longer be guaranteed by the tools of domestic demand management. State agencies and large bureaucracies were seen as failing to deliver efficiently; democratic institutions (for example, parliaments) as suffering from chronic overload. Electoral legitimacy was being withheld; parties became more fragile and were no longer functioning effectively as agencies for socialising into politics or to sweep up a range of issues and concerns (Keane 1998b: 126). Contemporary analyses suggested that:

> Weakening confidence in government leaders and political institutions in Western Europe, the United States and Japan was due to increasing demands from pressure groups and new social movements, the rise of protest demonstrations and civil disobedience. More polarised ideological and issue cleavages, combined with the apparent incapacity of national governments to mitigate the consequences of the international economic recession ... Nineteenth century institutions of representative democracy seemed unable to cope with twentieth century demands. (Norris 1999: 4)

These developments provoked much debate about 'rolling back the frontiers of the state'. Must the failures now diagnosed (and increasingly widely accepted) mean that the state should now withdraw from many of the functions that it had taken on, in the economic and social spheres and surrender these functions to the market, in which public goods could from now on simply be purchased? Or could the legitimacy of the public sphere be re-established by decentralising functions to local control, 'autogestion' as it came to be called on the French left? Was there another alternative, lying between the centralised state and the unconstrained market? If so, how could it be implemented, in such a way as to retain democratic legitimacy but provide efficient alternative means of delivering essential services and by whom? Could public goods still be delivered outside the market, but by different forms of agency?

These arguments have been systematically addressed in Paul Hirst's *Associative Democracy* (1994). Essentially, his argument is that the political system can best be revitalised by active promotion of civil engagement below the level of the nation state and the creation of new institutional forms (and revival of old ones) to perform the functions previously undertaken by the state – essentially, voluntary associations, especially those functioning through mutual aid. The crucial step is construction of an alternative 'architecture of associationalism', in which 'as many of the affairs of society as possible are managed by voluntary and democratically self-governing associations' (19). This implies at the least a coordinating function for the residual state and a common set of values that permeate the public sphere, but leaves on one side the problem of differential distribution of power and the capacity or willingness to act. This is illustrated by the crucial question of provision of welfare, on which Hirst argues that the free exercise of choice through participation in an association offers the greater reward of empowerment, rather than the illusory hope of equality of outcomes (170). He concludes:

> The civic culture of an associationalist society will have a different logic from that of democratic republicanism, one closer to liberalism in its giving primacy to an individual's right and capacity to choose. An associationalist welfare state would set common standards, it would enforce a thin but strong morality based on an ethics of freedom. (Hirst 1994: 202)

But how can this common morality – free *moeurs*, in Tocqueville's terms, however thin – be inculcated and sustained? As we saw in the previous chapter, some communitarians argue, with Etzioni, for communities to act as the guardians of morals, so that: 'they define what a society considers virtuous, provide approbation for those who live up to those definitions, and censor (sic) those who do not, thus reducing the need for policing' (2000a : 14).

Others, like Elizabeth Frazer, whose critique Etzioni is here attempting to meet, find this approach deficient in not providing explicit mechanisms for debate, choice and consent or safeguards for minority rights.

The gymnasium of democracy?

The original Tocquevillian idea of *moeurs* developed in democratic discourse has been immensely influential; and evidence to support it has been sought and often found in a whole variety of different situations. In recent times, the most often cited is probably Robert Putnam's analysis (for which see Chapter 3, above). The crucial element in the case that he makes for the importance of non-political activity is that actions undertaken outside the public sphere are nonetheless critical in creating the potential for democratic practice. In *Making Democracy Work*, he argues that:

> when individuals belong to 'cross-cutting' groups with diverse goals and members their attitudes will tend to moderate as a result of group interaction and cross-pressures. These effects, it is worth noting, do not require that the manifest purpose of the association be political. Taking part in a choral society or a bird-watching club can teach self-discipline and an appreciation for the joys of successful collaboration. (90)

But is this invariably so? As we saw in Chapter 3 (Bishop and Hoggett 1986: *passim*) many of those involved in these activities neither have nor seek any overt connection with a wider public sphere.

And if, in particular times and circumstances (Athens in the fifth century BC, Renaissance city states, nineteenth-century New England, twentieth-century northern Italy) civic participation was the rule, is that any longer the case? The significance of Putnam's reference to bowling is not that cultural changes have caused bowling as an activity to cease altogether or even decline, but that organised involvement in competitive leagues is no longer as significant as it once was: bowling has ceased to be a social activity and become a solitary exercise in personal skill. In the same way, in many western countries the (literal) gymnasium has become a fitness centre for individual body maintenance, not an arena for competitive games or training for team contests.

Putnam's extended portrait of the decline of civic America rests heavily on the notion of the moral value of participation. He deplores the development of politics without social capital, which he describes as 'politics at a distance' and the weaknesses of virtual organisations 'whose members never meet' (2000: 63).

Some reasons why non-political participation might be in decline in advanced western societies would include socio-demographic factors like higher female participation in the work force leaving less time to spare; or longer working hours generally. Other suspects include: shrinking of blue-collar employment and loss of membership of traditional working-class associations, like trades unions; mass communications and their impact on the content and manner of debate in the public sphere, becoming remote to the point of irrelevance (Habermas); excessive amounts of time spent on viewing television (Putnam); loss of civility in argument and in willingness to accept adverse outcomes in debate (Etzioni); inter-generational change: the approaching demise of the 'civic generation' born between 1910 and 1940 (Putnam again); 'post-materialism and extreme individualism' (Inglehart): lack of any need for commonality in an internet society which no longer requires physical proximity for intimacy; and the defection of the elites, sometimes to the point of literal departure to separate gated communities (Lasch). For Putnam himself, this is a case of 'Murder on the Orient Express', Agatha Christie-style: all the suspects are guilty (2000: 184).

Politics and the future of citizenship

Has the civic culture frayed beyond repair under these new pressures? The collection assembled by Pippa Norris under the title *Critical Citizens* (1999) and drawing on a number of international panel studies provides some evidence to support that proposition. In his essay, Russell Dalton summarises the situation as follows:

> We find that citizens have grown more distant from political parties, more critical of political institutions, and less positive toward government – this points to fundamental changes in the political orientation

of democratic publics over the past generation. The decline in political trust is most dramatic for evaluations of politicians and political elites in general. The deference to authority that was once common in many Western democracies has partially been replaced by public scepticism of elites. Feelings of mistrust have gradually broadened to include evaluations of the political regime and political institutions. (1999: 76)

This can be partly explained by the evolution of a 'post-materialist world view ' which emphasises self-expression rather than deference to authority (Inglehart, 1999: 242).

One response to what is often perceived as a decline in the stock of civic virtue has been to locate the problem in a crisis of citizenship and to deploy arguments for government intervention through a programme of civic education, as the Speaker's Commission on Citizenship (1990) argued for the United Kingdom and as Putnam proposes for the United States. Another is to revisit the issue of trust. Ken Newton argues in the Norris collection that 'the nature of social trust may be shifting from personal, particular or thick trust to a more impersonal, general or thin trust of an abstract nature'.

He adds:

> The evidence suggests that while membership of voluntary associations has some importance for the creation of social trust, their influence is generally weak, though not trivial. Social trust is most strongly expressed, not by members of voluntary associations, or even by their most active members, but by the winners in society, insofar as it correlates most strongly with education, satisfaction with life, income, class and race. For that matter social trust is the prerogative of the winners in the world. (1999: 85)

And the evidence he assembled from the World Values survey suggests that the role of social trust and participation in non-political associations is in any case likely to be only of marginal significance in producing political trust (Newton in Norris 1999: 184).

Sidney Verba, revisiting the civic culture thirty years later, but this time only within the United States, confirms that there is now (1995) an increasing class bias in participation, partly due to the increased weaknesses of traditional blue-collar organisations, like trades unions and among some ethnic groups. The solitary compensating factor is the role of religion, which provides the only truly democratic arena where political skills can be developed (and this only for some denominations). As a result, equality of outcome is not to be expected in the public sphere, as long as institutional involvement, knowledge and skills generates greater political activity. For

> experiences in the family, at school, and in the workplace and citizens' voluntary affiliations with non-political associations and religious institutions – a function of their socially structured circumstances and the constrained choices they make about their lives – affect the stockpile of time, money and civic skills available for politics. (Verba, Schlozman and Brady 1995: 271)

These findings have some important implications: chiefly, that although there is not much remaining of the gender gap which Almond and Verba found thirty years earlier, an ethnic gulf is opening up. And as a result 'the public's voice is often low, sometimes clear but rarely equal' (1995: 509). But Verba and colleagues also point to a continued vitality in civic voluntarism; a willingness to participate in political processes whether the commitment of time and money is strictly rational or not, in terms of realistic expectations about rewards. However, this willingness is modified by the lack of salience of specifically political issues for most Americans (1995: 79).

In considering these findings, we need to take account of a certain amount of continuing American exceptionalism, not just because of the far higher rate of participation in religious activities, which is the outstanding difference between the United States and other western democracies, but also the weaker role of political parties and their lack of a class base. Pippa Norris concludes that:

> One plausible view is that channels of political participation may be evolving rather than declining, if people are becoming more active in new ways. Compared with earlier decades, by the end of the century American citizens may not be joining the Elks or striking in trade unions or demonstrating about civil rights, any more than they are hula-hooping or watching sputnik or going to discos. But they may be engaging in civic life by recycling garbage, mobilizing on the internet, and volunteering at women's shelters or AIDS hospices. (1999: 217)

And she adds that similar changing patterns of civic engagement may be found in many western democracies where new social movements are challenging the political order. So in the longer term, globalism may ensure that American values do eventually become internationally dominant, but those will not be the 'old-fashioned' ones of class or political ideology. And where America also leads, in the sharp fall in participation in the electoral process itself – voting and active involvement in campaigning – other democracies also appear to be following. (In 2000, the closest Presidential election for a quarter of a century drew less than half the electorate in the United States to the polls). Yet if democracy is to be sustained, encouraging participation in non-political associations may not always be the best way to do it – and social trust generated outside the political arena does not appear to be readily transferable into it. Here, Robert Putnam's programme for civic re-engagement, which ends with a rhetorical flourish by inviting Americans to go on more picnics together, seems more than a touch naive.

Towards good governance?

One last issue remains to be considered: whether or not associations have a function in promoting democracy, does democracy provide a model of organisation for associations themselves? Their credibility, after all, does depend – to some extent at least – on providing a convincing representation in their own actions of democratic values.

The associational model tends to brush aside the issue of how far the customs and practices of associations themselves are democratic: in Hirst's account their external functions are differentiated but not their internal operating styles. Yet more recent developments, notably the rise of environmental bodies, have brought precisely this issue into sharp perspective. Selle and Stromsnes (1997) have argued that the way in which voluntary organisations conceive and execute their external role is inseparable from their composition and constitution. Organisations, they propose, 'may be distinguished in terms of whether they view members as a resource or a problem'; and they contrast traditional Norwegian associations, based on mass mobilisation and active membership with new-style issue-based organisations drawing on the passive support of dues-paying subscribers. The latter style may be more appropriate to modern conditions but it shapes not just the organisational form of the organisation (essentially non-participative) but its mission and the ways in which it is undertaken.

Secrecy and lack of direct accountability are often found among campaigning organisations which have to be able to conduct their campaigns on the basis of surprise – media-friendly events, like the carefully crafted direct action protests staged by Greenpeace or (less theatrically) Friends of the Earth which I will revisit in Chapter 6. So are the highly personalised forms of leadership that provide a convenient focus for media attention and the style (often drawn from business models) in which power is seen to be exercised. The lessons that are drawn by those involved from intensive participation in some types of organisation can often be not democratic but the habits of oligarchy or even despotism.

When challenged on these issues, some voluntary associations will respond by asserting that their activities represent participatory democracy in contradistinction to representative democracy with its manifest failure to engage the majority of citizens. This response might be more convincing if associations were able to demonstrate an active involvement of their membership not just in tasks like fund raising but in the setting of the organisation's own priorities. In my own experience, most voluntary organisations fail that test: the empty ritual of the Annual General Meeting is no substitute for engagement in defining positions on major public policies and strategies for addressing them.

So we return to the debates visited earlier, about the effectiveness of government and the function of associations as part of the democratic process. Andrew Green comments that: 'any conception of civil society and its role in democracy must incorporate a more sophisticated understanding of policy making' (1999: 10). This requires an analysis of the precise role that bodies operating outside the state can expect to play in framing policies and the form that interactions in the public sphere between those bodies and the state in its various manifestations have taken. Here, a distinction has to be drawn between lobbies, pressure groups and voluntary associations and different forms of activity, access and influence that can be secured.

Lester Salamon (1993) has taken an agnostic view of the interactions between voluntary associations and democracy. In his analysis, there is an imperfect and partial connection between the two, and the evidence will support a variety of rival propositions – an essential connection, a merely contingent one or outright opposition between the two. Much depends on the definitions employed, both of democracy and of the 'non-profit' sector. In different situations, voluntary associations of various kinds can help to facilitate or even implement the common will. Alternatively some of their interventions can obstruct its operation, or their activities can simply be marginal or irrelevant. But where the state's actions are intruding on the civic space, then certain associations in some circumstances can provide an essential counterbalancing element.

So, finally, is democracy a necessary condition for the existence of 'authentic' associations, or can they survive without a framework of law and citizen rights? And does democracy, in turn, require associations? Is the 'capillary' role of associations (as Almond and Verba call it) an essential factor in nourishing a healthy public sphere, bearing with it a refreshing trickle of information, messages about preferences and values, or merely decorative: or possibly even a potential obstruction to the efficient conduct of public business? And is liberty always and in any given circumstances an asset too priceless to be compromised in any way? A subject's duty to associate in totalitarian regimes becomes a right of citizens in democracies, but not an obligation. Those who have been personally involved in the transition from the status of subject to that of citizen may well have different attitudes to those who have been able to take the environment of democracy for granted. Which is why the next chapter will explore some aspects of post-war experience in East and Central Europe as an illustration of these and other questions about the nature of civil society.

Conclusion

In this chapter, I have set out to explore how far political engagement is an activity necessary to the functioning of a healthy civil society. The introduction and survival of democratic forms of governance provide the test bed, showing how the individual concept of civic virtue can mesh with a collective notion of the common good and be translated into action that can be sustained by formal associations operating at all levels in the civil society space.

As illustrations to support the argument, I have sketched the stages through which democracy has become established as a form of governance, the role played by associational activity in that process and the challenges that it has faced. In the twentieth century, democracy has shown both its weaknesses and its strengths, specifically in seeing off successive rivals in wars both hot and cold. In doing so, there has been a significant change of form and function, in which a crucial element has been the shifting relations between citizen and state and the ways in which relationships have been mediated through intermediate bodies of different kinds.

By the end of the century, concerns have begun to be felt about the continuing level of commitment to democracy and the weakening or even disappearance of crucial forms of associational activity, some of it related to economic, social and demographic change, others to a presumed shift in values, a loss of civic virtue.

The implications of these changes are not yet clear and the significance of some of them is contested: one test of the vitality of the concept of democracy and the importance of the part played by associations lies in the origins and outcome of the dramatic changes that occurred in the late 1980s in the former state socialist countries – the subject of the next chapter.

CHAPTER 5

Civil Society as Revolution?

There is a constant search for something that is neither a society of atomized individuals nor bureaucratic state. History has shown innumerable times that no path leads there, but rather that freedom, political pluralism and the market are the best tools to create a just, proper and solidaristic society. This conviction has driven my four-year polemic in favor of the market alone, of a standard system of political parties without national or civic movements, and, based in the same logic, has also directed my actions to create a society of free citizens, rather than the misleading idea of a so-called 'civil society'. (Vaclav Klaus, former Prime Minister of the Czech Republic, speaking in 1995, quoted by M. Potucek in *Voluntas*, June 2000)

Context: the cow that walked away

In 1989, the world changed fundamentally in East and Central Europe. After forty years of regimented state socialism, 'we, the people' peacefully overturned, in succession, all the structures of 'actually existing socialism', which ceased to exist with barely a struggle. The images that endure from that astonishing period underline how utterly unpredictable – incongruous, even – the events of those weeks seemed at the time. There were the huge crowds of East Germans jammed into the grounds of embassies in Budapest and Prague, their abandoned Trabis lining the roads; the first non-Communist premier of an eastern bloc country, Poland, taking his seat on the government benches of the Sjem; Vaclav Havel, translated in one dizzy leap from outcast dissident to President, walking out in trousers half an inch too short to meet visiting dignitaries at Prague airport. Most famously of all, the jubilant groups of young people hacking away with pickaxes, undisturbed, at the wall that had divided Berlin for their entire lifetimes.

These events were especially dramatic for the generation that had lived through the cold war in their overturning of fixed expectations about the future both inside and outside the system. As Andras Torok, Hungarian dissident (and future head of the National Cultural Fund) put it, it was as if a vast cow had been sitting on the meadow that was his country for half a lifetime, its imprint so deep that many people thought it had turned into solid rock: then, suddenly, 'the cow got up and slowly walked away' (1999).

But why should these events, however dramatic, be especially relevant for the theme of the present undertaking? Because they tested in a uniquely visible form the significance of civil society as a shaping force and the role of civic associations both in the transformation itself and in the post-transformation processes.

It has often been suggested (see Chapter 1) that the existence of the institutions of a free society (the rule of law, democracy, a free press and the market) is an indispensible precondition for the creation and subsequent vitality of civil society, in any meaningful sense. However, Anheier and Seibel in their discussion of the transformation and its significance have argued the opposite case: that the 'third sector' played an indispensible role in these events, suggesting that civil society doesn't appear as a consequence of the existence of these institutions but is a proximate cause of their creation. Precisely because the changes in East and Central Europe took place so swiftly and without apparent warning they should provide an especially good test of the validity of these rival arguments.

But before exploring them in any depth it is worth remembering that what took place in East and Central Europe at the end of the 1980s was not unique, even in the history of post-war Europe. There is a precedent, in the peaceful end of the southern European dictatorships – Portugal and Spain – a decade earlier. These events and the issues around the transition to democracy there and the creation of new institutions after a period of totalitarian rule of similar length have already been largely forgotten. This may perhaps be because of a residual sense of guilt in western countries that colluded with the continuation of fascist dictatorships in those countries after the end of the Second World War (supposedly fought to rid the world of fascism).

Perhaps more important, the cases of individual countries within East and Central Europe itself, Poland, Hungary and Czechoslovakia (as it then was), are different. The similarities are important and some generalisations fruitful; but their histories diverge in fundamental ways. In particular, it is important to grasp that pre-communist experience remains relevant – after all, it falls well within the lifetime of many still alive. Moreover, the nature of the communist regimes in different countries of the eastern bloc and their willingness to tolerate any deviation from the Soviet-derived model of state socialism differed substantially both between those countries and over time within them. Repression of dissent was more systematic after 1968 in Czechoslovakia and East Germany and more confrontational, at least latterly, in Poland than it was in the Hungarian case. There, the customary view that none of the dictatorships would tolerate any independent association and suppressed all attempts to create them, so that dissenters could only associate in secret, by word of mouth and samizdat, needs some modification.

The Hungarian example

Even the casual visitor to Hungary speedily becomes conscious of the burden of the past. To the inattentive ear, Hungarian history is easily reduced to a litany of disasters, oppression, occupations and military defeats (invariably heroic). Such an impression does not do justice to the fifty years of the dual monarchy, from the Compromise of 1867 with Austria that created it to the collapse of the Austro-Hungarian Empire after defeat in the First World War. Those years shaped Budapest in its modern form – the 'Chicago of Central Europe', with a rapidly expanding economy and public buildings to match and a vibrant intellectual life.

But the sense of grievance still lingers in the 'Trianon syndrome': expressed in visible representations of the historic lands of the Crown of Hungary lost by that Treaty after the end of the First World War. ('No, no, never!' was the official slogan of public rejection plastered over public places during the inter-war period). One legacy of this grievance was Hungary's participation in a further world war, again on the losing side. Russian occupying troops were a constantly visible reminder of that outcome and the fate of the 1956 rising against them an illustration of what would happen if cold war realities were not accepted. The cold war is over now and lost territories and 'separated brethren' are still hankered after; maps, posters, postcards and lectures in guidebooks press a case that some politicians are still prepared to take up. Other distinctive factors that need to be taken into account are the dominance of the capital, Budapest, in a small country and the occasional strong reactions against that dominance; and the communication barrier presented by language. (Hungarian usually proves almost impenetrable to all but exceptionally gifted linguists, and Hungarians of an older generation have reciprocal difficulties in coping with the new lingua franca of the region, business American).

But from the most brutal of all repressions in the Soviet satellite states, the crushing by Soviet tanks of the 1956 revolution, there eventually emerged, under Janos Kadar, installed by the Soviet Union as their compliant instrument, a unique form of compromise. This was clearly not a free society (it lacked plural political institutions, rule of law or a free press) but not a straightforward command economy or police state either.

The economy was part-modernised in the conventional state socialist sense, with the customary emphasis on heavy industry and the elite status of workers in it. It was subject until 1968 to the heavy hand of central planning and incorporated into the regional planning mechanisms of COMECON (the state socialist equivalent of the Common Market, with membership of all Central and East European countries in the Soviet bloc). But after 1968 the system was significantly modified, with the introduction of the liberalised New Economic Mechanism (NEM). The welfare system provided a basic level of care at nominal cost for the whole population but on terms that were ideologically loaded: poverty and unemployment could not and therefore did not exist under socialism: participation by citizens in planning or delivery of services was redundant and the concept of social work subversive. Whether, in sum, this system constituted modernity, in a Western European sense, has subsequently been much debated. The outcome of those debates can be summarised as being that it did, but in a distorted form.

As a result, to put it in very crude summary terms, in Hungary from the 1970s onwards there were spaces within the system left (or in some cases created) by this distorted form of modernisation. How were they filled?

Not by 'resistance' in the conventional Second World War model, discussed in the previous chapter. The legacy of 1956 was not sabotage in that sense – 'silk and cyanide', planting explosives on clandestine instructions from the BBC. There had been martyrs, and in due time their memory would be celebrated – for example, in the rather touching Imre Nagy memorial in central Budapest, with his trademark umbrella. And money from the Hungarian diaspora helped to keep some lines of communication open from the outside.

Other outsiders helped in this process: left-wing intellectuals from all over the world made the journey to Hungary, for a mixture of reasons: solidarity, remorse or simple curiosity. Researchers interested in the social and economic problems of the eastern bloc were frequent visitors; and some cultural products from the West, ranging from the plays of Sartre and Osborne to the music of the Beatles became available from the late 1960s onwards.

Nevertheless, Zsuzsa Ferge has commented that at this point: 'Totalitarianism adversely affected spontaneous micro-solidarities and atomised society by confining freedom to the innermost private sphere (if at all)' (quoted in Szaki 1999: 153). Most civil associations and foundations, which had a considerable presence in social policy in the inter-war years, had been abruptly closed down after the change of regime; from 1946 a series of regulations restricted the range to activities to 'social associations which qualified as politically innocuous' (Szeman and Harsanyi 2000).

Moreover, there was a lack in Hungary of other independent institutions that might provide a common space in which networks could form, as the Catholic Church had done in Poland. As Vajda and Kuti put it:

> Hungarian churches traditionally curried favour with the government. The rest of their credibility was lost when they were ready to cooperate with communist authorities. In contrast with their Polish counterparts, Hungarian citizens did not have an 'oppositional' Church which would have preserved some basic values and would have represented and protected their interests'. (2000: 158)

However, there were other channels into which resentment towards the occupiers and the Hungarian state socialist regime could flow and exploration of alternatives take place. If, to use Albert Hirschman's terms (see Chapter 1), the *exit* option was not a realistic alternative and *loyalty* was unthinkable, there were other ways in which *voice* could be heard.

One especially important development after 1968 was that the economic reform (NEM) provided scope for independent economic initiatives by small businessmen outside the official, planned economy (hence known as the 'second economy'). By the end of the following decade, there was

- scope for economic enterprise, especially after 1982, when it became easier, in Anheier and Seibel's terms, to take up 'the challenge of quasi-entrepreneurism' and
- some spaces of a different kind – for example, that occupied by what Torok calls 'egghead' intellectuals.

In style of operation, these come across like the 'internal exiles' among the Tsarist intelligentsia crossed with western dropouts (class of 1968, frozen in time) but with a distinctive Hungarian flavour:

> In this slightly cruel, utterly frustrating but only mildly totalitarian society almost everything was hazy and dreamlike; not only books but life in general was cheap ... political pressure forced eggheads to become members of a very close-knit society, whose members were going to live a life without any real responsibilities outside the family or their own spiritual circle. A critical spirit became one of their fortes, an uncompromising, seeming easygoing political spirit ... The typical egghead had some small job at a publisher or at a university or one or other think-tank of the academy of sciences or a theatre, or another language school but was also involved in some other odd job – like translating a long book of social science for some publisher (and many eggheads were involved in the underground press from the early 1980s on). (Torok 1999: 226–7)

Many of these 'long books' were in fact the products of western social scientists, which had a far-reaching influence on how Hungarian intellectuals, students and some politicians analysed and interpreted social problems and tried to develop alternative strategies. In this vein, Eva Kuti has described those intellectuals and professionals who were neither dissidents nor supporters of the regime:

> They did not organise (but sometimes participated in) manifestations, did not produce (though read) *samizdat* literature, did not revolt, but their everyday activities gradually undermined the system. These were the intellectuals who (together with the reform wing of the communist elite) developed the concept of the economic reform in the 1960s, introduced the reform in 1968, created thousands of quasi-market units within the state-run companies and even public institutions developed a variety of mechanisms for agricultural entrepreneurship, organised cultural events of (mainly hidden) oppositional spirit, established

seemingly neutral voluntary organisations, etc. *They went beyond the actual legal and political bounds very rarely, but frequently reached and sometimes managed to broaden them* [my italics]. (Kuti 1999: 4)

So in addition, there were by then:

- a significant group of reformist socialists operating from within the regime but attracted by western economic and cultural standards, and
- a new generation of younger people who had not experienced directly the traumatic events of the previous thirty years and consequently did not live in constant fear of their repetition.

This variety of approaches and institutions left individuals free to take advantage of economic opportunities and allowed them to indulge in less showy forms of resistance (like failing your Russian exams). As Torok emphasises, it also helped those involved to develop skills in evading and manipulating the system through networks of mutual aid – what the French call *'système D'* (from, Fr, *se débrouiller*, to disentangle oneself, resourcefully) and employed to good effect during the Occupation (Ousby 1999: 125). This was the opposite of the 'learned helplessness' of some stereotypes of life under Communism; but also productive of cynicism about institutions and public proclamations about concepts like 'the public good'. This aptitude in sceptical manoeuvre was not new; as Kuti demonstrates, it has deep roots in Hungarian culture, but nor did it cease to be relevant with the end of state socialism – *système D* also has uses under capitalism.

Individuals also became increasingly free to engage in different forms of association, not necessarily overtly political. The regime had created a variety of bodies explicitly to further its own political objectives – characteristically 'peace' organisations. But the scope allowed for 'innocuous' non-political organisations like sports and leisure bodies gradually expanded – including, more controversially, women's organisations. Eventually, after 1987, foundations were once again legalised. Though all these bodies were still kept on a tight rein by the regime, by 1989 their numbers had increased from 6500 in 1982 to 8500 (Cox and Vass 1995: 160).

Discussion of alternative political agendas begin to be increasingly significant in the 1980s, with some evidence elsewhere in East and Central Europe that the ice was beginning to melt (though in the Polish case the suppression of Solidarity in 1981 appeared to point in the opposite direction). Contacts of an informal kind with sympathisers in the West became more frequent. It is a curious and fateful paradox, as Ralf Dahrendorf has pointed out, that the Western European model attracted most attention in the mid-1980s, when possessive individualism at its post-war peak had elevated conspicuous consumption of consumer goods almost to the status of a religion. This accident of timing would have important consequences.

Transformation begins or, 'Living in Truth' – and afterwards

Mary Kaldor proposes the Polish dissident Adam Michnik as the first advocate in contemporary East and Central Europe of civil society as a transforming idea (1978), emphasising self-organisation, autonomy, solidarity and non-violence (*Independent*, 22 October 1999).

Less grandiosely, Jerzy Szacki suggests that 'people simply started to use it as a description either for the goal to be achieved or for the already visible results of the actions of the opposition in the form of a network of interpersonal relationships and institutions independent of the state' (1995: 92). He comments additionally that the term was used quite widely in Poland, and to a lesser extent in Hungary as a simple expression of opposition: what was not-the-state, not-totalitarian (an altogether more straightforward definition than some of those reviewed in Chapter 1).

Over the course of the 1980s, the little 'circles of freedom' (Istvan Bibo's phrase) in Hungary began to enlarge and become more significant (Jenkins 1995). The subjects with which they concerned themselves expanded – for example, ecology in the Danube Circle (1984), though this seems to have been in part a political umbrella of convenience under which more controversial topics could be aired (Bozoki in Cox and Furlong 1995: 38). Discussion of political philosophy continued. The future Mayor of Budapest, Gabor Demszky, who was deeply, though in his own account quite unheroically, involved in underground publishing, recalls a fellow dissident passionately proclaiming the importance of the ideas of J. S. Mill on the rule of law and civic virtues in a document circulated in samizdat (*Central European Economic Review*, November 1999: 24).

The circle of those involved also expanded – a dialogue was opened and continued with reformers inside the system, most of them members of what became known as the 'great generation', who reached adult life in 1968, to whom 1956 was barely a memory.

The Hungarian Democratic Forum (MDF) was created in 1987, originally as a discussion group, sharing new ideas and producing a declaration on democratic principles. By this stage, it is estimated that samizdat publications were reaching a readership of around 10 000 (Bozoki 1995: 42) and the participation in discussions was widening to include some 'revisionist' supporters of the regime. But these debates were still restricted to an elite; if there were divisions they were generational (Szalai 1999).

Transition proper began in 1988, when Janos Kadar was dismissed as the head of the Communist Party by the ruling party congress. As the pace of change increased, the process of civil society bodies transforming themselves into proto-parties began. Setting the objective as 'revitalisation of civil society', 'intellectual elites within the movements started to define the term 'civil society' in a political as well as an economic sense' (Bozoki 1995: 39). Struggles took place within MDF. Some wished to preserve the objective of setting out a new style, distinct from traditional politics – a 'third way'. But the majority preferred the option of translating the organisation into a mainstream political party. Other new parties were created outside the MDF, the SZDSZ, (Free Democrats or 'Social Liberals') and FIDESZ ('Young Democrats'), both set up in 1988.

The following year, 1989, saw the rapid development of a crisis of the system throughout East and Central Europe, precipitated by Gorbachev's reforms in the Soviet Union and his reluctance to intervene in support of the East German regime. The mass flight of its citizens to Hungary and Czechoslovakia from East Germany in search of a route to the West provoked a crisis across the region. Eventually, this was resolved when the Austrian frontier was opened by the Hungarian Government.

In a public speech (June 1989) the Young Democrat leader Viktor Orban boldly called for withdrawal of Soviet troops. But the risk of a repetition of the events of 1956 had already dissipated when in October 1989, Gorbachev's spokesman proclaimed the replacement of the 'Brezhnev Doctrine', which threatened recalcitrant satellites with military intervention, with the 'Sinatra Doctrine' – 'Every country decides on its own which way to take' (quoted in Dahrendorf 1990: 13).

A negotiated transfer of power, based on round table discussions between the emergent democratic groups and technocrats from the Kadar regime, followed. A new constitution and institutions were created: a largely ceremonial presidency, a parliament elected by modified proportional representation, a reformed legal system and code (including the right to free association and a free press), submitted for approval by referendum and proclaimed at the end of October 1989.

The solutions that had been devised were remarkably clear (and rapidly put in place), but in content and ideology profoundly unoriginal – hence the subsequent critique, that what had occurred had been a 'revolution without ideas' or a mere 'reformutation'. To which the British historian and close observer of these events, Timothy Garton Ash, retorted: 'The ideas whose time has come are old, familiar, well-tested ones. (It is the new ideas whose time has passed)' (quoted in Dahrendorf 1990: 24).

But one significant outcome of these developments was to leave committed representatives of civil society, who had helped to bring those well-tested ideas to the table, outside the process with no obvious political home to go to (see Bozoki in Cox & Vas 1995 and Miszlivetz & Ertsey in van Rooey 1998). Though the 'revitalisation of civil society' may have been an essential precondition for transformation, there was apparently little scope for the carrying over of their values or distinctive approach into the new settlement.

Szalai comments that the political change of system:

> swallowed up a large part of the reserves (of civil society) in the rapid formation of parties. Despite this, in 1989/90 some members of (civil) society still believed that it could ... actively and creatively help to shape their lives. However, the inner logic of the rapidly formed new political elite and expanding increasingly stronger economic elite led them to reject the idea of presenting any socio-economic alternatives that differed from their own, particularly the organisation of movements with such aims. The cultural elite meanwhile turned away from the idea of a self-organised civic society [and she instances the failure of the 'workers' council' movement]. In a wide section of society, therefore, illusions linked to the change of system are rapidly dispelled. (Szalai 1999: 66)

This view is contestable. Some of it seems to stem from a kind of 'instant nostalgia' for past common struggles, already detectable as early as 1990 (I encountered it in Prague in February of that year). There is also a question about whether the cultural elite did in fact turn away from the concept of civil society – and whether those who moved into the political arena (and there were many who did) constituted in every case an authentic elite.

Implementing transition

So Hungary entered the new universe of party politics, with the MDF now as a centre-right political party (free market liberals in economics and socially conservative) forming a government after the 1990 election. Pre-communist parties had found it virtually impossible to re-establish themselves: and former communists were routed at the poll.

Though deprived of the opportunity to contribute directly to events, the immediate post-transition period did provide a role for voluntary associations and foundations. To those observing and seeking to influence events from the outside, in the United States and the rest of Europe, these bodies were seen as having an important contribution to make to the democracy-building process and facilitating economic development – a view that did not necessarily reflect realities on the ground.

Internally, they were seen as an appendage (but an increasingly significant one) to the process of delivering welfare and as a source of funding for political enterprises. The new administration's initial decision had been to slacken regulation to the point where foundations would be given complete exemption from taxation. This concession ran until the end of 1991; and during those two years the number of foundations increased fifteen times, from 400 to 6 000. Among them were many 'rogue' foundations created as vehicles for the projects of individual political or economic entrepreneurs (Vajda and Kuti 2000).

Nevertheless, direct government support to the voluntary sector increased. So did external funding, from a variety of outside sources (the British Foreign Office and European Union among them); but principally from Foundations based in the United States (for example, Rockefeller Brothers, Charles S. Mott) and from funds created by the successful financial speculator George Soros, himself a refugee from post-war Hungary, whose activities had begun well before the transition, in 1984 but expanded dramatically after 1989.

Soros specifically set out to strengthen civil society and adapted his programme of grant giving to that objective. He had wanted to create a network of new organisations operating outside state control; but early experience after the change of regime convinced him and his advisers that a better way forward would be through partnership with some state agencies and emerging market organisations (Szeman and Harsanyi 2000: 85).

The pattern of funding by these outside agencies showed a different pattern of priorities from domestic sources, being directed mainly towards large organisations, Budapest-based and concerned with economic development and providing services to other civil society organisations ('intermediaries'). There has been some debate about effects of this funding; Eva Kuti says: 'the indigenous non-profit sector was developed enough to absorb the unexpected funds without seriously disturbing its organic evolution' (1998b: 12).

The Rockefeller Brothers Foundation were apparently especially sensitive on this point (see also Siegel and Yancey 1992). Others suggest that the activities of foreign donors created locally an intermediate (*comprador*, in Marxist terms) class, negotiating between the two worlds, 'speaking for the masses, "talking civil society", displaying the right liberal values, but divorced from their reality' (Miszlivetz and Ertsey 1998: 78).

The arrival of western advisors to assist associations in developing a new role was important in itself but also significant as part of a larger process of rapid change in culture and values common to all countries in East and Central Europe. This process was based in large part on uncritical importation of ideas from the West, often leading to a fundamental misperception of what could be achieved and its likely consequences.

Adam Michnik has described his Polish compatriots as wanting 'Western salaries and standard of living and Eastern prices and job security' (LSE lecture, November 1999). In the immediate aftermath of the change, most of them got neither – a Hungarian variant on this joke has Hungary as a country 'with Swedish cost of living and African salaries'.

It is hardly surprising that the general reaction in East and Central Europe after the first flush of sheer astonishment at what had occurred should have been to take maximum advantage of material opportunities. After all, when ordinary East Berliners came for the first time through the newly opened wall, the gift with which their hosts in West Berlin chose to greet them was a package of Deutschmarks to enable them to go shopping.

The opportunity for western consultants was too good to miss: the entry of the 'Marriotteers' (so termed after the Marriott hotel chain where they frequently stayed) followed almost immediately.

As a contemporary advertisement in the *Economist* put it: 'We will change your Marx into dollars'. Western governments and international agencies promoted a slightly subtler version of the same message.

What is perhaps more surprising is that relatively sophisticated politicians should also have believed that transition could be accomplished without undue stress. Vaclav Klaus, economist and first Prime Minister of the new Czechoslovak republic proclaimed that 'we need an unconstrained, unrestricted, full-fledged, unspoiled market system and we need it now' (quoted in Szacki 1995: 147). His subsequent efforts, as he recorded them in a speech quoted at the head of this chapter, were directed to ensuring that market values retained their primacy in the face of critics arguing for a more prominent place for those of civil society.

Shock therapy along these lines, ending price control and fixed exchange rates and breaking up large public sector monopolies was common to all the East and Central European countries and in most cases initially as much shock as therapy (though not in Czechoslovakia, where Klaus the politician behaved a good deal more prudently than his rhetoric had suggested).

On the feasibility of such a rapid transition to a market economy, Szacki comments:

> A unique experiment got under way consisting of planning and rapidly building a capitalist order whose main feature elsewhere was that it was supposed to develop spontaneously and without any pre-conceived theoretical assumptions. In the post-communist world, capitalism had to be invented and put into practice in the reverse order to its entire previous history. (1995: 221)

As he points out, this was precisely the kind of 'utopian social engineering' for which the right has always criticised the left (an issue that I will be exploring in more detail in Chapter 8).

The advocates of unconstrained markets were on stronger ground in emphasising the apparently unconvincing character of the alternatives on offer, notably, the impossibility of finding a viable 'third way' to promote. As Dahrendorf suggests, the spectacle then presented by the principal candidate, Western European social democracy – even in its Scandinavian redoubts – was not exactly reassuring. It is difficult not to feel that the timing was unfortunate for those whose ambitions for the future were not captured in Klaus's 'unrestricted, full-fledged, unspoiled market system'. But by the end of the 1980s, the West as well as the East were about to discover the weaknesses in that neo-liberal paradigm. Tax cuts and rich pickings from privatisations lost their gloss as Western European economies descended into recession, accompanied by large-scale job losses and a chronic sense of insecurity among the employed. But warnings were not heeded and in any case the declining prominence of civil society organisations meant that there was only a restricted audience for an alternative message. A few hoarse prophets of doom croaked in vain. The willing adoption of a liberal political model had been almost universal; but so was the acceptance that in the apparent absence of any viable alternative this must necessarily be linked to a neo-liberal economic programme.

The transition was in some respects less difficult for Hungary, in that there was some preparation for this process in the promotion of business enterprise in the final period of the previous regime. Indeed, many of the elite were able to make a painless transition from the old system to the new, notably in the banking sector (Szalai 1999: 43), although this continuation in powerful positions of figures from 'former times' was not unique in East and Central Europe.

There followed a rapid and uneven transformation to a form of market economy.

The system evolves: a reconstitution of liberty?

The period between 1990 and 1994, when the centre-right government led by the MDF was in power can be viewed from a number of different angles.

In terms of political change, it can be seen as providing an index of the performance of the newly created democratic institutions. At the end of this period, the country passed one admittedly crude, but fundamental test of viable democracy, a peaceful transfer of power, when members of the former ruling party, now repositioned as Socialists (MSZP) won an absolute majority at the next election, though electing to govern in coalition with the Free Democrats (SZDSZ). Electorally, this was not just a reaction against the economic constraints imposed by the first post-transition government; this 'spectacular return of the late-Kadarist technocracy' (Szalai 1999: 225) in alliance with the democratic opposition represented by the Free Democrats could also be seen as a willingness to contemplate an alternative approach to policy (as expressed in some of the documents prepared by the opposition before the election, like the 'Democratic Charter' aimed at the MDF Government's aggressive cultural and media policies).

The period can also be assessed in terms of economic change. The role of international agencies, especially the World Bank, was crucial here (Ferge 1999). Privatisation (then seen as an indispensible item in the neo-liberal reform package) was driven through and the role of banks rapidly expanded, though these initially remained predominantly under state ownership. Given the country's chronic state of indebtedness, the attracting of significant foreign investment was a prime objective of policy: and, once political stability had been established, substantial progress was made in this direction. But a key condition for securing support from international financial agencies was the additional item in the neo-liberal package – reduction in public spending. This meant not only the rapid ending of price controls, which was an intrinsic element of social policy under the former regime; but also a broader assault on what was described by critics as a 'premature welfare state' (Kornai, quoted in Ferge 1996b: 4).

These changes had major implications for social policy. It was clear that reconstruction of the existing system of welfare would have to be undertaken: acute structural problems within the system were manifest by the end of the 1980s. But, as Zsuzsa Ferge has pointed out, these 'reforms were not based on a liberal political criticism of social policy but on a neo-liberal economic approach' (in Szalai 1999: 153). The attitude of outside advisers was clear: the system of welfare introduced by the former regime was inappropriate to the economic needs of the country and prohibitively expensive. Ferge quotes the World Bank's judgment (1994) that 'since neither the revenue effort commensurate with high spending nor a large fiscal deficit represent sound macro-economic strategies, an expenditure cutting strategy is necessary' (1996b). The resulting reform process (as she has subsequently analysed it) was designed to 'cleanse' the existing system of its solidaristic elements and scale down the coverage and wherever possible the level of benefits. In that process, the role of the central state in the provision of welfare was substantially reduced and occupational welfare virtually eliminated (Ferge 1996b: 9).

In the longer term, these changes can be seen as an attempt to banish collectivism by denying the legitimacy of state action except in extreme cases of relief of destitution and ensuring that welfare, at least, should become more a matter of individual or family responsibility. Ferge quotes the former Hungarian finance minister in the MSZP–SZDSZ coalition: 'In this change the decisive factor is the (increased) responsibility, ability of adjustment and self-provision of the individual. The aim can be attained only if we do away with the false sense of solidarity... welfare policy should focus in the future on the indigents and defenceless': (Laszlo Bekesi, quoted in Ferge 1996b: 1). These developments, initiated under the centre-right government and made a central plank of policy under its Socialist-Liberal successor, connect with a fourth arena of change, in values.

As already suggested, the issue was not whether to reconstruct attitudes from scratch: the notion that Hungarians needed to be taught entrepreneurial skills (a problem that seriously exercised consultants in the former Soviet Union) is a paradigm case of a redundant exercise. But scepticism about institutions had been deeply engrained in the culture and persisted after the change of regime, although at least one attitude survey (SOCO) suggests that the idea that this translated into wholesale distrust of the state and all its activities may be over-simplified.

A new role for the third sector?

The revival of the associational sector proceeded rapidly, driven partly by outside funding but also by the efforts of large organisations operating within the country – the Hungarian Red Cross, the knights of Malta charitable service. The main problem they faced was that as the state divested itself of responsibilities, especially in welfare, a rapidly widening gap opened up which foundations were unable to bridge. Logic demanded partnership and the only logical partner was the state – local government, in particular. Further problems then arose of the capacity of state organisations and the willingness of non-state organisations to trust them.

As Vajda and Kuti put it:

> very few (if any) of the Hungarian governments were completely trusted by citizens. Although the variations in number and depth of conflicts between state and citizen were wide over history, there was always some need and mostly also some opportunity for independent citizen action. Both co-operation and mutual distrust were essential features of the history of state-non-profit relations. (2000: 159)

Government saw the third sector of associations and foundations as important in facilitating the 'modernisation' of state welfare services – for which often read, cutting by substitution (as in the social services law of 1993). But state policies towards the sector were also inconsistent (Kuti 1996), largely because they had been driven by different forces: by fiscal pressures deriving from economic reforms; by a pull towards centralisation in policy-making, though with some gestures towards decentralisation at the outset; and by reservations about democracy not being perceived as efficient; and foundations often being seen as corrupt (sometimes correctly) and frequently as 'useless'.

As a result, different approaches were adopted towards the third sector by different government departments. Eva Kuti in her analysis contrasts the 'Germanic' approach of the Ministry of Justice, 'eager to develop legal schemes in order to more closely control nonprofit organisations' (1996: 135) and the neo-liberal perspective of the Ministry of Finance, seeing voluntary action as an expression of individual enterprise. The outcome for government policy as a whole, as she describes it, was a

> confused conglomeration of civil society rhetoric and tightening state control; liberal economic and etatist legal approaches; establishment of large government foundations, increasing direct subsidies and shrinking tax advantages. (Kuti 1996: 136)

Confusion lay on both sides: the question of the future role and development of the third sector after 1990 was problematic for the associations themselves. The rhetoric of the period of transition suggested a number of possible roles, apart from the straightforward delivery of services – for example involvement in policy development. Much of the activity in this area had been captured by the new elites in the reformed political system and retained there. Eva Kuti suggests that a 'problem-solving approach' by associations 'can be quite fruitful, can efficiently influence the decisions of the "professional policy makers" and can result in some kind of control of the changes in the welfare mix' (1996: 139).

But Miszlivitz observes that the new political leadership after the moment of transition was increasingly resistant to any notion of active participation in the policy-making process: 'they argued that continued grassroots mobilisation was unnecessary, if not dangerous, to the new democracy: and that the well-articulated field of political parties provided an efficient arena for the completion of ideas' (in van Rooey 1998: 76).

This was not how many of the outside agencies funding develop-ments after the transition saw things: the definition of 'democracy' in the European Union and British government ('Know How') pro-grammes contemplated a much broader role for 'NGOs', including campaigning and advocacy (both 'defensive' and positive). This area of activity was also evolving but was disputed terrain, not just for the reasons given by Miszlivitz but because of conflicts between the pre- and post-transition organisations, especially among organ-isations concerned with women's issues.

The legal context

The scope for effective action under these different headings depended largely on the legal context. After the period of experi-ment with minimal regulation had thrown up an excessive num-ber of scandals the then opposition parties became fervent advocates of reform (Kuti 1996: 132–3). Pressure for change of the legal framework within which the third sector operates was even-tually addressed after the MSZP–SZDSZ Government, which had committed itself in its election programme to a new comprehen-sive legal framework, had come to power.

However, the proposals for reform were slow in coming for-ward and there were a number of false starts, with proposals drafted by rival expert groups. When draft legislation was finally produced in 1996 the proposals were bitterly resisted by the non-profit organisations themselves, who saw the proposal, based on the English model, with an organisation along the lines of the Charity Commission monitoring the functioning of non-profit organisations, defined by a test of public benefit, as a threat to the independence of the sector. A new bill was then introduced, pre-pared by a panel of experts, changing the conditions for getting and keeping public benefit status and dropping the notion of an agency to monitor the sector's activities. This version also ran into severe criticism, this time from the government side; but given the need to deliver on the 1994 commitment to legislate in time for the forthcoming elections, a compromise version was agreed which deleted most of the remaining provisions for monitoring and accountability and this passed into law in December 1997.

Two features of particular interest in the final version are the attention given to the relations between non-profit organisations and the state, extending specific privileges to organisations supplying services that would otherwise be provided by the state and the explicit distinction between political and non-profit activity. The codification of public benefit in terms of a check list of specific activities is an interesting – and problematic feature of the reform, as revealing for what it includes (the promotion of 'Euro-Atlantic integration', activities relating to 'Hungarians living beyond the borders'), as for what it omits (religious activities of all kinds). The latter is the result of an attempt by the churches to insist on distancing themselves from lay voluntary organisations and having separate systems of regulation.

The churches were also initially sceptical about another important innovation, the so-called '1 %' Law introduced in December 1996, which gave taxpayers the right to nominate a charity of their choice as the recipient of one per cent of their total tax paid. The taxpayers themselves are not direct beneficiaries: the money in question has already been paid to the tax office. But the system provides a powerful incentive for organisations, as potential recipients of the one per cent, to make themselves and their activities known to taxpayers. In practice, the amount of money raised in this way has not been large. But the scheme has not simply provided an additional source of revenue. It has opened up an additional channel for support through which small grassroots organisations and local foundations based out of the capital have been able to obtain funding on a basis that is, as Vajda and Kuti put it, 'slightly more equitable and significantly more democratic' (2000: 179).

Developing welfare policies

On the wider policy scene, neo-liberal economic policies continued to be pursued by central government, especially after 1995, when a package of economic measures (the 'Bokros package') was introduced, specifically intended to reinforce the minimalist concept of state welfare through substantial cuts in social services. As Laszlo Bekesi put it 'social policy cannot take the place of distribution according to achievement and of providing for oneself; that is, it cannot offer protection, and cannot offer guaranteed security, to defend the living conditions and the financial standards of the middle strata' (quoted in Ferge 1996b: 7). This tends to reinforce Erzsebet Szalai's rather cynical explanation that:

> an attack on the state education and health care systems only became possible and necessary when the elite managed to become independent

of these – their income enabled them to send their children to private schools, to turn to private health care in Hungary or abroad, to afford frequent foreign holidays etc. – and when the amount of resources required to stop the gap between the elites and the majority … reached such proportions that it would have seriously affected their position of power. (1999: 149)

These developments had important consequences for the third sector's welfare role, not least because the decentralisation of responsibility for delivery of welfare set up opportunities for new relationships between the third sector and local authorities. Istvan Sebesteny comments that 'significant parts of local government did not recognise the possibilities and advantages hidden in co-operation with the non-profit sector until 1996. Some of them believed that financial support to NGOs was only a one-way charity action and not a bilaterally advantageous collaboration' (Sebesteny 1999: 6). However, as he demonstrates, after that date things began to change quite rapidly and a 'contract culture' started to take hold. (The extent of this process – and some of the residual suspicions associated with it – was very evident in 1998, when I took part in discussions of contracting with representatives of local government and third sector organisations in Budapest's wildly over-ornamented *Jugendstil* Town Hall).

Szeman and Harsanyi show that reciprocal relationships evolved rapidly in the second half of the decade as both sides shed their mistrust and worked out ways of dealing with the expansion of responsibilities caused by the withdrawal of services for the neediest. They conclude:

> It has not yet been made clear in Hungary when and to what extent the non-profit sector has a role of substituting for the state which is withdrawing or where it is rather a matter of supplementing, making use of the advantages of pluralism by separating the financing and operating service providers. Policy-makers and observers frequently speak of the latter, but in reality the case is more often the former. (2000: 163)

So by the end of the second democratic government's period in office, the third sector was becoming firmly established, if sometimes on insecure ground. The Hungarian Statistical Office's analysis shows a rapid upward trend in the creation of new organisations. There were around 48 000 by 1997, one third of them foundations but the majority membership organisations. Most foundations work in the fields of education, health and social care; while membership organisations were heavily concentrated in sports and recreation. Advocacy was a growing field: 'philanthropic intermediaries' still operate on a relatively modest scale. The sector supported just over 50 000 paid staff and involved 380 000 volunteers; funding was drawn, in order, from 'income generated by basic activities' (one third), investment and business (a quarter), government support (22 per cent) and donations (CSO – Hungarian Statistical Office – 1999).

Outside influences on the sector were beginning to fade away and an authentic 'indigenous' agenda has started to emerge. The belated appearance of effective intermediate bodies now provides a channel of communication and advice on policy between government and the association world. Some of the persistent weaknesses are also clearer: there is no clear perception of the longer-term implications of relationships with state ('short sighted rationalism'); a lack of cooperation within the sector, and problems of transparency and accountability. There are also continuing problems of a shortage of resources, and sustaining the level of volunteering.

The 1998 Election closes this stage: the victory of the Young Democrats (FIDESZ), in coalition with the Smallholders' Party represents a reversion (in part) to earlier policies from the immediate post-transition period; but with the same neo-liberal economic sub-text. The eccentricities of the new administration's approach to the third sector is part of a larger pattern of attempting to delineate a new non-statist but nationalist approach, with 'subsidiarity' as a key organising concept and voluntary associations praised for their 'flexibility'.

Civil society a decade after the transformation

What functions does civil society now perform, a decade after the change? On the basis of the evidence cited, it is possible to provide an interim assessment of performance against four claims sometimes made for civil society, but one which leaves more questions than answers behind. Once again, Albert Hirschman's categories may be helpful here.

• Has the engagement of civil society helped to complete a 'modernisation' process, straightening out the kinks in the deformed model that was immediate pre-transformation Hungary? The trajectory now appears to be towards normality, in the western democratic sense – through progressive legitimation of the new institutions and a stable national identity not compromised by fissures of class and religion. But, if so, there are still questions to be asked about how the future role of civil society in such a 'normal' environment is best defined. (Hirschman 1970)

- Has civil society assisted in the process of building democracy – did the networks that existed from 'former times' before the transformation of civil associations into political parties help or hinder in the process of transition? Ralf Dahrendorf's question was whether 'we, the people' could learn how to govern. In fact, it is debatable whether they were ever seriously offered the opportunity. In some respects, it has been merely a matter of an established elite moving from one role to another, as Szalai would seem to suggest, with her references to a 'great generation' manoeuvring successfully and retaining the substance of power. Meanwhile, what has happened to Torok's 'eggheads'? Have they opted out again (Hirschman 1970) or simply developed other roles and interests? What became of the workers' organisations? Genuine gains made for women in earlier periods in fields like child care and abortion law reform seem to have been put at risk or even lost as a result of the transition. (see Ferge 1997).

- Does civil society now have the capacity to hold power to account? (Hirschman 1970). What became of ecological protest, once significant in Hungary (the Danube Circle) and now so powerful in some western countries – as demonstrated in the Brent Spar episode (see Chapter 7). Are the dismissive references inquisitive visitors hear to 'the inevitable gypsies' just a ritual spasm of guilty conscience? Or are assertions about 'minority rights' really coded references to the significance of Hungarian minorities across the borders?

- What has been the significance of welfare reforms, especially those made after 1995, for the future role of civil society? Should organisations operating there have resisted these reforms more vigorously, as in the case Zsuzsa Ferge cites of the pensions reform, which could be seen as an attack on inter-generational solidarity? Could it have done, given her conclusion (in 1996) that 'it will take some time until civil society becomes strong enough to defend itself and the rights, social rights included, that it considers essential' (1996b: 15). And there must be doubt about whether the capability exists in civil society to cope with the consequences of changes in welfare. Szeman's and Harsanyi's analysis shows that there is evidence of a developing focus on homelessness and other visible 'casualties of reform' – but probably not at a level sufficient to match the emerging scale of the problems, even where effective partnerships with local authorities have been created (2000: 144).

So is civil society, at least in its expression as voluntary associations, at risk of becoming simply an appendage: a convenient mechanism of substitution for state welfare services? Are the partnerships that have been formed with state organisations merely flags of convenience for this process?

The current distribution of activity and political profile of the association sector suggests that a pattern of activity has begun to stabilise in what could be described as a 'mixed economy of welfare' but one that has distinctive Hungarian features (Kuti 1998a). These are progressively being exposed by the withdrawal of foreign funding and the winding down of direct outside involvement in areas like the promotion of democratic institutions and values.

Future directions

Remembering how the events of 1989 in East and Central Europe took the entire world by surprise, it would be prudent to frame any forecast of future developments in exceptionally tentative terms. History, in this region above most others, cannot be taken to be at an end. But it seems safe to assume that any sketch of likely lines of development over the next decade should take into account the following factors:

- Globalisation and in particular the influence of information technology; and the continuing impact of the international business community's expanding activities especially in the light of the extent of foreign investment.
- The likely consequences of accession to the European Union. These include the equal opportunities element in the Treaty of Rome, and the influence of European social policy, including the Social Chapter of the Maastricht Treaty and rights for minorities (in the Amsterdam Treaty). Jeffrey Sachs is on record (1996, quoted in Ferge 1999) as warning that the high social

costs would be damaging to prospects for the economy and implying that Hungary should seek to opt out of them.
• The possible impact of greater involvement with other cross-border bodies, in the rest of East and Central Europe, Europe as a whole (in the Council of Europe sense) and even 'global civil society'. (The consequences of NATO membership and the sharp impact on the new members of events in the former Yugoslavia – notably, the bombing of Danube bridges in 1999 – have been largely overlooked in Western Europe).

What are the wider lessons of developments over the past decade, which might help identify future trends that may determine the prospects for civil society?

First, that the importance of history cannot be over-stressed. This brief account has found no space for description of the nineteenth-century roots of some civil organisations, for example, those founded under the Habsburgs to promote Hungarian cultural and linguistic objectives. Nor for the distinctive cultural legacy of Hungarian Protestantism, unique in the region. But these are only illustrations of some of the particular elements in Hungarian civil society with deeper historical roots (there are some parallels here with Putnam's account of Italian civil society summarised in Chapter 3). More recently, the contours of the state socialist period are still clearly visible and some still are influential – especially in the continued importance of *système D*. This is well described in slightly over-indulgent style in Torok under the ironic title 'privileges' and now seen by its critics as a means of perpetrating the influence of an elite in fields like cultural policy (Borocz 2000).

All this feeds into the issue of national values and 'character'. There seems to be a generation effect here. The 'great generation' (the 1968ers, now in their fifties) appears well equipped to cope with the transformation: their younger successors now take the market for granted and operate easily and profitably in that arena (though without commanding much admiration from their fellow-citizens for doing so). Both groups have gained substantially from the new individualistic universe: but society as a whole is beginning to experience the full effects of the withdrawal of the safety net once provided (however imperfectly) for those without sufficient 'privileges', in Torok's sense – the elderly on state pensions, the young without marketable skills.

As an abstract value, democracy now appears to be almost universally accepted: but there is less enthusiasm for its wider implications. Reforms since transformation tend to have been top down: civil society has not been trusted to make a positive contribution or accepted as a legitimate critic. Vaclav Klaus's view, quoted at the head of this chapter that civil society is an artificial and unnecessary construct is one held widely by politicians across the region. One symptom of this attitude is that the state that has emerged is not very trusting of outsiders, with politicians taking a rigid view of democracy as representative, not participatory. There is a common suspicion that behind this front there lurks a state that still has, in Zsuzsa Ferge's phrase, 'Bolshevik genes'. Would reform have taken a different path if the state had been prepared to adopt a more open and consultative style; or was civil society simply not strong enough to respond effectively or too mistrustful to wish to do so?

Another factor is the influence of economic elites, which has become rapidly stronger. Szacki (1995) has described market liberalism, in an inversion of Marx's famous phrase as 'the spectre that is haunting Eastern Europe'. One symptom is that the 'reunification of language' that observers like Ralf Dahrendorf called for in 1990 has now taken place; universally, in East and Central Europe, it is business American. Given the continued absence of any effective rival, though the credo of market liberalism has a few influential doubters (including now, George Soros) there is a vacuum of ideology, including religion, except perhaps in the case of Protestant Pentecostal sects.

This can be seen positively. East and central Europeans have 'refused Utopia' (just as Dahrendorf hoped they would) by rejecting elaborate ideologically-based alternatives in favour of pragmatic reforms. But the dominance of neo-liberal economic policy is leading to lost solidarity and levels of anxiety arising from insecurity. Pessimism returns: cynicism remains; *système D* flourishes. Another symptom of change driven by economic transformation has been the near-collapse of old subsidised high culture, as widely foreseen. The consequences can be seen in two ways: either the emergence of a new, plural culture with wider choice and multiple entry points (Torok) or a tide of uniform Americanisation, driven by the lowest common denominator of popular music and sport on identical television channels, leading to an accelerated version of the process that Robert Putnam indicts (see Chapter 4) – a passively consumed mass culture swamping active citizen participation.

In this it is important not to lose sight of the question of size. In the case of Hungary, it's important not to forget how small a country it now is, both geographically and in terms of population. Networking is easier but can be excluding and well as inclusive – perpetuating intergenerational hostilities and intragenerational resentments (there is an echo here of the Republic of Ireland: where party politics used until recently to be based on who shot whose grandfather).

Conclusion

So finally, how is the issue raised at the outset to be resolved? Was civil society cause or consequence of the changes that occurred in 1989? Anheier and Seibel (1992) are clearly right in arguing that a form of civil society (constrained by the absence of civil liberties but nonetheless clearly identifiable as such) was a significant factor in shaping and promoting change in the particular form in which it emerged in Hungary. But civil society organisations had less influence over the eventual results and, a key paradox, have not been able to influence outcomes in significant areas of social policy. This has remained true more recently, despite circumstances being much more favourable to the operation of civil society in both its oppositional and provider roles. This must lead to speculation about whether the operation of markets – at least in the form in which they have been installed in East and Central Europe – is necessarily favourable to the development of a strong civil society and the political and cultural environment that would sustain it.

CHAPTER 6

Civil Society and the Market

The only thing worse than being exploited by capitalism ... is not being exploited by it' (Joan Robinson, economist, quoted by Michael Edwards, *Future Positive*)

Introduction

In this chapter, I will be exploring different aspects of the interpenetration of voluntarism and the market – patrolling another frontier zone (see Figure 1.1). There has always been a significant amount of exchange of values, organisational forms and techniques between organisations based in the market sector and those operating in what we described earlier as the 'civil society space' (some of this history is described in Chapter 2). But the importance of these relationships has greatly increased over the last two decades of the twentieth century, for two main reasons.

The first is the increase in the quantity and diversity of activities taking place within civil society, largely as a result of the changes in the role of the state already charted in earlier chapters. This has sometimes been presented as a process of wholesale withdrawal from functions that the state had taken on during the period of expansion of its role described in Chapter 4. The truth, as we saw there, is rather more complex: a matter of redefinition rather than retreat, in the case of most developed countries, although more fundamental changes have been occurring in most of the ex-communist countries (described in Chapter 5) and in many parts of the developing world. Uneven though this process may have been, China being still a notable exception, these developments have presented voluntary bodies with a whole range of opportunities for expansion of their activities. In doing so, they have also greatly increased the occasion for contact with business, as potential models – or rivals.

The second reason for the increased importance of relations with the market for organisations operating in the civil society space is the rapid expansion in the volume of market activity and the impact that this has had across the entire world – the phenomenon now generally known as 'globalisation'. This has been most immediately visible in the rapid growth in the activities of multinational corporations. Beginning in the 1960s, these organisations have expanded not only the range and reach of their activities but also their forms of governance, some developing fully multinational systems of organisation and control, others retaining ownership and control in the centre, in the developed world, but diversifying their sources of production. High profile brands like Nike, Coca Cola or McDonalds command universal recognition, reinforced by global advertising and constant media attention to their marketing programmes. This expansion has formed a key part of the development of a global economy, increasingly characterised by free movement of goods and services (but not labour) and especially by the vastly extended influence of the operations of finance capital made possible by the introduction of new technology allowing instant access to relevant information. As George Soros, who has made a huge fortune speculating in this new arena, summarises the outcome:

> The result is a gigantic circulatory system, sucking up capital into the financial markets and institutions at the center and then pumping it out to the periphery either directly in the form of credits and portfolio investments or indirectly through multinational organisations. Capital brings many benefits, not only an increase in productive capacity but also improvements in the methods of production and other innovations, not only an increase in wealth but also an increase in freedom. Thus countries vie to attract and retain capital and making conditions attractive to capital takes precedence over other social objectives. But, [he adds,] the system is deeply flawed. (1998: 102).

[I shall explore some of the reasons for this judgment later].

In this chapter I set out to examine some of the main implications of these developments for organisations and individuals in the civil society space, operating in the context of a contracting state sector and markets expanding both nationally and globally. Cumulatively, what this has meant is that any organisation operating outside the state seeking to influence the direction of events in the public sphere or expand its activities in delivery of services on any scale must consider how to make and sustain relationships with the institutions of the market.

This will raise a number of questions. First, what are the likely consequences of increases in the volume of contacts and level of interaction with markets on voluntary organisations operating in the civil society space: which values do they carry into new relationships; what will they encounter there, what can they expect to gain from them and what will they put at risk? Second, what particular characteristics do voluntary bodies have that will equip them to cope with a changing environment both within and outside the civil society space? What are they best – or least – fitted to do in these new circumstances? Third, how should the consequences of these interactions be seen and what potential is there for influencing developments in the market sector, so as to align them more closely with the overall goals defined earlier – principally, the creation and maintenance of the good society. These are all questions that voluntary associations need to address not as an option but a necessity.

Change and evolution in the market

After the end of the cold war, a sequence of rapidly accelerating changes took place internationally, driven on by the powerful thrust of what came to be called 'turbo-capitalism'. Many of those directly affected by the energies released by this process initially held what can only be described as romantic views of the capacities of markets, enhanced by the glamour of the new technologies now being employed there. The phrase 'the magic of markets' was frequently employed, without irony, to explain these new developments. Those bewitched were, understandably, most often found in countries that had intimate experience of the failure of rival modes of organisation. They either had not seen or did not wish to see what the flaws in the alternative might be. In a phrase much used at the time, what they wanted was 'market, no adjective' (see Chapter 5).

This romanticising of the market was accentuated by the circumstances in which the texts of classical liberalism had been conned, often in clandestinity, in the 'free universities' of East and Central Europe. But it was already common in neo-liberal doctrine – witness Enoch Powell's assertion that he was frequently on his knees 'thanking God the holy ghost for the gift of capitalism'. Many of these accounts of the virtues of capitalism are necessarily dogmatic, in the strict sense. One example, which will serve among many from the beginning of the decade of market triumphalism immediately after the fall of the Berlin Wall in 1989, is the work of the American Catholic sociologist Michael Novak.

> Markets, [he argues] have a centripetal force; their inner dynamic aims at mutual, civil, reasoned arguments. Markets do not drive people apart into alienation; on the contrary, they drive them toward closer contact with one another, even from the antipodes. Markets are extraordinary social institutions, rich with tacit understandings, traditions, conventions and valuable lore. Open to the world, they bind humans together in thousands of visible and invisible filaments of choice. They are one of the great works of human reason ... [And so ...] democratic capitalist societies [keep] the space of civic life open and alive, so that within it many social energies may thrive and even boil. (Novak 1990: 14–15)

An essential point for our present purposes is Novak's determination to assert that civil societies are not collectivist, because the essence of civic communities is that they are composed of free *individuals*, each separately 'capable of reflection and choice and thus inalienably responsible for his or her destiny' (32).

The individual, empowered in this way rather than through participation in collective decision-making, forms the key element in the new structure, as in Margaret Thatcher's notorious comment about there being 'no such thing as society, only individuals and their families'. (This was widely misunderstood, because it was intended not as description but as exhortation, to accept duties and meet responsibilities). Even the poor can 'become the agents of their own development' (Novak 1990: 33) because the market provides the capacity for freedom of choice to be exercised. The state's functions can then wither away to those safeguards necessary to guarantee that this freedom will be exercised and in a morally acceptable way – that is, by adherence to 'Judeo-Christian' values. Politics become a question of individual consumer choice; and 'trickledown' from the pool of wealth accumulated by the most prosperous – and any additional contribution they choose to make as charity – will provide solutions for the 'social question', chiefly the residual problems of poverty.

It scarcely needs saying that outside the United States at the end of the two most prosperous decades of its existence the reality is often rather different, especially when markets 'boil over', to adopt Novak's image. But before attempting to make any judgments on the performance of global capitalism we need to go a little further in the direction of exploring the ways in which it now presents itself as a potential partner – or indeed rival – to voluntary action, and also assess the consistency of the values with those of voluntary organisations who may seek to enter into partnership with commercial undertakings or seek to compete with them.

The imprint of the market on philanthropy

What markets do best is to make selected individuals wealthy. As a general proposition, those fortunate enough to be well placed on entry through their skills, natural aptitudes and other assets (primarily location by class and geography) will be those who emerge the wealthiest (Galbraith 1993: 92). However, the dynamic of capitalism requires that in order to provide the essential motivating element there must be some possibility that individuals will prosper without these advantages, through honest toil – or simply by luck. Every tadpole, to employ Tawney's image, must believe that they have a sporting chance of becoming a frog and leaving the stagnant pond (ultimately even to become a prince).

Until recently, capitalism has also mandated certain forms of behaviour for those that have succeeded, with or without a head start and whatever the means they may have employed to do so. Specifically, success in the marketplace provides individuals with the resources and opportunity to exercise their philanthropic instincts, as we saw in Chapter 2. The wish to do so has in the past often stemmed from the religious impulse, as in the example given there of Quaker philanthropy, the so-called 'Chocolate Conscience' or in the form of voluntary 'tithing'. But the form that it has taken, in the Anglo-Saxon context, has also been strongly marked by the application of business principles; 'joint stock' philanthropy in the eighteenth century and 'five per cent' dividends from investing in charitable housing in the next. (This has a feebler echo in the late twentieth century in one per cent donations by successful companies to charity from their profits.)

Philanthropy has traditionally helped to confer a particular type of immortality on the successful businessman, through the custom and practice of leaving legacies for charitable purposes. This has been an activity carried out at all sorts of different scales and with different ends in view, ranging from the Easter dole for elderly parishioners commemorated in the porch of the parish church to the funding of the largest foundations with gifts of shares and property, some of them operating internationally with incomes larger than many nation states (Carnegie, Wellcome, Rockefeller, Ford and now Bill Gates). Behind the legacies and life-time gifts lie a wide diversity of motives that illustrate the different characteristics of philanthropists: insiders celebrating and perpetuating their status (livery companies, masons); outsiders trying to obtain entry for their compatriots by reinforcing mutual aid or promoting assimilation; individuals seeking atonement or salvation, gongs or royal patronage.

These are values more securely embedded in some societies than others. Michael Novak's rhapsody on the 'commercial republic' of the United States seeks to persuade us that the founding fathers did not merely foresee the necessity of sustaining morality within the operations of a dynamic capitalist economic system, but enshrined that message in the Seal of the United States, still to be seen on the back of the dollar bill. This symbolises (he tells us) the 'institutional shape of democratic capitalism' in the pyramid at the centre and the role of providence in benevolent scrutiny epitomised in the eye that tops it (1990: 2).

Certainly in the United States the existence of corporate philanthropy on a substantial scale has for long been an established standard feature of the social system and has often helped to determine developments on the ground and sometimes also the shape of public policies in fields like arts and culture and latterly social and environmental policies as well. However, this engagement has been less marked in some other societies and circumstances – in Britain for much of the twentieth century, the contribution of business has tended to be little more than a token rent on commercial success, or a useful supplementation of local benevolence. Despite the example of the Quaker firms and some local employers like the glass manufacturers Pilkington, there has been little evidence of the level of corporate benefaction and active community engagement normal in the United States.

In the late twentieth century, different patterns of corporate governance have begun to evolve in Britain. In some respects, these developments have been favourable for the development of constructive relations between business and voluntarism.

The modernising impulse has produced a concern with corporate image, often leading to selective high profile sponsorship of charitable activity. New trusts and foundations have been established by major players in the financial markets – for example, banks and building societies. There have been other stirrings, the creation of a 'Per Cent' club under the patronage of the Prince of Wales, based on the donation of a fixed proportion of profits to charity. There are hints of the development of a new model philanthropy based on addressing a 'triple bottom line' where firms seek to add environmental and social as well as economic value through their activities. (See *Financial Times* 'Visions of Ethical Business', 1 October 1998). 'Corporate social responsibility' is now a well understood concept, though not one universally accepted by all major players. One that does recently told its shareholders:

> We continue to play an active role in the world that surrounds our operations. During the year we contributed over £10m to the community, mainly through cash donations, staff secondments and matching pound-for-pound the funds raised by employees. Additionally, we have contributed £12m to the Children's Promise, a fund raising event to mark the millennium. Our environmental policies also made progress … And our social responsibility goes further – ensuring our premises are safe for staff and customers, enabling all groups within the community to have equal access to our operations and working with suppliers worldwide to make sure their employees are well treated. Of course, these measures also benefit shareholders. They make our operations more efficient, our workforce more inspired (*sic*), our brand more respected and our customers better served. (Marks & Spencers Annual Report 1999: 14)

[A cynic – or an M&S shareholder – might say that this is a paradigm case of a firm trying to satisfy every possible objective except the key one: making profits.]

But these developments have run alongside the emergence of certain other factors in the private marketplace that are producing an environment that is altogether less friendly to civil society and the values of most organisations operating there. The extreme case has been the emergence of predatory capitalism (James Goldsmith-style), with its endless casualty lists of assets stripped, jobs shed and firms closed. But in the Anglo-Saxon economies there has been a common pattern of decline of traditional ('family firm') approaches and a developing threat to mutualism, in part as a result of the growth of multinationals and loss of local roots. This has become a new universe of contract, not custom, the driving down of costs by downsizing and outsourcing to the cheapest sources of supply, justified as promoting shareholder value, and conferring on senior executives what appear to be disproportionate rewards for successes that often prove to be ephemeral. In the United Kingdom, the role of the City of London as the centre of finance capital has been crucial: what critics sometimes called 'casino capitalism' propelling the search for short-term profit at the expense of long-term investment.

These values are in many respect the precise opposite of those that drive many (though far from all) individuals and voluntary associations operating in civil society. These are usually taken to include: importance attached to the non-monetary value of goods and services provided to meet need, altruism as the animating motive for individual actions and satisfaction measured not by monetary reward but in reciprocal affection.

But given that engagement (as I argued above) is inescapable, how well equipped are voluntary organisations to engage with a competitive private market in which characteristics apparently antipathetic to these values are increasingly common, if not dominant; and what particular assets do they bring to the encounter?

The economics of voluntary action

For most economists – certainly neo-classical ones – the question about the distinctive contribution of voluntarism is usually posed as an attempt to identify the form of organisation best equipped to supply public goods and how that task is most effectively undertaken.

One reason often advanced for suggesting that non-profit organisations should play a more prominent role in delivering public goods is simple market failure (Salamon 1993). This can be seen in cases like the supply of care and provision for those – like, for example, the elderly – unable to afford to pay for them in the marketplace. If the government also fails to deliver, the non-profit sector comes in as the provider of last resort, thereby performing an essential (but also a residual) role.

Rational choice theory views non-profit organisations more positively. Their selection as a provider is seen as the outcome of the demands of individuals seeking solutions to their problems in a market economy and searching out information on how best to do so. Henry Hansmann extends the argument by presenting non-profit organisations as being viewed as more trustworthy: the constraint on distribution of profits acts as a 'crude but effective signal' to potential consumers. Otherwise, especially in the area of human, services, the potential purchaser of the service will not have the experience necessary to judge in advance the quality of what is being provided, either comparatively or absolutely. In Hansmann's analysis the non-profit distribution constraint provides that basic information about quality (Anheier and Kendall 2000: 3).

Other analysts (James 1987) suggest some additional grounds for extending the argument in favour of non-profit organisations. Transaction costs may be minimised if the potential consumer can be confident that the non-profit form can guarantee quality. One reason for believing that this may be the case would be instances where voluntary organisations are composed of coalitions of stakeholders with the providers of the service (who have a vested interest in securing good quality outcomes) among them. Another would be organisations belonging to distinct religious or ethnic groups, looking after and accountable to 'their own'. These have additional reasons for underwriting the standards of the goods and services they provide and additional means of doing so, through rituals that reinforce mutual trust or sanctions that deter individuals from breaching it.

However, Anheier and Kendall suggest that arguments based on trust may lead in different directions that do not necessarily favour spontaneous voluntary action. More efficient state regulation and inspection, regardless of provider, may reinforce consumer confidence; so might professional control and self-regulation; cooperative and mutual provision outside the non-profit sphere or free market solutions generated spontaneously but including customer guarantees and protection beyond the crude market sanctions of complaint or exit. They comment that:

> While short term opportunistic maximisation of shareholder value may characterise the for-profit sector in some contexts, economy-wide institutional and social factors can emerge as controlling forces that keep market opportunism in check. One example would be small business owners whose motives go beyond profit and include other goals such as independence, 'craftsmanship' and professional fulfillment. (Anheier and Kendall 2000: 5)

And even within the main corporate sector, there are cultural models that differ from the American version espoused by Novak, which may shape behaviour within the market in different ways. The social market economies of 'Rhenish capitalism' or the Confucian models of commercial enterprise in South East Asia do not give automatic priority to profit maximisation or shareholder interests as against communal or family concerns.

Finally, within the non-profit sector itself, organisations may behave differently in their provision of services but for reasons not connected directly with their non-profit distribution status – for example, preferential fiscal regimes, state subsidies to voluntary bodies, involvement of volunteers in their labour force.

In sum, arguments based purely on economic theories for supposing that non-profit organisations will necessarily be able to operate at an advantage linked specifically to their status when supplying goods and services in the public arena should be treated with caution. (Lester Salamon and Helmut Anheier's tests of validity of rival explanations on the basis of data assembled in the Johns Hopkins studies proved inconclusive.) In practice, cases of 'philanthropic failure' are sufficiently common to undermine any automatic presumption in their favour. This is a more or less inevitable consequence of the environment in which they increasingly have to function. As Salamon comments on the process he defines as 'marketisation':

> there are doubtless advantages to be gained from a greater degree of competition in the social marketplace. Like government agencies, non-profit organisations can become insulated from their target populations and insensitive to their needs. A dose of client-driven, customer-conscious discipline of the market can therefore produce positive results. At the same time, however, there are serious risks ... Consumers of services in this field are often not the same people as those who pay, severing a link that is crucial for the market's operation. As for-profit firms enter the social market, moreover, they will inevitably siphon off the more affluent customers, leaving non-profits with the most difficult and least profitable cases, If non-profit firms are forced by this competition to behave similarly, the focus of attention of the non-profit sector will also shift increasingly toward those able to pay, leaving the disadvantaged with few places to turn. Finally, as scarce management talent in the non-profit sector is forced to focus increasingly on the management of for-profit commercial ventures, the time and attention required to oversee the central operations of the sector will suffer. (1993: 37)

Yet despite these practical concerns and the anxieties about values raised earlier, there are grounds for supposing that the market-based approach has an important positive contribution to make – for example, where efficiency and quality of goods and services are the desired characteristics.

Adapting to the market

To adopt an approach which is based on market-like behaviour but conducted within the civil society sphere necessarily involves raising issues around values. In his recent study of the generating of community wealth in the United States, *The Cathedral Within* (1999), Bill Shore describes the hesitations among non-profit organisations when invited to enter a competitive market for goods and services whose scope has been dramatically increased by the withdrawal of the state. This is a process that has developed more rapidly there than in other western democracies: Lester Salamon refers to: 'A striking expansion of commercial activity on the part of nonprofit firms, blurring the distinction between non-profit and for-profit providers and raising serious questions about who will serve those in need' (1993: 17).

Shore's answer takes the form of a passionate plea for the wholehearted adoption of market approaches to assessing costs and calculating benefits and in the process the demolishing of what he calls 'the wall between for-profit and non-profit' (1999: 137). This would involve thinking in a longer-term way about objectives and seeking to construct organisations with long-term life expectancy. In this process, skills learned in the marketplace will be needed to add value and build organisational capacity. But above all there would need to be a basic value change: Shore describes one organiser beginning workshops with non-profit executives by inviting them to recite repeatedly after him the mantra: 'profit is good' (1999: 213). And he reinforces his argument, in classic American business-school instruction-manual style, with case studies of successful adaptation by voluntary organisations of all sizes, in every kind of environment.

But the tools of business don't come value-free. Shore's argument is that their use is a necessary though not a sufficient part of the process of change: but he skates over the internal difficulties frequently caused by the introduction of (for example) business approaches to recruitment and remuneration. A charismatic leader is his simple prescription for solving all such problems. Such leaders are, of course, immensely appealing to the outside world but often less effective when it comes down to deploying basic management skills.

Externally, voluntary organisations seeking to replicate market conditions in their own operations inevitably find themselves heavily involved in questions like image and marketing, reflected in concern to 'rebrand' organisations and find logos and slogans that catch the changing moods of a fickle public. It involves new promotional strategies, hard sell of the product, struggling for increased market share or at least securing a niche position as provider (Bruce 1994). It means adopting this year's new business vocabulary, talking of customers, 'drivers' for change and being focused, on a hitherto undiscovered passion for excellence. Above all, it means competition for the resources that will provide the essential support for these strategies (the equivalent of the test of black ink on the single bottom line that shows profit or loss).

In this process, pick and mix is not always a realistic option. Competition and the devices designed to secure success in the contest sit uncomfortably with the traditional values of many older voluntary organisations – altruism, unpaid service to the community as a whole. William Beveridge famously remarked in his account of voluntary action that the business motive was 'a good servant but a bad master'. Many of the developments of the last twenty years must have seemed to some of these organisations like a Beaumarchais farce – what happens when the servant gets out of hand and becomes a Figaro, calling the tune?

There are other perspectives on closer engagement with business and the marketplace that do reflect an alternative ('civil society') approach: these range from simple rejection of business values and approaches to attempts to define an alternative position in which profit is not the dominant objective but efficiency is nonetheless achieved. Where altruism remains the distinctive ingredient, this means identifying means of doing things in a manner that properly reflects that priority. Adalbert Evers comments that:

> It is clear that economic considerations about 'institutional choices' usually fail to consider systematically the degree to which strategies of voluntary and non-profit organisations are influenced by 'ideological' factors. Far from being merely 'irrational' features, they point to the special nature of such associations which separate them from business organisations. (1995: 165)

Alternatives to the market-without-adjectives

On the domestic side the search for alternatives implies exploring different models of economic action based not on neo-classical economics but on alternative perspectives in which the main motive force is neither laid down by the state nor led by business values (Leadbeater and Christie 1999: 11).

The term 'social economy' is familiar usage elsewhere in Europe (Vienney 1994): but in Britain it has tended to be treated as a marginal area: the preserve of cranks and what are dismissed by the would-be hardheaded as 'do-gooders'. This, though, is the arena in which much of the original thinking about the distinctive contribution of the third sector is now taking place.

Dissatisfaction with the quality of what is on offer through the state and the cost of what can be obtained through the market have been major forces in generating these alternative approaches to service delivery. In this model, citizens are not passive recipients of services, from whatever source, but themselves become co-producers, mixing financial and non-financial resources in order to do so (Laville 1998).

As an approach, this has a long history (for which see Chapter 2); in its modern form it emerges in Britain in the 1960s as a means of making good deficiencies in the services for families with young children. The absence of adequate state provision for care of children below school age has been a marked feature of the British scene, in contrast to countries elsewhere in Europe. At the end of the Second World War, when large numbers of mothers left the workforce – with official encouragement – after the emergency conditions had ended, the state's commitment to providing crèches evaporated. The quality of commercial child-minding services was generally too low and the cost too high to provide a viable alternative for conscientious parents. The gap was filled by the creation of self-managed pre-school play-groups.

This movement grew largely spontaneously on the basis of mutual exchange; its value was eventually recognised, though not for a long while – I well remember in the mid-1960s hearing a government representative at a conference telling delegates that care of 'ordinary' pre-school children 'could not become the state's responsibility'. Eventually, funding support did become available and this activity was eventually absorbed into the mainstream of provision in the classic pattern of voluntary sector innovation followed by state adoption (Leadbeater and Christie 1999: 25).

But the application of the principles developed in the process – free exchange of skills and shared responsibilities – has spun off in a number of different directions. The demonstration that money might not be the only viable basis of exchange generated an interest in barter and schemes based on local exchanges by tokens (LETs). Co-production has taken a literal shape in the self-build housing associations that involve members directly in the construction of their own homes. The scale of these operations is small but the impact ripples out as schemes demonstrate their value not just in extending choice in provision of housing but as a unique means of acquiring and using skills.

Once past the stage of demonstrating that these activities are not simply the preserve of eccentric simple lifers but adaptable to modern social circumstances, the issue of scale arises. In economic terms, self-help has always been an established activity, especially in the context of newcomers attempting to cope with the problems of entry to a complex new system and survival within it. As we saw in Chapter 3, migrant groups frequently run quite complex systems of mutual assistance, enabling members of the group to draw upon capital from a common pool at crucial stages in their family's life cycle – starting a business, renting a house, education, care of the sick.

However, these activities operate at an intimate scale between those who have a well-established basis of mutual trust – reinforced, as suggested earlier, by communal sanctions that can be imposed where necessary on those who fail to meet their obligations. There remains a question about whether this type of operation can translate on to a larger scale and become not just a matter of personal support for a transitory period but a permanent source of assistance, available for investment and innovation.

Hence the current interest in the development of credit unions. These build on the model of spontaneous sharing of access to resources already common in working-class areas going beyond the traditional pooling of savings in the 'Christmas Club' and attempt to provide a secure source of short-term loans that can divert business from loan sharks – private credit companies operating at prohibitive rates of interest, which are often now the only source of credit in highly deprived housing estates that have been deserted by orthodox financial services – banks, building societies and insurance agents (Leadbeater and Christie 1999: 62–3). Here, there are lessons to be learned from parallel experience with micro-credit in the developing world and in particular the success story of the Grameen bank in Bangladesh.

More ambitiously, community trusts and foundations attempt to support local community-based voluntary activity by pooling resources assembled from a variety of donors – state, individual, corporate and charitable. By operating close to local situations they can reach underrepresented groups and help inexperienced ones through the process of establishing themselves and acquiring a secure longer-term base. Because they are locally based they can assess need on the basis of local knowledge and minimise the risk of picking up the latest fashionable activity and the expense of what is unsustainable. They are also able to encourage effective corporate philanthropy by helping donors to invest in a permanent resource but without the burden of investigation and management.

These initiatives have achieved substantial momentum; but they also face dilemmas of control and accountability and critical mass. For example, in order to grow, should such organisations federate up or franchise down? They need access to additional capital and revenue sources if they are to extend their activities and make an effective contribution to addressing significant policy issues like urban regeneration. Their capacity to build assets and invest to trade and create employment requires them to act entre-preneurially and to enter the marketplace as potential competitors to state and market-based organisations.

There is an issue here around how far addressing mainstream policy questions is likely to compromise the distinctive character-istics of community-based enterprises. An alternative approach would not exclude attempting to demonstrate their capacity to address existing social and economic issues, but stress the poten-tial community-based economic development bodies possess to enter new arenas and tackle questions of sustainability; green issues, cultural initiatives and uses of new technology for commu-nity benefit. However, to do so effectively may be not so much a matter of developing new techniques as refurbishing old ones.

Occupying the middle ground: mutuality in Britain

As we have already seen (Chapter 2), there is a longstanding his-tory in Britain of mutual aid and cooperative forms of provision. In the late nineteenth century these formed a well-established out-let for working-class enterprise and provided necessary support, in the absence of state provision, for the welfare of the working population and their dependants.

It was this tradition of mutual aid that Beveridge celebrated in *Voluntary Action,* taking the friendly society ethos and its organisational form as the epitome of the self-reliance of citizens in freely chosen association. Although the state pre-empted many of the functions of friendly societies in Britain as a result of the welfare reforms after the Second World War, the practice elsewhere in Europe, especially in France, was rather different. There some of the tasks discharged here by the state – 'assurance and social protection' – are still performed by mutuals and cooperatives (Vienney 1994: ch. 2).

In Britain, mutuality survives, but in a skewed distribution. The friendly societies are 'a shadow of their former selves' (Leadbeater and Christie 1999). The largest remaining representatives are now building societies and insurance companies; but their own position is now under continuous threat as a result of the changes that have taken place since the 1980s, which have led many of them to abandon mutual status. This has sometimes been the result of decision by management but increasingly the change has been enforced by the activities of 'carpetbaggers': entrepreneurs who persuade members to vote for demutualisation in order to obtain 'windfall' conversion bonuses. Membership has not proved to be an effective defence against these assaults: other techniques have had to be deployed, like the Nationwide Building Society's stipulation that a condition of new membership should be compulsory donation of windfalls to charity.

The other traditional form of mutuality is the Co-operative movement. This represents the best known distinctive contribution that this country has made to theory and practice of common enterprise. (This has spread across the world: I well remember my surprise at encountering in Puerto Rico in the late 1960s the 'Rochdale' taxis that commemorate in their name the birthplace of the movement.) But in the twentieth century the market share of the Co-op as a retailer has declined steadily (it is now down to 6 per cent of the whole if groceries are taken separately). Leadbeater and Christie provide the full story: the partial exception is the success of the Co-op Bank set up by the Co-operative Welfare Society on the basis of promoting ethical banking and investment – and Co-operative funeral services.

Nevertheless, there is still a substantial range of cooperative and mutual enterprises (what Stephen Yeo has termed CMEs) in existence and some evidence of a revival of activity, linking traditional strengths with new ideas and practices An example of this revival is the work of the mutuality task force led by the Oxford, Swindon and Gloucester Cooperative Society, which has used the traditional policy of distributing a proportion of the trading surplus to promote social development.

But taking the established mutuals collectively, there are still tensions around their roles: the successful rivalry of their commercial competitors, inadequate 'product differentiation' (Leadbeater and Christie 1999: 61); the need to have access to capital markets. The adoption of market values risks eroding their distinctiveness: it is no longer possible to identify benefits for the users of their services clearly enough or establish the nature of the 'cooperative advantage'. Membership has always been the key distinguishing characteristic of the sector; but in itself this has not provided a sufficient defence, especially when allowed to become moribund through lack of engagement of members. Their decline in the recent past can be read as one sort of warning of the consequences of interpenetration of the market and voluntary sectors.

The established mutual sector contains another important example of the consequences of blurring of boundaries. This is the case of housing associations, though here the tensions around their role are different: these arise from the fact that they have become the inheritors of the local state's functions in the housing market, to cater for the housing of the least well off. The introduction of private finance into their operations from 1988 changed the way in which housing associations did their job, changing their position on management of risk and moving them out of the rehabilitation of existing property towards construction of new housing schemes.

However, at the same period almost all local authorities stopped building new housing and were thereafter progressively less able to meet local housing needs, beyond their basic minimum statutory obligations. Housing associations were thereupon called on to fill the breach (and in so doing inherited many of the local authorities' problems over management and quality of services).

The Housing Corporation's 'Housing Plus' scheme, launched in 1994 represents an attempt to cope with the consequences: it is intended to help associations promote sustainable social housing which contributes positively to the community. In order to do so effectively, Michael Young and Gerard Lemos have argued, the principle of mutuality needs to be invoked: they propose the introduction of a Mutual Aid Compact. In their analysis, housing associations should provide support at the local level for some the initiatives already mentioned (specifically credit unions and LETs) but also formally require new tenants to enter into a commitment to provide mutual assistance to create and sustain the local community (Young and Lemos 1997: 78).

But in parallel with these attempts to reclaim the value of mutuality, similar forms are also being deployed in new contexts, making use of up-to-date technology. A frequently quoted example is the development of Internet/Linux software where innovation was driven by informal collaboration involving a 'club' of participants primarily interested in technical problems for their own sake rather than profit and exclusive ownership.

In summary: mutuality does in theory offer an alternative between market and state in which the voluntary impulse finds a natural outlet. Membership and the commitment that goes with it helps to build trust; collaboration involving different stakeholders can produce 'win-win' situations and the outcome can be to produce a healthier sense of community (Leadbeater and Christie 1999: 11). There is space for experiment and potential for marrying up the traditional strengths of mutuality with some of the 'new economy' ideas about harnessing market energy to social objectives.

On the other hand, it is far from clear that mutuality in practice always provides an effective means of delivering services that can provide better outcomes than those that can be delivered by the market or even the much-abused state. For all the talk of empowerment, the quality of what's provided by mutual endeavours at local level, morally excellent though that effort may be and rewarding for those that take part in it, still often falls below the standards that those receiving it are legitimately entitled to expect. There is a risk here of perpetuating the poverty of expectations among the poor that Bevan warned about.

Future relations: separation or synthesis?

What is certain is that relationships between the market and voluntary associations will develop and extend. However, the terms on which relationships will develop are less clear. Traditional relations, in which business is seen by associations simply as another charitable donor, may be on the way to exhausting their potential, even if the potential patrons may be becoming relatively more prosperous. This can be illustrated by the search for sources of new money among the new rich, and their propensity to follow past patterns when they do give: now there is a sudden proliferation of internet millionaires with no clear notion of where to put their money – as long as they are seen to be doing it. (Bill Gates' apparent uncertainty about his objectives is one example; witness his foundation's sudden switch from techno-charity to health care.)

A more interesting line of argument may be to reverse the question: what can the market take from voluntarism, beyond the superficialities of corporate image building?

Early western capitalism and charity had common roots that were nourished by religion, as Novak is eager to point out: he is less keen on the divergences that followed as the capitalist enterprise gathered steam and entrepreneurs became less inhibited in their morality – and behaviour. Some of the common themes: ventures for mutual benefit; sharing of risks; trust in both the informal and formal senses, with the careful line drawn and entrenched in English charity law about who is to benefit and on what terms; stakeholding and stewardship; the binding force of religious sentiment (not just 'Judeo-Christian'), cooperation as an alternative style; the development of longterm relationships, loyalty and reciprocity.

Business forms do not exclude informality: social networks and family connections are still significant and not only in 'ethnic business' – compare the account Paul Thompson gives of the way in which transactions were conducted in the 'Old' City of London (in *Middle Class History*) before the gentlemen financiers were swept away by the international financial operators. Social responsibility still runs with the grain of some forms of business activity, not against it. Not all entrepreneurs are necessarily Novak-type individualistic profit-seeking or impersonal turbo-capitalists of the kind whose consequences Soros fears. But efforts to engage with voluntary action need to be seen as part of mainstream activity and not as an appendage. As the clothing company *Timberland* puts it in their statement of objectives:

> We do not give money to charity. Instead we try to create a return. We create value for our customers, the community and the non-profit organisations we work with, The traditional notion of philanthropy is not adequate. It is not smart or wise to approach social problems with the financial leftovers of companies. (Quoted in *Financial Times*, 1 October 1998: 7)

What common ground can now be staked out, where differences of values can be reconciled? Potential candidates include developing new approaches to generating community wealth (Shore 1999); recognising the legitimacy of social entrepreneurs and enabling them to function more effectively; introducing more effective means of trading to raise funds that don't scupper the mission; and evolving more sensitive means funding of new enterprises. A 'new mutualism' may have a future as alternative means of service delivery (Leadbeater and Christie 1999). Collaborations that involve some measure of cross-boundary cooperation on sustaining and reinforcing the open society (Soros 1998) are certain to remain important.

There will always be a debate within voluntarism about 'contamination' by the market. Anarchism and rejectionism will not evaporate. There will still be many organisations operating within civil society who will not (and many who need not) engage with business. Equally, there will always be a debate within business about the relevance of engagement with voluntary associations, between those are prepared to adopt an approach like Timberland and those who see profit as the only legitimate goal of business. Out on the fringes lurk the individualist ultras. This is where libertarian extremists like the anarcho-capitalists (see Lemieux 1988) can be found, whose acute pessimism about human behaviour leaves no space for altruism and where self-interest is the only guide to action.

Conclusion

This chapter began with some questions, the answers to which should by now have begun to emerge. The number and intensity of relationships formed across the frontier between civil society and the market have increased substantially, at least in the Anglo-Saxon countries, over the last two decades. But the various forms that the different interactions with markets that have been described here have taken don't lead to the conclusion that contamination of mission and values is automatic. It is wise for voluntary associations to be wary about some of the consequences of adopting some techniques in campaigning and competition: but the risk here is not necessarily the adoption of commercial values but of something more fundamental – competitive instincts at the basic human level?

In any case, most voluntary associations have a sufficiently strong sense of their own identity and purpose not to succumb to wholesale transformation of their values. They bring assets of their own to the transactions with the market and some of this may spill over into the changes now occurring in the business sector – the revived interest in the value of human resources and 'people-centred management'. At the same time, it is important not to lose sight of the role of market organisations as potential rivals in significant areas of service delivery.

This leaves a range of possible responses to the challenge posed by developments in the marketplace. Those recognising some of these apparent drawbacks but wishing to use the potential of capitalism – its energies and the stimulus it provides to innovation – seek to turn it in the direction of greater cooperation. Michael Edwards makes this case persuasively: I will return to it in the next chapter. As I have described in this one, this approach could lead to the promotion of an alternative 'social economy', embodying a different set of values, either through adaptation of existing institutions or through creation of new ones. Here, the use of skills and approaches to innovation on display in the marketplace have clear lessons – hence the current interest in the United Kingdom in 'social entrepreneurs', which stretches across the political spectrum.

Many voluntary organisations operating outside the 'civil society space' are already quite capable of efficient delivery of good quality services – the 'exceptional growth and transformation' of the UK sector testifies to that. Those who function as the sector's 'boosters' are fond of arguing that this represents the maturity of voluntarism. But in order to look other sectors in the face, on their own terms, this requires the value of voluntary activity to be assessed by measures like the level of job creation and contribution to the Gross Domestic Product – neither of which capture the essence of voluntarism. There are legitimate concerns that there are distinctive characteristics at risk if profit is accepted as a central objective: we should not be too hasty in rushing to take our places in the pews in Bill Shore's 'Cathedral Within'. Profit is not automatically good for voluntary associations or as a motivating principle for those who work in and for them.

What is needed at this point is a sober exploration of the uses and abuses of markets as they function in the public sphere, both in their own right as generators of wealth and alternative providers of services or as the means of communicating alternative approaches that might improve the performance of other organisations, through the application of 'market disciplines' or management techniques. The new context for these activities and the source of changes that have sharpened the issues is the phenomenon of globalisation, touched on at the start of this chapter and a persistent presence in the wings at earlier stages in this book. This deserves more detailed examination.

CHAPTER 7

Civil Society and Globalisation

As the violation of justice is what men will never submit to from one another, the public magistrate is under the necessity of employing the power of the commonwealth to enforce the practice of this virtue. Without this precaution, civil society would become a scene of violence and bloodshed, every man revenging himself at his own hand whenever he fancied he was injured. (Adam Smith, *The Theory of Moral Sentiments*, 1759, quoted by A. Skinner in his introduction to *The Wealth of Nations*)

Globalisation, as David Held remarks, is (yet another) 'much-contested word'. There are those who would wish to see it as an entirely new phenomenon, representing a drastic break with the past, promoted by a new politics (a single hegemonic superstate, the United States) and empowered by a new economy based on new technologies. Others prefer to point to continuities, rather than changes. Societies have always been interconnected; in some senses the current extent of connectedness represents a reversion to the past order (for example, the relative stability of the era of imperial geo-politics in the latter half of the nineteenth century) rather than the creation of a new one (Hirst and Thompson 1996).

As Held argues,

Globalisation is best understood as a spatial phenomenon, lying on a continuum with 'the local' at one end and 'the global' at the other. It denotes a shift in the spatial form of human organisation and activity to transcontinental or interregional patterns of activity, interaction and the exercise of power. It involves a stretching and deepening of social relations and institutions across space and time such that, on the one hand, day-to-day activities are increasingly influenced by events happening on the other side of the globe and on the other, the practices and decisions of local groups and communities can have significant global reverberations. (1997: 253)

The impact of globalisation also depends crucially on the perspective from which it is viewed – specifically, the location, both spatially and in class terms, where a new global elite that resides at the apex has a grandstand view. And although globalisation as a process has a very long reach, it also exposes the issue of power – who has the capacity (the leverage) to control events and which individuals or organisations simply experience the outcomes without having the capacity to change them.

The detailed impact of the current phase of globalisation can be explored along a number of different dimensions. The most dramatic have been the economic and political developments of the last two decades. Trade is one example: the growth of international trade now far surpasses the levels reached at the end of the nineteenth century; and although barriers to a perfectly open global economy still persist, the linkages are multiplying steadily. As Held puts it: 'national economies are enmeshed in a pattern of increasingly dense and competitive international trade' (1997: 255).

But it is the growth of global financial flows that has been the most spectacular development. The liberalisation of capital markets has meant that currency speculators (which may mean a George Soros but can also be a twenty-five-year-old empowered by new technology) can cause the collapse of a national currency or severely injure it, with all the associated damage to the economy and society of the country concerned. Characteristically, this effect is produced by bringing about a panic charge of what Thomas Friedman calls the 'electronic herd' of stockbrokers, bond and currency dealers, mutual and pension fund executives, merchant bankers, individual investors and the financial advisers, analysts and journalists who swarm about them (1999: 93ff.).

In this new environment, the role of multinational corporations has become far more significant and the extent of their influence on events across the world has become much greater. As Held summarises it, 'MNCs account for a quarter to a third of the world's output. 70 per cent of world trade and 80 per cent of direct international investment. They are essential to the diffusion of technology and they are key players in international money markets' (1997: 256).

All these developments have important political implications. Obituaries of the nation state are certainly premature; but political decisions taken at national level and policies adopted there are increasingly subject to modification, correction or even complete shipwreck as a result of events at the global level. Nation states are increasingly incapable of setting limits; and the civic culture associated with them has thinned out as a diversity of new influences is brought to bear.

To complete the earlier quotation from George Soros (p. 139):

> As long as capitalism remains triumphant, the pursuit of money overrides all other social considerations. Economic and political arrangements are out of kilter. The development of a global economy has not been matched by the development of a global society ... The relationship between center and periphery is also profoundly unequal. If and when the global economy falters, political pressures are liable to tear it apart. (1998: 102)

After the near-collapse of communism and the alternative modes of organisation that went with it, national boundaries now have an uneven application. Multinationals can leapfrog them: technology empowers interventions (like internet finance trading) that disregard them, which can have drastic consequences across whole regions. Many health and most environmental issues do not respect them either. Organised crime evades them. But people – flesh and blood human beings – seeking to escape the pressures of poverty and take advantage of new opportunities are still often unable to cross them.

In the developed world, globalisation has had an impact at a number of different levels. It has promoted an enhanced form of individualism based in part on the new technology which has permitted ambitious young people with the right mix of skills and resources to escape from the traditional career pattern in large organisations and launch themselves as individual entrepreneurs ('me, plc'). For others who have gained in a more passive style from the prosperity globalisation has conferred on their particular societies, it has also helped to promote what J. K. Galbraith calls the 'culture of contentment', eliminating the need to question the means, accepting the ends as a reflection of their just deserts.

In some contexts, it has provided governments with the opportunity (or pretext) for drastic reductions in public sector activities. Thomas Friedman calls this 'donning the golden straightjacket', essentially, the full market-dominated neo-liberal kit, tailored to meet the situation produced by 'the democratizations (*sic*) of finance, technology and information', which have 'blown away all the walls protecting alternative systems' (1999: 90). This would generate a kind of hyper-subsidiarity in which all intermediate agencies have been eliminated and charity is finally assigned the residual supporting role as a safety net that neo-liberal theory attaches to it – and one that also materially benefits the charitable. 'Give to charity', urged the American ambassador at a meeting of the Hungarian United Way that I attended at the hideous Marriott Hotel that disfigures the banks of the Danube immediately opposite the Castle Hill 'and you will ensure that your own taxes remain low'.

Thus we have a situation in which the dynamic of relationships is constantly changing. For voluntary organisations, this involves dealing with an expanding – and a rapidly mutating – market on the one hand and on the other with a state sector whose role has been substantially modified and in many crucial respects diminished. But the market still needs the state to perform certain key functions that allow commercial transactions to take place – maintaining public order, providing an 'appropriate' legal and regulatory framework.

Global institutions

On the terrain of this 'New World Order' there are a number of key institutions that operate at the global level. Some have responsibilities explicitly linked to the world economy: the World Bank, the IMF, the World Trade Organisation (WTO), the OECD; although the outcomes of their interventions, some consequences of which we have already encountered in Chapter 5, have a far wider impact. Others have a different remit: political, military, legal or humanitarian: the United Nations (UN) and its associated agencies; NATO; the International Court of Justice, other 'regional' bodies (the European Union and its various satellite activities). The architecture of this system is complex; many of the structures were built up in response to developments like the traumas of two successive world wars and the rivalries of the cold war and still bear the marks of their origins (Edwards 1999).

A diverse set of values underpin the operations of these bodies. Some of them are partly about holding member states to account (at least in theory); about human rights enforcement; and sometimes moving towards pooling some aspects of sovereignty. There has been cautious and uneven progress in all these directions, compromised in many cases by the weaknesses of some institutions and the lack of commitment to some key objectives of the most powerful member, the United States. But the outlines of a global system of regulation and even control are beginning to emerge, however partially and imperfectly.

But the activities of international organisations are also driven by liberal capitalist notions on the 'right' way to manage domestic economies. As crudely but forcefully expressed by Thomas Friedman in *The Lexus and the Olive Tree*, it is all about doing it the American way.

> What is going on in the world today, in the very broadest sense, is that through the process of globalisation everyone is being forced towards America's gas station. If you are not American and don't know how to pump your gas, I suggest you learn. With the end of the cold war, globalisation is globalising Anglo-American style capitalism. It is globalising American culture and cultural icons. It is globalising the best of American and the worst of America. It is globalising the American revolution and it is globalising the American gas station. (1999: 308)

Do these values in fact transfer successfully to the global scale? As we have seen in our earlier discussion (Chapter 4) one of the key elements in a successful system is that of trust. How far can that extend to the new environment? Does it depend on physical proximity, on eye contact, on a ritual exchange of prescribed words followed by a (firm) handshake? Clearly the universal impact of American culture can help to establish a set of common values; although those who pay lip service to these values from expediency may in practice help to subvert them, either unintentionally or deliberately (Held 1997: 258).

What is clear is that the international institutions that attempt (so far with very mixed success) to manage the global economy do so on a basis that habitually replicates the formulae of the Anglo-American model of capitalism: a freeing up of the labour market – or, otherwise expressed, an end of job security and trade union power – greater scope for entrepreneurial activity by deregulation, reduction in the range and cost of state welfare services by privatisation – all the elements in Friedman's 'golden straightjacket'. Packages of assistance to countries whose economies experience difficulty in the new environment have habitually been made contingent on the application of these basic principles, sometimes known as the 'structural adjustment': by and large, governments in need of help have accepted them. Unfortunately, the results of these interventions have not been what their initiators expected – or what those on the receiving end were told that they would be. As Michael Edwards summarises the position:

> almost all the independent research that has been carried out agrees: there is little evidence of significant structural change in the economies of the adjusting countries, the competitiveness of non-traditional exports, the efficiency of production or levels of savings and investment – all the things that would have to change to make the economy stronger in the long run. [Furthermore]...the social costs were immense. Inequality increased in nearly all cases and poverty in most, especially among poor people in rural areas who lacked the assets as skills to take advantage of market incentives and in the cities, where the axe fell heavily on people in government jobs and on others whose wages fell in real terms against a background of rising food prices. Those who did not have relatives to fall back on were affected especially badly, and women bore the brunt of coping for their families. (1999: 116–7)

As a result, there has been some movement away from this position, even in the World Bank itself, where there is now talk of a new 'Washington consensus'. One symptom of this change that has become increasingly evident is the inclusion in the range of factors when countries are being assessed of a concern with the presence of civil society. The World Bank's interest in this topic suggests a new set of questions for international bureaucrats: can we lend where a viable civil society doesn't exist: does its presence provide good security for loans or a guarantee of the right outcomes? Should we assess the quantity of social capital in debtor nations as well as their conventional financial reserves?

Counterbalancing globalism

Some countervailing pressures against the advance of globalisation, at least in its crudest form (Friedman's gas station formula) do exist. One is the persistence of nationalism; another, connected but distinct, the continuing strength internationally of religions that offer an alternative world view – what Ernest Gellner (1994) calls an 'umma' – to the 'Judeo-Christian' values taken to be universal by the advocates of the neo-liberal paradigm. Certain forms of such religions are sometimes denounced as 'fundamentalist' by those who do not share these beliefs or have no wish to understand them. Others are 'extremist', in the sense of having an explicitly political agenda to be pursued without inhibition or geographical restriction – illustrating the 'global reach of violence', though often undertaken by individuals on their own initiative, much assisted by the use of new technology (Friedman 1999: 326).

Not all these nationalisms have taken a traditional form. Some are revivals of those suppressed in the Versailles settlement after the First World War: but others represent new aspirations, sometimes linked to religious revivals. These have led to a proliferation of liberation movements of all kinds, new ethnic conflicts, some on the basis of association around identities once barely recognised, even by those who now claim them; exclusions of all kinds and in extreme cases expulsions or even genocidal massacres.

Another series of global developments cluster around the theme of democracy. One of the striking developments of the late twentieth century has been the revival of democracy at the national level as a form of governance. But there are questions about how genuine this always is (much apparently democratic practice is a superficial façade) and whether how far democratic principles can be applied outside the framework of the nation state. This question is especially relevant for voluntary associations, one of whose main functions, as we have already seen, is frequently taken to be the underpinning of democratic institutions and practices where they exist (see Chapter 4) and their promotion where they do not (see Chapter 5).

David Held makes a persuasive case for an extension of democratic principles to the global arena as a form of 'cosmopolitan' democracy that would involve 'the development of administrative capacity and independent resources at regional and global levels as a necessary complement to those in local and national politics' (1997: 263). And the Kosovo episode in 1999 when NATO intervened on behalf of the Kosovar Albanian population expelled by the Serb authorities demonstrates a qualified willingness to adopt these principles in practice as a basis for intervention. This has sometimes been called 'armed humanitarianism'; the record in the post cold-war period also includes some spectacular failures elsewhere in the Balkans and notably in Somalia, which had the long-term consequence of extinguishing any enthusiasm in the United States for future involvement in such enterprises – at least at ground level (Shawcross 1999).

But if there is indeed a 'global public space' that will continue to require intervention in some form to mediate in conflicts, are there other alternatives to the blind workings of the global market, or the intermittently effective functioning of international institutions still mainly dominated by nation states and in particular the most powerful of them all, the United States? In the first case, the global market's capacity to discourage active conflict is unproved: 'Friedman's law', that no two countries with McDonald's franchises will go to war with each other (1999: 374) was instantly shown to be false by the Kosovo episode. And the commitment of the United States will never be complete, but always conditional on the consistency of any proposed action with their own perceived national interests – as their politicians are frank enough to acknowledge, at least to domestic audiences as when the Secretary of State, Madeleine Albright, warned that the United States would 'pursue its national interest' if the UN Secretary General came up with deals that 'we don't like' (Edwards 1999: 175).

Non-governmental organisations: their international role

The term 'NGO' (the form to which the cumbersome description 'non-governmental organisation' is now habitually shortened) is of comparatively recent origin (1950) (Dichter 1999: 38); but voluntary or charitable organisations working outside national boundaries have a much longer history. If we set aside as a special case the most ancient of all, the Roman Catholic Church and its various orders, the Red Cross, dating from the mid-nineteenth century and the need to cater on a non-partisan footing for the needs of war casualties and prisoners, is perhaps the best known (Moorehead 1999). Save the Children, founded by Eglantyne Jebb after the First World War to deal with famine and the families of war victims is another early example (Moorehead 1999: 281–2); but the paradigm case (certainly the best known in the United Kingdom) is Oxfam, formed by Quakers in 1942 to provide food and clothing for the inhabitants of Nazi-occupied Greece. The pacifist humanitarianism of all these earlier organisations set the initial tone for activity in the immediate post-war period. This was transitional action, designed to provide emergency relief for immediate consequences of wartime devastation and to supplement where necessary the actions of national governments and the newly established international relief agencies acting under the auspices of the UN (UNRRA, UNICEF, UNHCR, eventually UNDP, United Nations Development Programme) to address the pressing problems of starvation and resettlement of refugees.

This role expanded in scope and extended to developing (or, as they are now usually described, 'Southern') countries as they began to emerge from the colonial period. Alternative approaches to relief of poverty in these countries began to be developed. Some organisations repatriated some of the lessons that they had learned in that process to their own domestic environments. (As we saw in Chapter 3, in the United Kingdom Voluntary Service Overseas (VSO) begat Community Service Volunteers.) But in the world of international NGOs, as in the other domains described earlier, a period of rapid growth in the level of activity in the field of aid – and changes in the roles being performed there – began in the 1980s and has continued up to the present.

This growth can be measured most simply in the increased numbers of development NGOs based in 'Northern' countries and operating internationally and the growth in the size of their budgets. But this has not just been a matter of increased scale of operation. There has been a parallel process of growth in the extent and level of activity of organisations based in the South and operating locally – what are sometimes termed GROs (for grass roots organisations) (Edwards and Hulme 1995).

There have also been fundamental changes in the environment in which all kinds of organisations operate, some of which have already been touched upon. The first and perhaps most important shift has been in the political context within which NGOs operate. Since the end of the cold war, what has sometimes been called a 'New Policy Agenda' in the areas of development policy and aid transfer has come into being. As Edwards and Hulme put it: 'This agenda is not monolithic – its details vary from one official aid agency to another, but in all cases it is driven by two basic sets of beliefs organised around the two poles of neo-liberal economics and liberal democratic theory' (1995: 4).

As a result of the first, the NGOs have become the preferred means for service provision in deliberate substitution for the state and on the grounds of their greater cost efficiency and sensitivity to the needs of the poorest. As a result of the second, NGOs have become the chosen vehicle for the development of a 'counterweight to state power protecting human rights, opening up channels of communication and participation, providing training grounds for activists and promoting pluralism' (Edwards and Hulme 1995). With the end of the former regimes in East and Central Europe, this responsibility has also extended to NGOs operating in those areas (see Chapter 5). In many cases, they have become the chosen agents for the promotion of civil society, as national governments and international agencies like the World Bank conceive of that term – though there are now indications that some governments, like the UK's DfID (Department for International Development) may prefer to fund civil society organisation direct and cut out the NGO middlemen.

In many of the areas where NGOs operate, state structures have progressively proved themselves to be inefficient and bureaucratic, fragile in the face of rapid economic changes, undermined by emerging ethnic conflicts or corrupted by unscrupulous politicians ('kleptocrats'). This has presented third sector organisations with a set of demanding new challenges. As Lindenberg and Dobel express them:

> Should NGOs try to function as a substitute for the state and provide basic health services, teachers, schools, water or sanitation? Ironically, without a state to actually provide services or security NGOs face the task of how to rebuild communities and provide service often without the effective public power needed to sustain them. The issues of service and relief often stand in conflict when an NGO addresses human rights abuses. If NGOs advocate against the abuses, they can endanger their access to the country and people who need help as well as endanger their own staff on the ground. This dilemma opens up the broader strategy of advocating for a global protection of a people's civil economic and political rights while balancing a commitment to serve those locally in most need. (Lindenberg and Dobel 1999: 11)

Along with this redefinition of roles, there has also been a substantial change in funding patterns. Not only has NGO funding from governments of OECD countries increased rapidly (within 1975 0.7 per cent of all such aid passing through NGOs, in 1985 3.6 per cent and in 1994 5 per cent); but private funding has also grown at an even greater rate and is now the principal source of funds for development activities. (Dichter 1999). Alongside these developments, 'global altruism' has come to be an increasingly significant factor: a series of well-publicised natural disasters have provoked an unprecedented level of private giving, greatly enhanced by the part played by high-profile public figures, most of them from the entertainment industry. This type of celebrity-fuelled activity has added substantially to the potential for fundraising by NGOs but the attention it attracts is also by its nature volatile; unpredictable in its extent and duration and open to manipulation and patronage (the use of images of starving children adding to the stereotype of local helplessness).

In these new circumstances, NGOs have found themselves attempting to cope with a variety of issues and adopting a range of different styles in order to do so. As Michael Edwards puts it NGOs 'have always been both market-based actors, providing services at a lower price than the commercial sector, and social actors, representing particular nonmarket values and interests on the political process. These two identities have radically different implications' (1999: 28).

The persistence of poverty has necessarily remained a central preoccupation, especially since political changes after 1989 have frequently had the result of increasing levels of need in certain parts of the population, notably those distinguished from the majority by their age, class or ethnic origin (like the Roma throughout East and Central Europe). Conflicts arising from these rifts have sometimes produced humanitarian catastrophes on a scale comparable to natural disasters, of which events in the 1990s in former Yugoslavia or in Rwanda are key examples.

These events have raised issues about the legitimacy of all interventions from outside; relations between national governments (donor and recipient) and international relief agencies; and the place of grass roots organisations, increasingly unwilling to act as 'water-carriers' for northern NGOs. There are maverick organisations like *Médecins Sans Frontières* (MSF) who prefer to try to steer clear of all direct involvement with governments and criticise those that do for practising a 'form of moral paralysis' (Moorehead 1999: 710).

Perhaps even more fundamentally, it raises questions about the consequences of those interventions that have taken place. Are NGOs actually more efficient as distributors of aid and providers of services, or can commercial undertakings operating under contract perform these functions as well or better? Can NGOs cope effectively with emergencies with political elements; and are they capable of demonstrating that they have made an impact on the political reform process, in the direction of greater democracy and participation?

The conclusions that Edwards and Hulme offer are not very encouraging. They find:

- no empirical study that demonstrates a general case that NGO provision is cheaper than public provision. Even where NGO service provision is 'low cost' it usually fails to reach the poorest people, although it may still reach more than the government or commercial agencies; and
- little impact on political reform: partly because NGOs themselves (as non-representative organisations) have failed to develop effective strategies to promote democratisation.

What can be done about these deficiencies? Improved accountability; more open negotiation with other stakeholders; institution building for the longer term and appropriate audit procedures; but above all, development of a broader agenda for international cooperation built around negotiated rules and standards (Edwards 1999).

How likely is that in the present situation? What tactics might best serve the interests of those for whom NGOs, at their best, are trying to cater?

Alternative perspectives on the global market

Direct challenges to the New World Order have been one of the main preoccupations of the new social movements we encountered in Chapter 3. Over the past decade they have expanded their campaigning role and the range and effectiveness of their interventions. (This function is linked with but distinguishable from the facilitating and advocacy role of international development NGOs).

There are a number of different themes around which action by new social movements has coalesced: environmental issues; feminist concerns and human rights more broadly construed. These concerns were made visible at a number of international gatherings – Helsinki, Rio, Beijing, Cairo – where they have secured an increasingly high profile through engaging the attention of the world's media. Action has taken a variety of different forms: some of it designed to secure greater accountability of institutions operating at the global level or achieve policy change by consent; some of it explicitly oppositional, designed to secure a fundamental change in current economic policies or the abolition of some of the bodies associated with them. Viewed together, these developments are generally taken to signal the appearance as an independent actor of a new entity, 'global civil society'.

The rejectionist strand has become increasingly visible: the innovative use of modern technology converted a local protest by the Zapatista opposition movement in Mexico against the policies of the World Bank into a virtual rally conducted on the Internet, a precedent rapidly followed by other organisations. In 1999, police mishandling of protesters at the meeting of the WTO in Seattle gave huge coverage internationally to images of direct action taken against international finance capital and international organisations.

Environmentalists have become adept at using publicity to embarrass governments and multinational corporations. Greenpeace has proved especially skilled at this exercise and has acquired a worldwide reputation for giant killing as a result. Their confrontation with Shell over the proposed sinking of the Brent Spar oil platform in the North Sea ended with a decisive victory for the NGO over the multinational. Both sides learned lessons from this episode. Shell proclaimed their adhesion to the ranks of socially responsible business and submitted themselves to verification of their good environmental intentions by audit. Greenpeace used the mix of direct action and publicity that had worked so successfully in this case – and greatly expanded their membership in the UK from 80 000 in 1987 to 420 000 in 1995 and funding base – to address other targets in the international business sector (for example, Monsanto and their role in the introduction of genetically modified (GM) crops). Opponents of American cultural hegemony have singled out McDonald's, ostensibly on environmental grounds but in practice as a highly visible scapegoat, given the global popularity of the product and instant recognition of its trademark 'golden arches'. The firm's attempt to silence critics by recourse to the law courts has backfired disastrously – another instance of the destabilising power of the World Wide Web, which gave the original critique posted there far wider circulation than it could ever have expected to achieve by old-fashioned print publication.

Yet the Brent Spar conflict, which looked like a defining episode, has also had its downside for campaigning NGOs. The evidence deployed so effectively by Greenpeace turned out to be seriously flawed: the group had overestimated by a factor of thirty-seven the amount of hydrocarbons in the oil rig which might have leaked into the sea. Some observers saw a pattern developing: environmental groups, in particular, were continually bidding up dangers and using crude exaggerations of risk to scare up support. In a scathing critique [on these NGOs], Michael Shaw Bond quoted the comments of the executive director of one charity working in the South: 'In their anti-corporatism they've become anti-technology, anti-science, anti-informed discussion. They do not like complexity, just the black and white' (2000).

And Shaw Bond extended this criticism to argue that confused lines of accountability and lack of transparency in operation (Greenpeace is a particular case in point) was drawing international NGOs into 'ambulance-chasing' behaviour, anxious to be seen by their donors at the scene of the next major disaster, where press and television have congregated, at the expense of working in a less dramatic fashion over longer time spans in areas where the need may be greater.

Conclusion

In this chapter, I have explored some of the implications of the process of globalisation and the rapid extension of its reach over the past twenty years, despite some countervailing pressures. I have described the parallel development of international institutions and the uneven progress made since the end of the cold war towards the creation of a global political order. The most influential of the international bodies have been those concerned with the management of the global economy, the World Bank and the IMF. The impact of their activities has provided a new context for the activities of NGOs, many of them originally established after the Second World War with a short-term aim of relief of poverty, but now frequently entrusted with a wider mission of propagating democracy and helping to establish and sustain civil society. As they attempt to discharge these missions, NGOs have encountered increasing criticism of their methods and the effectiveness of their performance – some of it well justified. At the same time, the level and intensity of challenges to globalisation by other non-profit organisations has increased rapidly. Their critique has mainly been addressed to the activities of international agencies and multinational corporations and has in its turn attracted criticism both for the quality of their analysis and their campaigning tactics.

Taken together, some of the evidence I have deployed suggests that rather than concentrating on performing on a global stage, non-profit organisations may often find better scope for their distinctive contribution at the local level. Internationally, this would mean paying more attention to helping to develop 'global civil society' as an alliance between a range of widely differing bodies with varied agendas, operating at different levels but facilitated by new technology, that can provide a counterweight to the excesses of global capitalism. Locally, this means facilitating grass roots organisations and embracing solutions that embody mutual aid, like the micro-credit movement. Eventually, when put together, these approaches might provide the synergy through which the local becomes global, just as for feminists the personal became political.

In his stimulating polemic, *Future Positive*, Michael Edwards sets out his objective as being 'humanising capitalism, [which] means recreating rationality on the basis of caring' and in that process it is civil society 'tarnished, as all heroes are, by the real world demands of compromise, pressure to reform, and internal failings' that is nonetheless 'the indispensable innovator, facilitator, bridge builder and counterweight; providing channels for accountability and communication in the good society; supporting poor people to organise and fight for their rights; experimenting with new social and economic models; and helping to underpin the norms of an emerging global polity' (1999: 231).

Even in the summary account provided here, it is clear still how far there is to go to reach that destination: but better, perhaps, to travel hopefully than arrive – which takes us off on the voyage to Utopia, which is the subject of the next chapter.

CHAPTER 8

Civil Society and Utopia

An acre in Middlesex is better than a principality in Utopia. (Thomas Macaulay)

Introduction

The aspirations of those who argue for the significance of civil society and an enhanced role for its institutions and values are often described as 'utopian'. In this chapter, I will be exploring some alternative types of Utopia and argue for the relevance of including utopian models of thinking and the outcome of utopian experiments in discussion of civil society theory and practice (both global and 'local').

In his immediate response to the events of 1989 in East and Central Europe, Ralf Dahrendorf wrote:

> We must beware of Utopia, (which) is in the nature of the idea a total society. It may exist nowhere but it is held as a counter-project against the realities of the world in which we are living. Utopia is a complete alternative and therefore of necessity a closed society. Whoever sets out to implement utopian plans will in the first instance have to wipe clean the canvas on which the real world is painted. This is a brutal process of destruction. All this applies to the Utopia of the middle way as it does to all others. (1990: 56)

Dahrendorf's hostile reaction is based partly on the real life experience of the citizens of countries that endured over forty years of 'actually existing socialism'. But behind this critique lie other, more fundamental objections to whole notion of utopian theorising, that go beyond the deformed practice whose consequences we have already touched upon (in Chapter 5).

Nevertheless, in this chapter I shall try to establish that analyses that deploy utopian values and the experience of attempting to apply them have relevant lessons to provide for the civil society debate. Specific issues on which I believe these ideas and their applications have a distinctive contribution to make include the theory and practice of leadership, alternative modes of association and their implications, ways of realising the potential of feminism and the debate on virtue – how it can best be inculcated and sustained. This should help to establish whether the civil society project itself can properly be categorised as utopian.

But before I do so, there are a number of difficulties to address. The terrain covered by Utopias is vast and the literature on them (and their presumed opposites, 'dystopias') correspondingly extensive. In his recent anthology of utopian writings, John Carey describes how in setting out to make his selection his search engine produced 577 entries under this title for him to review – and this is certainly a gross underestimate.

The concept of Utopia also covers an immense range of topics and a wide variety of forms. Frontiers are contested: what may seem to one observer to fall far inside the boundaries of Utopia is another person's practical undertaking. Values are passionately debated – the same project may be paradise to one, hell to another. Definitions are accordingly fluid and in order to make discussion manageable a large number of exclusions will be necessary. For this chapter, I will concentrate on ideal models of potential future societies and the values and arrangements that are called up to sustain them.

The geography of Utopia

Several recent commentators have undertaken mapping exercises in which they have not just charted the territory but attempted a taxonomy of Utopias (Goodwin 1978, Kumar 1987). These descriptions are perhaps best organised as polar opposites – the first and fundamental distinction being between Utopias as a general category matched on the other side by dystopia, where the best of intentions produce the worst of outcomes. This opposition reflects the swing between optimism – essentially about the potentialities of human beings and their capacity to control their surroundings for benevolent ends – and pessimism, the enduring power of the old Adam of original sin. Some Utopias look backwards, to a golden age (a classical Arcady, or paradise before the fall), others forward to a radiant future (*'les lendemains qui chantent'*, as French Communists used to say; 'tomorrows that sing'). But the devil lurks in both: *'et in Arcadia ego'*, the Renaissance engravers portray him saying, as he peers through the Arcadian shrubbery ('I can be found here, too'). They can be all-embracing – a future that beckons for humanity as a whole – or operate on the smallest scale, around a handful of people doing good in a mundane, private capacity.

Utopias are often conceived of as urban – a city of the just, of the saved, on a hill – or they can be rural, seeking to return to the (presumed) innocence of nature in the wild. They are usually collective, building on the essence of sociability, the 'natural' impulse to associate; but they can also be individualistic. Some see these as the ultimate dystopias: for William Morris, 'the absence of fellowship is death'. They are frequently cast in egalitarian form; but utopias are also sometimes quite rigidly hierarchical – critics of different sorts have called both types dystopias. They can be based on the discoveries and potentialities of science, but are also sometimes humanistic or in some instances deliberately anti-scientific. Finally, contrary to a widespread notion, they can be dynamic as well as static, though the means by which any Utopia can improve on presumed perfection remains a matter for puzzled debate.

Because some exclusions are necessary, I will not be drawing upon Utopias founded on religious millenarianism – Utopias of religious ecstasy and paradises: Eden, the Isles of the Blessed or Valhalla. In strictly theological terms, both Christian and Islamic, such a state cannot exist on earth: it is the prerogative of the Supreme Being and awaits us, if we are worthy or fortunate enough, only beyond the grave. However, theological orthodoxy has not inhibited many individuals intoxicated with what they take to be divine inspiration from making numerous attempts to construct paradise on earth founded upon their religious beliefs (there are examples from sixteenth-century Anabaptist Münster up to contemporary Taliban Afghanistan). But the values that animate these enterprises are ultimately impenetrable to outsiders. We may observe their consequences, which are often dramatically dystopian (like the Jonestown mass suicides) but the lessons of these episodes are not readily transferable outside the closed circle of belief.

I have also excluded the utopias of the age of European expansion and discovery. There is a whole archipelago of utopias from this period, presented as narratives of voyages on which expeditions encounter island worlds with strange and wonderful – or sometimes terrible – customs and practices. More's original *Utopia* (1516) is the archetype: it is typical of the genre that it is impossible to find agreement on whether it's intended as an absurdist satire (like Swift's flying island of Laputa in *Gulliver's Travels*), as a fantasy (as in Shakespeare's *Tempest*?) or designed to be taken seriously as a set of precepts for human behaviour. As More himself put it: 'the truth, as if smeared with honey, might a little more pleasantly slide into men's minds' (Kumar 1987: 24) . But what, then, are we to make of his dismissive attitude to conventional religion and assault upon materialism – gold in his Utopia serves only to make handcuffs and pisspots. Indeed, was More's coinage 'Utopia' itself an ironic pun, the meaning poised ambiguously between *eu-topos*, the good place, and *ou-topos*, nowhere?

These utopias are customarily presented as traveller's tales, where fact and fiction blend, destined for an audience that lacked reliable criteria for distinguishing between the two. Such travellers often encounter or even bring back with them a Noble Savage (a stock device of eighteenth-century authors descending from Crusoe's Friday) to confront and satirise 'advanced' European civilisation – a device revived by Huxley in his *Brave New World* (1932).

At the other extreme, I will also pass lightly over constitution-building projects that are sometimes cast in thinly fictionalised form. These can be useful intellectual exercises in rehearsing arguments from first principles that are intended to inform contemporary political debate. They have their place, from *The Prince* and *Leviathan* onwards; and I will touch on them where the argument requires. Finally and more frivolously, I won't deal with 'counter-factuals' – similar universes which exist in parallel with the real one, based on divergences stemming from alternative outcomes of actual events. These can be a useful intellectual tool as well as merely entertaining – a discovery now being belatedly made by historians, a generation after the social scientists. Nor, by extension, will I employ science fiction; not out of intellectual snobbery – this literature contains many entertaining and some thought-provoking utopian works – but simply because the field is too vast.

And the main body of literature cited will be Anglo-American (there is much else, especially in French; but I will arbitrarily exclude it at this stage) and mostly twentieth century. These omissions mean passing over much dross but also some key political science texts, several excellent novels, two of the great texts of nineteenth-century English socialism (William Morris's *News from Nowhere* and Oscar Wilde's *Soul of Man under Socialism*) and the most successful utopian text of all, in terms of copies sold and discussion provoked (Edward Bellamy's *Looking Backward*).

Oysters and omelettes

Even when the field is reduced in this way, there is still a substantial body of argument that maintains that it is either impossible or undesirable to use utopian modes of thinking. This stream of thought might be termed Utopia-denial and there are three main currents within it: the Marxist, the liberal democratic and what might be termed the '1989ers' – those who had first-hand experience of the dystopia of state socialism. There is also a postmodernist critique which could constitute a fourth. Frederick Jameson comments that: 'Utopian discourse should not be seen in terms of representation: it can only be a form of: "neutralisation" which suspends the logic of antithesis and contradiction and offers the imagination full play' (Kumar and Bann 1993: 2).

As we saw in Chapter 4, Karl Marx himself was notoriously hostile to contemporary utopian socialists – Fourier, Owen, Saint Simon – maintaining that they were incapable of understanding the grand dialectic of history and that their experiments were ill-founded attempts to short circuit the necessary stages of the historical process and come prematurely to terms with capitalism and capitalist modes of thinking. (An approach based, as Marx put it with his customary charm, on 'the illusion of seeing the dirty bourgeois as a priest' (quoted in Goodwin and Taylor 1982: 73).

The liberal democratic critique proceeds from the opposite assumption, that utopianism by postulating an attainable and permanent state of perfection negates the potentiality for choice and change. This case is perhaps most formidably deployed by Karl Popper's *The Open Society and its Enemies* (1945), in which he argues forcibly that the promise of achieving perfection involves costs that can never be worth paying (quoted in Kateb 1963: 56). The same point is made by Isaiah Berlin in a slightly more restrained, college common-room style, in his late essay on utopianism;

> if one believes this doctrine (of human perfectibility) to be an illusion,
> if only because some ultimate values may be incompatible with one

another, and the very notion of an ideal world in which they are reconciled to be a conceptual (and not merely practical) impossibility, then, perhaps, the best one can do is to try to provoke some kind of equilibrium, necessarily unstable, between the different aspirations of different groups of human beings – at the very least to prevent them from attempting to exterminate each other, and, so far as possible, to prevent them from hurting each other and to promote the maximum practicable degree of sympathy and understanding, never likely to be complete, between them. (1991: 47)

Not exactly 'a wildly exciting programme', as Berlin himself adds – though perhaps a realistic one, in its careful minimalism.

Where Popper and Berlin see a totalitarian potential in utopian theories, the 1989ers' critique blames utopianism for what they have experienced in reality – in its most extreme form, a tyranny that could only obtain its objectives by gross illegitimate intrusions on freedom. It is these critics who coined the formula: 'Utopia = gulag'.

George Kateb's '*Utopia and its Enemies*' (1963) provides a thorough examination of all these forms, subdivided between critiques of the means and of the ends. His anatomy of the criticisms finds answers to most of the main charges – the unattainability of Utopia, its intrinsic tyranny and its inflexibility as a concept. He also turns the tables on the critics by exploring the pathology of anti-utopianism as well (1963: 233). Fear of the exponential extension of technical and human potentialities has implications that are threatening not just to religion but to all conservatives (as in H. G. Wells's alarming concept of *Men Like Gods*). He also points up the contrast between the anti-utopians' squeamishness about utopian means and their ruthlessness in accepting existing suffering and injustices as legitimate ends. These 'natural' phenomena are seen as serving the social function of the grit in the oyster that forms pearls – the exact equivalent of socialist utopian's rationale for ruthlessness in means, that eggs have to be smashed to make the perfect omelette.

But Kateb himself sympathises with those critics who are concerned with the exclusion from Utopia of some facets of reality:

a society of peace, abundance and effortless virtue [he remarks] would seem to have no room for a number of things we in the real world now cherish or respect. The struggle against great odds, against scarcity, against infirmity of will, the chance to do a great deal with a very little, the occasion to display certain virtues or habits or characteristics which only a dark world gives, are all, in theory, eliminated from a utopian society. (1963: 230)

Yet he also dismisses most past utopian experiments which have addressed these issues – 'actually existing Utopias', predominantly in the United States – mainly because they have been limited in scope and transitory in time and have generally been perceived as having been unsuccessful – even catastrophic – in their outcomes. However, despite the appearance of failure, there are lessons to be drawn there for the civil society debate that should not be neglected. In the next section, I set out to identify some of them.

The communitarian moment

> Of all the relations that ever I see
> My old fleshly kindred are foulest for me
> So bad and so ugly, so hateful they feel
> To see them and hate them increases my zeal
> O how ugly they look!
> How ugly they look!
> How nasty they feel!
> (Shaker hymn, quoted Kanter 1972: 90)

It has been justly observed that a crux issue in utopianism is original sin: the issue of whether the potential for perfecting human nature exists here on earth. Those who assert that all human beings are fallen sinners are not likely to accept the feasibility of the utopian project on this side of the grave. Even the Calvinist elect accept limits on their capacity to reproduce in the here and now the ultimate state of heavenly bliss for which they have been chosen.

Nineteenth-century utopianism was born of Enlightenment optimism about realising man's full potential and buttressed by discoveries of natural science, reinforced in turn by the confident assertions of positivist social science about human behaviour. As Saint Simon put it: 'The Golden Age of the human race is not behind us but before us; it lies in the perfection of the social order. Our ancestors never saw it; our children will one day arrive there; it is for us to clear the way' (quoted in Kumar 1987: 45).

Twentieth-century communitarianism, whose central significance in the civil society context was examined in Chapter 3, is by contrast pessimistic about humanity's ability to manage its own affairs – and propensity to sin. It proceeds from the observation that abundance has not produced happiness even in the highly developed societies of the West and seeks to reassert traditional values as a means of correcting deviant behaviour by calling upon the sanctions that traditional communities and families based on monogamous marriage can deploy. At first sight, it may seem surprising that in constructing this agenda its advocates have not drawn on the communitarian experience of the previous century.

As Christopher Clark shows in the book that gives this section its title, at the 'communitarian moment' – which he defines as the 1840s, shortly before the American Civil War – every sort of would-be utopian community was to be found all over the United States. They included Fourierist phalanxes, Owenite socialists, Icarian elysia, Rapp's harmonists, Oneida perfectionists, Hutterite brotherhoods, Amana colonies and Shaker communities, to cite only the best known examples. Some of these were religious, often millennarian; some individually perfectionist and based on novel forms of relations between the sexes. Some were economistic, based on new industrial processes and modes of trading or production: what Clark calls 'an attempt to harness capitalism's ability to coordinate human activity to a higher moral purpose and so create cooperative rather than competitive, social conditions' – a theme also especially relevant to the circumstances of the late twentieth century (1995: 14). Some were quite simply communist.

Some vignettes from this extraordinary moment in American history may help to illustrate this diversity. For example, there were the gentle and harmonious Shakers, quoted at the head of this section vituperatively repudiating their natural families in the name of their community. (Not exactly the tone that 'Simple Gifts' might lead you to expect!). Or Robert Owen addressing both houses of Congress and two presidents on the importance of his experiments in socialism, before going on to denounce private ownership of property and marriage in what he described as a new Declaration of Independence. There is John Humphrey Noyes' vivid metaphorical description of the birth control methods that allowed promiscuous sexual intercourse and sanctioned eugenic breeding in the Oneida community. Noyes, subsequently the author of a history of American socialism, attracted George Bernard Shaw's warm approval for his experiment in communal living. Shaw comments in *Man and Superman* that he had 'proved that Communists, under the guidance of a Superman … and caring no more for property and marriage than a Camberwell minister cares for Hindu caste or suttee might make a much better job of their lives than ordinary folk under the harrow of both these institutions.'

But, Shaw adds 'when he [Noyes] came to the end of his powers through age, he himself guided and organised the voluntary relapse of the Communists into marriage, capitalism and customary private life, this admitting that the real solution was not what a casual Superman could persuade a picked company to do for him, but what a whole community of Supermen would do spontaneously' (1949: 238).

And then there was the Book of Mormon, on whose fantastic foundations a vast social and economic enterprise was in due course to be elevated, creating in Salt Lake City a unique model of civil society in which mobilisation of collective energies is built upwards from the base of the extended family, within a religious framework that mandates cooperation.

To present day communitarians, these episodes are apparently simply a largely forgotten chapter in American history. Amitai Etzioni, introducing *The Spirit of Community* to a British readership, explicitly repudiates any suggestion of American roots and identifies the source of new communitarian thinking as Ancient Greece and the Old and New Testaments (1995: 4). (Reciprocally, there is no mention of his work in the communitarian historians' encyclopaedic *America's Communal Utopias*.) For other commentators, these episodes contain lessons that are still relevant for the current debate on the form and values of civil society. The sociologist of management, Rosabeth Moss Kanter, has provided a helpful analysis of success or failure among these widely varied communities, which helps to answer some questions about the characteristics that helped to make utopian experiments work.

She shows that the survival rate among these groups was greatly enhanced by the building of commitment to the community through:

- Common material sacrifices (common ownership of property and other goods and sharing of outcomes, both negative and positive);
- 'Mortification' (a system providing for mutual criticism freely conducted between members of the community): but not on a basis that denies their individuality, as some military institutions seek to do (although some communes did put their members into uniforms or their equivalent);

- A coherent ideology (regardless of its actual content); and effective means of reinforcing it – group rituals and festivals and above all communal education.
- Clear leadership structures and support and special status for leaders (ultra-egalitarian groupings were not functional, at least at this period).

Most of these characteristics are fairly – but not entirely – predictable and clearly still apposite to the health of bodies in current civil society. It would be right to add that the criteria for success that Kanter employs are not exactly subtle (essentially, duration of the survival of the community concerned, not the quality of life there or success in achieving defined objectives). Subsequent reviews add an extra criterion:

- The capacity to change (the presence of what has been termed 'developmental' communitarianism). Some utopian communities became businesses, as Shaw correctly describes Oneida doing, others conventional religious communities, others still model municipalities (Kanter 1972: 145).

Nineteenth-century communitarianism didn't necessarily reject the world. Clark's study shows how the Northampton Association acted as a focal point for the abolitionist movement in New England, both as a source of ideas and of shelter – for the African-American apostle of abolitionism Sojourner Truth, for example. The communitarians did have descendants – some survivors of the original foundations, sometimes very successful ones, which had adapted and changed to fit new environments, others, especially in the 1960s, that are revivals of older forms or developments of new ones. The movement had relations elsewhere, in the kibbutzim of Israel, at least in their idealistic phase. And separate communities continue to appear for a diversity of motives – age, religion, and in the late twentieth century wealth, psychic development and therapy – for example, drug and alcohol rehabilitation, as in the 'Synanon' community, whose methods are luridly portrayed in the autobiography of a former member, the jazz alto saxophonist Art Pepper (1979: 392 ff.).

Science and technology

One of the major changes that diverted the course of community-based utopian experiments was the rise of industrial capitalism and development of new technologies – railroad, steamships, the telegraph, mass production – all driving on the process of rapid urbanisation and creating an industrial proletariat whose aspirations ran in different channels.

The impact of technical innovation at its high tide in the second half of the nineteeth century is neatly epitomised in H. G. Wells's *A Modern Utopia* (1903). Wells himself originated as a scientific rationalist, largely self-educated, convinced of the limitless potential of the new discoveries of science and the necessity of bringing them under the right form of direction. This should set out to release individuals from the highly visible constraints and distortions imposed on the lives of many of them, during the (presumably transitional) capitalist period of human development. Wells had a brief phase as a Fabian socialist but rejected their gradualism and 'gas and water' emphasis on reform from the municipal level upwards. The Webbs in turn disliked his erratic enthusiasms and his philandering; he repaid them with interest in a cruel caricature in his later novel *The New Machiavelli* (1911).

A Modern Utopia is barely fictionalised though vigorously presented. Wells (re)introduces a leading theme of utopian thinking – salvation by developments in technology, which he traces back to Francis Bacon's *New Atlantis* and whose future extensions through the twentieth century he vividly but, as actual developments in the real world proved, largely mistakenly imagines. The benevolent management of the consequences of change would be guaranteed by a corps of selfless managers, operating under the Rule (a form of self-denying ordinance) and known as the Samurai. The potentiality for conflict would be minimised by the institution of world government (this Utopia is universal) operated by the Samurai without the intrusion of politics. And the leading principle for his Utopians, their 'cardinal belief', is an explicit repudiation of the doctrine of original sin (1903: 288)

The resulting society would be organised on a eugenic (but not racist) basis; it would be vegetarian; there would be no private property and common sexual relations; and efficient management of abundant resources would eliminate poverty (which answers the social question). In an elaborate metaphor, Wells describes the state as developing energy and affording employment which will 'descend like water that the sun has sucked out of the sea', to fertilise all aspects of human activity so that: 'the State is for individuals, the law is for freedoms, the world is for experiment, experience and change; these are the fundamental beliefs upon which a modern Utopia must go' (1903: 95).

These were themes that preoccupied Wells for most of his life and to which he returned frequently but with less optimism as the twentieth century progressed. The implementation of his programme was to be entrusted to what he termed an 'Open Conspiracy' of well-placed sympathisers: and his ideas, though not his detailed policies did enjoy some influence – for example, he played a substantial role in preparing the ground for agreement to the Universal Declaration of Human Rights.

The opposite pole to that Utopia is normally taken to be Aldous Huxley's *Brave New World* (1932). Huxley's future pushes Wells' eugenic theme to its limits with humanity artificially bred and cloned in five immutably fixed categories with tasks divided between them: from the alpha administrators to the epsilon drudges. The system is stabilised by manipulation of personality by consciousness-altering drugs and sexual licence, inducing mindless hedonism in the subject population. Technology has produced material abundance: continuous consumption, fuelled by advanced advertising techniques, keeps the system stable – and maintaining stability is the prime purpose for which the system exists. The leading theme of Huxley's account is that achievement of Utopia is only feasible by distortion and crippling of humanity's aspirations and 'natural' feelings. His new world is post-Freudian and posits an unlimited capacity to manipulate human behaviour.

The Savage (not in this case Noble) introduced into this world has it explained in suitably chilling terms by the supreme manager of the new world state, Mustapha Mond:

> The world's stable now. People are happy; they get what they want and they never want what they can't get. They're well off, they're safe; they're never ill; they're blissfully ignorant of passion and old age; they're plagued with no mothers or fathers; they've no wives, or children, or lovers to feel strongly about; they're so conditioned that they practically can't help behaving as they ought to behave. (Huxley 1932: 261)

The curious mixture of wordy moralising and worldly cynicism Huxley puts into his mouth leaves an odd aftertaste (Mond, as George Kateb points out, is a lineal descendant of Dostoievsky's Grand Inquisitor).

Clearly, this is a dystopia and on the basis of *Brave New World* alone, Huxley can be fitted comfortably among the critics of utopian thinking. But there are some reasons for believing that the fit is not so comfortable after all. David Bradshaw's re-examination of Huxley's other writings at this period shows that Huxley was not initially a critic of Wells' utopianism but an active sympathiser, even to the point of endorsing his sceptical attitude towards democracy. *Brave New World* itself is capable of more than one reading – Utopian ambiguity again, assisted by Huxley's own rereading of his text in 1946; and there is a persistent rumour that American college students in the 1960s read it in exactly the opposite sense to the apparently intended one, as a paradise for drug users (Kumar 1987: 264). And, finally, Huxley himself produced at the end of his life an out-and-out Utopian fantasy, *Island*, in which the polarities of *Brave New World* are explicitly reversed.

What conclusions can be drawn for the civil society debate from this first pair of texts? There is the recurrent theme of irresistible advances in technology providing a shortcut to a conflict-free future, where material abundance would make choices unnecessary and eliminate moral dilemmas. At the time that Wells wrote, the Catholic critic G. K. Chesterton put his finger on the omission of the moral dimension in utopian thinking which has carried through into the civil society debates of the end of the twentieth century. ('They first assume that no man will want more than his share and are then very ingenious in explaining whether his share will be delivered by motor-car or balloon' (quoted by Kumar 1987: 28).)

A broader, but still pervasive theme is that of progress: willed advances in the human condition made possible by wholesale modernisation of institutions of all kinds and to the recasting of human behaviour into predictably rational patterns that eliminate wasteful inefficiencies. In effect, this neuters civil society bodies by depriving them of their advocacy role and making the space for innovation which they might still occupy redundant.

But the attraction of constructing this rational New Model of Humanity was a theme dear to revolutionary regimes of both left and right. Leon Trotsky offered a particularly optimistic variation on it in his *Literature and Revolution*, quoted at length by Kumar:

> Man will make it his purpose to master his own feelings, to raise his instincts to the heights of consciousness, to make them transparent, to extend the wires of his will (*sic*) into hidden recesses and thereby to raise himself to a new plane, to create a higher biological type, or, if you please, a superman. (1987: 64)

No doubt Shaw approved! In the 1930s and 1940s developing these potentialities became a favourite exercise of propagandists of all kinds: but some of the most chilling utopian sketches in English are those of the 'progressive' scientists (J. D. Bernal, J. B. S. Haldane) seeking to implement the task Stalin set them, by acting as 'engineers of human souls'.

A counterweight to this optimism about the potential for change is the emphasis on the need for leadership, and the rights and duties attached to that role. It was the evidence of abuse of leadership coupled with the shock to belief in the inevitability of progress inflicted by the First World War that had led Karl Mannheim to proclaim the impossibility of Utopia in the twentieth century. Yet there were those who were prepared to make the attempt: we can perhaps best categorise them as 'planners'. They are especially relevant to the evolution of civil society in the second half of the twentieth century because planning, at least in its Western European variant, seeks to demarcate the limits of the public sphere and define what should be taken as the state's responsibility there and what can remain contested.

Planning as Utopia

Huxley and Wells both present the need for systematic planning of resources, human and material, as a general subsidiary theme of their analyses and make this a prime responsibility of the benevolent or machiavellian controllers of their new world order. However, in English terms, this approach is more usually associated with the Fabians, whose caste of managers is less formidable, morally and intellectually and whose powers are granted conditionally, not absolutely.

There is no systematic Fabian Utopia as such: their gradualism eschewed such grand gestures. But there are ideal constitutions and also, to their shame, the Webbs' catastrophic misreading of Stalin's Russia, published towards the end of their joint lives as *Soviet Communism: A New Civilisation,* the title shedding in its second edition the fig-leaf question mark of the original.

But what has been termed 'middle opinion' produced in the 1930s a plethora of designs for living that can be legitimately grouped together: what critics like Correlli Barnett have subsequently called the 'New Jerusalem' syndrome. The planning projects of this period were often referred to, half seriously, in these terms: we have already encountered some of the practical outcomes of the attempts at rational planning and its impact on voluntary organisations in Chapter 2. However, utopian planning is probably better seen through the specific lens of a particular form of activity, as opposed to the broad sweep of 'political and economic planning'.

Architecture provides a particularly revealing way into the debate. The 1930s saw a flowering of ideas for a more rational approach to human habitation – better design of 'Machines for Living' (Le Corbusier's description of housing) and the active use of physical ('land use') planning on principles derived from systematic theories of human behaviour and patterns of economic development (drawn in essence from Freud and Marx) to improve living conditions in large cities.

The career of Berthold Lubetkin can conveniently stand for much of this approach. Born in Russia, brought up at the heroic period of the revolution, he left the Soviet Union for Berlin after producing the first of a series of all-embracing proposals for recasting the built environment ('the Polytechnic of the Urals': much admired, never built). Thence he went to London, where he formed the architectural cooperative TECTON. The practice's first commissions were for zoos: the Penguin Pool for the London Zoological Society and Dudley Zoo (this was the subject of some ironical comment). These were followed by two well-received developments of private flats using the new technology to build upwards (High Points I and II): and the provision of public facilities for working-class clients – notably the Finsbury Health Centre. Lubetkin's career ended abruptly after the Second World War when his appointment as architect–planner of Peterlee New Town foundered in unresolved conflicts over priorities (upholding clear principles of modern design against messy practices involved in maintaining the local mining industry).

The work of Lubetkin and his colleagues rests on a number of assumptions: that planning could produce a good quality environment and access to common amenities at a high standard (provided where possible on a communal basis in satellite towns, funded and managed by the state). Also, that construction of new housing on best modern principles could be extended to the entire population by use of new techniques of mass construction (building high and saving land that could be employed to better advantage for communal recreational facilities). Education was a key element in this programme; well-equipped schools with advanced technical facilities providing residents with the skills, while public transport (preferably by monorail) would provide easy access to 'clean', technologically advanced employment. These are the principles of *'Garden Cities of Tomorrow'* (one of John Carey's selected Utopias), as Ebenezer Howard originally conceived them, translated into practice.

The optimism inherent in this approach rests on environmental explanations of deviant behaviour: advocates were fond of contrasting these new planned communities with the 'slums' and their effects on mental as well as physical health and distortion of human personality. Unlike Octavia Hill (for whom see Chapter 2), they believed that 'the pigsty made the pig'. It followed that to improve material circumstances would transform behaviour. Successful improvement of the environment through planning also provides longer-term incentives: communal engagement of all those affected in an enterprise for collective advantage; active citizenship in its ideal form.

Such an approach depends crucially on the citizen body being prepared to place their confidence in public institutions and those who manage them. For this purpose, it is not necessary that the managers should be austerely rule-bound samurai or masters of diabolically cunning sleight of hand: merely honest, efficient and disinterested. It is not unfair to those public servants who have been all three to say that on balance the evidence shows that twentieth-century public bureaucracies have neither won nor deserved to win the confidence of citizens. (Nor is it necessary to accept neo-classical economists' public choice theories in their entirety to believe that the self-interest of bureaucrats is often the explanation for this failure.)

There is also a practical issue around accountability, addressed in prospect by Huxley when discussing a possible British Five Year Plan, in the Soviet Russian model. As he put it: 'the ideal of our planners is a coordinated government democratically controlled. A noble ideal. But in practice how far is coordination (if it is to be brought about in so short a period as five years) compatible with democratic methods? That is the uncomfortable question' (Bradshaw 1994: 219)

The natural counterpart to this utopian image of planning is sometimes taken to be George Orwell's *1984*. But Orwell's biographer Bernard Crick argues (convincingly, to my mind) that *1984* is not really a dystopia but a satirical portrait of immediate post-war Britain (1948), with the BBC, Orwell's much disliked former employer, portrayed as the Ministry of Truth. However, this is a portrait skewed by Orwell's intense anti-communism, precipitated by his first-hand encounters with Stalinist excesses in Catalonia during the Spanish Civil War, which led him to involve himself in cold-war polemics.

A coarser version of the behavioural approach, this time cast in utopian terms, can be found in the psychologist B. F. Skinner's *Walden Two* published in the same year (1948). Here, benevolent managers reappear, using less drastic techniques of control than Mustapha Mond. derived from behavourist psychology to achieve a state of 'general tolerance and affection': modest but incremental progress towards a small scale Utopia. Leaving aside the effectiveness (and indeed morality) of the techniques themselves, there is an uncomfortable emphasis on the redundancy of democracy as a device for managing the process, which is seen simply as a technical task.

A far more subtle and substantial critique of utopian planning can be found in Michael Young's *Rise of the Meritocracy, 1870–2033* (1961). Here, Young postulates a peaceful reorganisation of society through the categorising of human ability to create a world where careers and rewards are exactly calibrated to scientifically assessed intelligence, using standardised IQ tests (this dates from before their partial discrediting as tools after the exposure of Cyril Burt's manipulation of data). This satirical dystopia, which is eventually brought to an abrupt halt under the impact of a feminist revolt, is constructed as a subtle extension of trends clearly perceptible in post-war Britain. Too subtle, in fact: the key term 'meritocracy', coined ironically by Young, passed almost at once into common use, employed as a political slogan designed to justify rewards for the deserving – on their own estimates of their desert.

In practice, the most important anti-planning text was F. A. Hayek's *Road to Serfdom* (1944): the curious feature here is that this became really influential only when the circumstances in which it was produced (the apogee of the European dictatorships) and to which it was mainly applicable had long since passed. Hayek holds that planning is both infeasible, because the plurality and complexity of information necessary to make decisions defeats any formal apparatus set up to manage it and immoral, because it involves the state in taking decisions in areas where it has no right to operate (property, redistributive taxation).

Hayek's wholly justified concern about the abuse of power by the dictators caused him to believe that the connection between one of the means they had employed (planning) and the end for which they used it (totalitarianism) was an automatic one with inescapable consequences. As a result, he mistook milk and water English social democracy for a tyrannical Orwellian INGSOC – an error that inspired Winston Churchill's ill-fated 'Gestapo' election broadcast in 1945, with Clem Attlee cast as the least likely future gauleiter it would be possible to imagine. As Kateb comments, these arguments had carried the case against planning 'to absurd lengths' (1963: 60). But the debate around freedom and planning set Hayek off on a series of reflections on how to ensure that the particular aspects of liberal capitalism to which he attached importance could be preserved, best expressed in his *Constitution of Liberty*.

This line of thinking has subsequently produced a series of 'counter-Utopias', pessimistic about human behaviour, yet strongly committed to reducing the role of the state to a 'small, fierce' core with the protection of property and preservation of civil liberties as essential tasks: a classical liberal agenda, in its nineteenth-century form, customarily drawn from J. S. Mill in his pre-socialist phase.

The best known of these is probably Robert Nozick's *Anarchy, State and Utopia* (1974) This seeks to entrench rights and duties with a minimal state – not quite a night watchman but with few daylight duties apart from acting as guarantor of law and sole possessor of the right to force. Beyond that everything remains negotiable and the market is the device through which this negotiation takes place, for goods, services and provision of welfare.

Nozick's approach answers many of the basic criticisms of utopian thinking – his ideal society is dynamic, based on consent, and provides for negotiated exit. It is a kind of affiliated Utopia of Utopias: Barbara Goodwin has described it as the 'only true empiricist Utopia' (Goodwin and Taylor 1982: 51). However, it is not without its critics, even on the right. For there, further down the same branch line, lurk the anarcho-capitalists (David Friedman, Murray Rothbard). For them, as for classic anarchists, the state is simply immoral: there are no circumstances whatsoever that can justify its continued existence (Lemieux 1988: 117). But the mechanisms that they substitute for the state are not based on voluntary association – as William Morris's consensual anarchism in *News from Nowhere* is grounded in fellowship – but are simply and solely those that the market provides. There are no transactions that cannot be legitimately conducted there: the rule of law can be achieved by purchase through the marketplace and delivered by contract in the same way as any other goods and services.

The use of force to resolve disputes cannot be legitimately confined to any one user; rather, it should be freely available to be employed (by those who can afford to purchase it) for any end for which they may require it. Like Maoists, the anarcho-capitalists believe that in the last analysis power grows out of the barrel of a gun. Their ultimate avatars are the survivalists of the mountain states, waiting in their remote cabins to blow away in the sacred name of liberty any federal agent who strays into their sights.

The experience of utopian attempts at planning exposes important issues around civil society and relationships with the state. It helps to define the role and purpose of public intervention and the forms that it can take, and establish whether these function with or against the grain of civil society, how consent is achieved and maintained (a crux of the planning debate) and how the adversarial role of voluntary associations can be fitted 'neatly' into the planning matrix (see Chapter 4). Counter-utopias that set out to limit the role of the state contribute to the debate by mapping the contours and functions of a minimal state (as some theorists have tried to do) and the implications for free association of the state's withdrawal from certain activities.

The enthronement of the market as the principal alternative has major implications for civil society, some of which were explored in the previous chapters. It has had some significant practical consequences – for example, the tendency among some of the wealthy to withdraw from involvement with their fellow-citizens into privately maintained 'gated communities'. But the principles on which this disengagement is based also require closer examination.

Utopia, Ltd.

We have already arrived once before at 1989 and 'the end of history' – a slightly overheated interpretation of the consequences of the collapse of state socialism in that year and the severe damage inflicted on the social democratic project, the 'Keynesian Welfare State' – though from a slightly different perspective. As I have already argued, much of the writing and debate about the role of the market in the immediate post-1989 period seems in retrospect to be romantic, not realistic. Indeed, it is often to a large extent utopian. These views of the market, propagated by those in the West to audiences in the East eager to be reassured that the notions that they had of the wonders of capitalism were accurate, were sometimes moralistic (see Michael Novak's descriptions of the market, cited in Chapter 6) but more often took the form of endorsement of the promise of material abundance on a global scale and opportunities to share in it open without reservation to all willing to grasp them. This image is perhaps best summarised in a phrase of Francis Fukuyama's, that now: 'we cannot picture to ourselves a world that is essentially different from the present one, and at the same time better' (quoted in Kumar and Bann 1993, 6).

All these themes are strongly reinforced in the current literature on management, the current flavour of which is mostly Panglossian in the extreme. All's now for the best in the best of all possible capitalisms. Ambitious younger managers need only their energy, a basic vocabulary and toolkit of simple concepts and limitless self-belief to equip them to act as consultants carrying the message to the less fortunate, wherever in the world they are to be found – though it is important not to tarry and become caught up in the consequences. (An imaginative recent reviewer of these texts has suggested that an illuminating way to reread much of this material is to treat it as science fiction.)

So is this not merely the end of history, but finally the end of Utopia with it? Responses to Fukuyama's challenge have tended to be framed as flat denial: presenting liberal capitalism not merely as a false or premature Utopia but often as a dystopia.

The ecological critique falls into this category. There is a well-established tradition of gloom-laden warnings of the downside of the search for abundance, the rapid depletion of natural resources, the death of species, global warming precipitated by pollution and damage to the ozone layer. There are utopian alternatives that are based on care of the natural world: Morris's *News from Nowhere* is one well-known example. But these tend to be constructed on a small scale and to be based on withdrawal in time and space from current realities to the comfort of the remote, nicely epitomised in Ursula Le Guin's fine science fiction novel, the *Dispossessed*.

More cutting still are some criticisms of the damage to established systems of values done by consumerism spinning out of control and what is seen as the vulgarisation that has accompanied it. This critique of the destruction of imagination by the elimination of diversity paints a powerful image of a world in which consumption impoverishes, summoning up, in John O'Neill's satirical account, the image of a 'McTopia'. This, he argues, produces a process in which: 'McTopia finds itself accommodating

McFamily as each institution responds to the intensification of exploitable time in late capitalist societies' and produces the paradoxical outcome that: 'America is the only country in the world where the rich eat as badly as the poor – a demonstration effect that serves to underwrite the globalisation of McTopia' (quoted in Kumar and Bann 1993: 137).

Postmodernism carries the argument a stage further still by using Disneyland as a utopian template of the postmodernised world: providing, as Kumar puts it, 'a range of cultural experiences drawn from different times and places which one can mix according to taste' (1993: 76). (And in fact Disney have themselves constructed their own ideal community in Florida). Meanwhile, the French philosopher Jean Baudrillard has assured us that the end of masculine Utopia has indeed arrived, and woman, being a living Utopia, has no need of man; and (of course) that the year 2000, like the Gulf War before it, has not taken place.

Much of the direct opposition to the utopian images projected by the New World Financial Order has already been reviewed in the previous chapter. As we saw, possibly the most effective critique is that of Popper's disciple George Soros (*The Crisis of Global Capitalism* 1998) and his account of finance capital's operations as destructive of relationships at all levels and inflicting unsustainable damage on the Open Society, a view expressed more directly on the streets of Seattle and Washington in 1999.

Finally, the ultimate expression of the utopian notion of new liberating technologies can be found in the World Wide Web. The Internet is sometimes held up as instant democratisation, exemplified by its use as a means of linking a vast population across the world, unobstructed by political boundaries, to an immediately accessible source of free exchange of ideas and information. But in practice what we've seen has been a rapid decline from a technology created outside the market, to its ready exploitation for e-commerce uses and as a basis for feverish financial speculations, to widespread abuse – capricious damage inflicted on users by viruses and more disturbingly still, the use of the web to promote race hatred and spread child pornography.

Conclusion: civil society as Utopia?

Even a limited selection from the literature on Utopia like the one I have just given provides some new perspectives on themes that are directly relevant to the civil society debate. All of them raise issues that advocates of the importance of the civil society perspective must necessarily address. For example:

Leadership

Utopia both as imagined and in practice is full of examples of charismatic leadership and the strengths and pitfalls associated with it. Issues like the context within which leadership is exercised, the support for leaders, the role of 'elders', rotation of elites as opposed to the creation of closed castes and succession mechanisms all resonate with the civil society debate. So does accountability of leaders, plural or singular and the mechanisms for securing change without fracturing the organisation or secession. The developmental cycle commented on by analyses of utopian experiments also has relevant lessons (especially for southern NGOs). And if politics are 'the serpent in the Utopian Eden' they have also been portrayed in the same light by those who would like to see civil society as a zone free of political conflict, safeguarded by fixed and unchallengeable rules.

Association and community

Utopias offer a menu of different forms of association – from complete informality and equally shared roles and risks to the philanthropic but regimented 'factory village' regimes of employers like the Quaker chocolate magnates. Some utopias begin with association: Saint Simonite utopian socialism is explicitly about new forms of association; others end by reverting to more familiar ones and repudiating their experiments. A contemporary commenting on the later history of the nineteenth-century Northampton Association, which transformed itself, like the Oneida community, into a commercial undertaking observes that 'enlightened and liberal selfishness became as it usually does a beneficence, to which a weak communism was as the dull and cheerless gleam of a decaying punk (sic) to the inspiring blaze of the morning sun' (Clark 1995: 215). But a key question is how resources, even when separately assembled, can be devoted to the common interest and whether mutuality can be carried into action through cooperation: the Mormon experiment has interesting lessons to offer here. The market enters here as the potential guarantor of a sufficiency to share – or perhaps as another kind of serpent?

Gender and equality

Many utopias are egalitarian, in theory. Crass inegalitarianism is commonly the mark of a dystopia, one respect on which Orwell's *1984*, with its division between the membership of the Party, inner and outer and the residual 85 per cent of the excluded proles fits the pattern exactly. But in practice inequality creeps in, especially on issues of gender. Actually existing utopias were prepared to make gestures in the direction of equality which were for their time comparatively radical, although there were feminist critics both at the time and subsequently of Owenite harmonies (for which see Barbara Taylor's *Eve and the New Jerusalem*). However, as Barbara Goodwin sardonically observes, complete gender equality is properly utopian in the nowhere sense of that term:

> only a utopia can present us with an image of a society in which women's liberation has been accomplished. No actual, existing society can serve as such an image, since there is no working example (it would be argued by feminists) of the elimination of male dominance. (Goodwin and Taylor 1982: 249)

In the circumstances, it is perhaps not surprising that some of the most effective feminist texts, in terms of the ways in which the issues are presented, are fictional or even science fictional (for example, Marge Piercy, Margaret Attwood, Ursula Le Guin).

Virtue and optimism

The utopian repudiation of original sin leaves a gaping space. Since the perfectibility of human nature cannot be taken as given but must remain achievable, the question of means becomes acute. The utopian menu begins with education and the philosophy of progressive schools is founded on the optimistic assumption that the right kind of instruction will equip the future citizen with the values that will dispose them to put their extended knowledge to virtuous use. (Witness the philosopher Bertrand Russell's willingness while at the height of his powers to commit himself to running a small school). The beneficent modification of attitudes by other means is explored in the behaviourist utopia of Skinner, an alternative many of us would find profoundly dystopian. Building institutions that support virtuous behaviour (for the pessimistic, the law; for optimists, sensitive, incorruptible and efficient bureaucracies) provides one alternative route, participative democracy another. This, too, is a theme – the inculcation of civic virtue and the values of citizenship (for which see Chapter 4) – which is central to the viability of civil society.

The American example

The concept of America as the once and future Utopia is omnipresent in both the utopian and civil society literature. It echoes through the early vision of the new-found-land where mankind (sic) could make a fresh start by building a shining city on a hill. It was reaffirmed in the revolutionary period, as in Thomas Jefferson's concept of a pastoral Utopia, but one that was 'the product of design, enterprise and toil' (Kumar 1987: 74). It was a fundamental driving force in the social experiments of the communitarian moment, as it is in the 'remoralisation' agenda of the new communitarians. Tensions remain between the assertive claim to the pursuit of individual happiness (and freedom to capture it, through the acquisition of material possessions) and the 'powerful affiliative drive' of American democracy, so frequently remarked upon by observers from Tocqueville onwards; but there is also a fundamental optimism about the possibility of reconciling them.

Utopianism is as American as cherry pie; but the problem with cherry pie (however well baked) is that it is dished up in only one flavour. American cultural imperialism is an old complaint of Europeans (it goes back at least to Baudelaire!) but new technologies and the unprecedented power of the media of communication adds a new urgency to the concern about the elimination of diversity and unthinking imposition of culturally specific values. If George Steiner is right 'the future of the world is California' – where the state spends more money on prisons than on higher education.

Finally, to the extent that it reflects elements of these five (and indeed other) utopian assumptions and makes the claim to resolve the problems that they raise, civil society itself can legitimately be characterised as a form of Utopia and must confront some of the criticisms of utopian modes of thinking outlined in this chapter. I will address some of the implications in the final chapter. Meanwhile, although I do not myself carry a Utopian passport I believe, with Oscar Wilde that we need at least an occasional visit to Utopia to have a fully rounded picture of the world and its possibilities.

CHAPTER 9

Civil Society in the Twenty-first Century

> I see us free, therefore, to return to some of the most sure and certain principles of religion and traditional virtue – that avarice is a vice, that the exaction of usury is a misdemeanour, and that the love of money is detestable, that those who walk most truly in the paths of virtue and sane wisdom take least thought for the morrow. We shall once more value ends above means and prefer the good to the useful. (J. M. Keynes, *Essays in Persuasion*)

An American century?

Perhaps no question mark is now necessary. At the moment, the strength of the American economy and hegemonic reach of the 'military-industrial complex' that sustains it means that the institutions, values, culture and language of the United States seem certain to become increasingly dominant as the twenty-first century progresses. True, there have been until quite recently passages of doubt and uncertainty, before the current economic boom swept all before it. Disturbing parallels were drawn with the British (even Roman) Empire at its apogee and subsequent decline. But as I write (November 2000) there seems no immediate prospect that the acceleration of turbo-capitalism, fuelled by new technology, will slow down. As the hyperbolic celebrator of all things American, Thomas Friedman, asserts:

> America at its best takes the needs of markets, individuals and communities all utterly seriously. And that's why America, at its best is not just a country. It's a spiritual value and a role model. It's a nation that

is not afraid to go to the moon, but also still loves to come home for the Little League. (1999: 378)

But as his fellow-American David Landes points out, the divisions of the cold war have been succeeded by a gap (between North and South) which has implications that may in the long run be even more serious:

Here is the greatest single problem and danger facing the world of the Third Millennium. The only other worry that comes close is environmental deterioration, and the two are intimately connected, indeed are one. They are one because wealth entails consumption but also waste, not only production but destruction. It is this waste and destruction, which has increased enormously with output and income, that threatens the space we live and move in. (1998: xx)

If Friedman is right (and he may well be), if we wish to address these problems we can only do so by following the American way – even we think that going to the moon was a rather childish ambition and have no Little League in which to hone our small children's competitive instincts.

Alternatively, we might want to argue that one-size-fit-all is not a good prescription for the twenty–first century and that solutions to problems experienced at different scales and in various forms should be tackled in ways that satisfy the priorities of the societies in which they are being addressed. Tackling 'the needs of individuals and communities' doesn't necessarily mean adopting solutions on the American model, made in the United States. Globalism could mean diversity, not uniformity, a celebration of local difference, not a vast melting pot.

So I will conclude by reflecting on the implications of these developments and their likely future trajectory for the issues that have been explored in the course of this book and by asking the question:

In the American century, what will the future of civil society be; will there be a place at the table for the voluntary sector and where will it be set and by whom? Alternatively (or additionally) is there scope for a *New Philanthropy*, perhaps even in a new form – turbo-philanthropy?

The assize of neo-liberalism

One of the major questions, still not finally resolved, is whether the values of liberalism and the range of interventions that it sanctions will be fully adequate to the challenges that the new century will throw up. Any response to that question (even a provisional one) depends upon disentangling the two strands in liberalism, the political and the economic. Although its advocates tend to collapse them into one another, as Stephen Holmes shows, their agendas don't necessarily coincide. With this qualification, since the neo-liberal agenda rests essentially on American values, it seems appropriate to set the test established by the Founding Fathers: how far does it help to facilitate *life*, *liberty* and *the pursuit of happiness*?

Albert Hirschman, in his *Rhetoric of Reaction*, points to a whole sequence of arguments advanced against innovation, including the inevitability of destruction once embarked on the slippery slope of change – a phenomenon he calls after the refrain in Victor Hugo's *Les Miserables: 'ceci tuera cela'* – 'all this will kill that off'.

The critics of the New World Order are full of such assertions, that turbo-capitalism and its associated technology will kill the biosphere, distort the economies of the most vulnerable countries and impoverish their population, destroy distinctive national and regional cultures, subvert democratic institutions by removing the power of decision-taking from the people, eliminate all sense of community and belonging and subvert the family by isolating individuals through treating them as economic units.

Partisans counter with statements about the unique capacity of the global economy to satisfy aspirations of every kind. So that if *life* equals standard of living then, Amartya Sen (not a partisan but a balanced commentator) concludes: 'there is extensive evidence that the global economy has actually brought prosperity to many different areas of the globe. The productive and economic benefits of global integration can scarcely be denied' (Sen, *Observer* 25 June 2000).

If *liberty* means freedom to choose what and when to consume, the market can deliver that for most citizens of developed countries, in profusion. Here, the main conundrum, even in these most favourable of circumstances, is the compatibility of the economic and political agendas, of free markets with democracy – which is not always so evident as the protagonists of neo-liberalism assert. It is perfectly possible, in the American century, for a partner in Goldman Sachs to buy his way into the US Senate by spending $25m on political advertising. Elsewhere, the story can be still more discouraging: witness the corruption of democracy by business in many East and Central European countries.

The pursuit of happiness remains the great imponderable. Behind the babble of much communitarian discourse lurks the recurrent anxiety: will affluence prove capable of satisfying those needs that are not simply material, or will it subvert the traditional simplicities of human relations? Robert Putnam believes that sufficient stocks of social capital, prudently amassed and sensibly allocated, will help to address the problem that he (and others) detect of a steady decline in rates of satisfaction among Americans in the age group below the 'civic generation' of over fifty-fives. He comments, whimsically, that 'the Beatles got it right: we all "get by with a little help from our friends"' (2000: 334).

And perhaps money will after all buy us love? The American novelist Jane Smiley recently commented that:

> Capitalism has an excellent reputation, among fans of the free market, for disseminating goods and information and moulding the lives of consumers in ways that best serve both the system and individuals. If this is indeed the case, then late capitalism has evidently decided that what is best for us and our children is serial monogamy, frequent changes of employment and a high degree of instability. It has decided that, on balance, it is best for all adults to work rather than one designated gender to stay at home with the children … It has decided that the individual's relations to society will be less and less mediated through the family and more and more experienced directly. Fans of the free market would say that we should embrace rather than resist what capitalism has decided. (Smiley, *Observer* 25 June 2000)

What contribution can faith-based activity (but which faiths? what activities?) make towards sustaining coherence in the face of such upheavals? Putnam's answer is to try to harness the energies of religious organisations in the United States to 'new pluralistic socially responsible' goals (2000: 409), but conceding that much of that energy is to be found among Christian fundamentalists and 'tolerance of unbelievers is not a virtue notably associated with fundamentalism' (410). Friedman's response is to dissolve into sentimentality by encapsulating the future in the scene of a multi-ethnic Judeo-Christian Christmas. (The possibility that for some this image might be excluding, not inclusive clearly doesn't occur to him. Very American.)

Some implications for civil society

What does all this imply for the future of civil society? The continuing dominance of a single set of values would certainly have some profoundly significant implications. This is evident when we return to the Walzer agenda summarised in the opening chapter. His approach is one which, having set down different approaches to action in civil society, offers a guarantee of pluralism and presents civil society as a project of projects, none of which necessarily have priority.

But the adoption of the liberal paradigm necessarily means that others must be excluded. Clearly the Marxist is; some aspects of the Conservative nationalist one are too; and although it is broadly consistent with the communitarian approach and with a religious paradigm, at least in certain forms, liberalism is at war with the republican programme in certain crucial respects around the authority of the state and the legitimacy of its role in civil society and the supremacy of the market over politics.

Even if we rephrase the objective in terms of achieving the common public good, as Barry Knight would wish to do, there are conflicts around both means and ends still to be resolved. Which are the agencies, public private or voluntary, best equipped to promote and sustain it; where will their accountability to fellow citizens lie and how it will be exercised – how 'transparent' will their operation be? As for ends, Robert Putnam asks: 'Don't we face in the end a painful and even arbitrary choice of values – community or individualism, but not both? Liberty or fraternity, but not both?' (2000: 354). For him, restocking with social capital provides the means of washing out these dilemmas: others may be less sanguine about that solution.

Can the centre hold?

More specifically, in the first chapter and subsequently, when employing the wide angle lens to explore the diversity of different functions performed in civil society space and along its boundaries, I identified a series of issues that illustrate the importance of pluralism:

- in Chapter 2, civil society as an arena in which voluntary action could form relationships with the state that would supplement – perhaps even eventually supplant – the state's role, in particular as a means of delivering welfare;
- in Chapter 3, the civil society space as one in which activity at a small scale facilitates linkages between families and groups (both formal and informal) that can build and sustain communities and create social capital;

- in Chapter 4, civil society as the public sphere, in which the means of creating and sustaining democracy, evolving rights and responsibilities of citizenship are forged; and as an illustration;
- in Chapter 5, a healthy civil society as a crucial factor facilitating transformation from a totalitarian regime and helping to sustain the democratic system that succeeded it; and
- in Chapters 6 and 7, civil society as a space in which social movements can mount challenges to certain features of globalism;

To which I should add the potential, explored in Chapter 8, for devising new templates for civil society – some frankly utopian, others as an outcome of adopting or adapting new techniques or technologies.

The evidence is reviewed at length in the main body of the text; so for now I will only refer to some key conclusions – those that are especially relevant for a twenty-first century that may evolve on the American model.

The evidence in Chapter 2 showed that in England, at least, voluntary action has acted as the state's partner, that over time this partnership has been broadly beneficent and that it retains the potential to adapt. But if there is to be change, on whose terms will it be made? The crux here is less on the civil society side but over the boundary, with the state and its functions. If the American model does become dominant, the prospect is of a rapidly diminishing role for the state and the likelihood of ever tighter limits on its functions in welfare will draw voluntary bodies further on, into the discharge of functions once abandoned to the state. This means that there are likely to be more challenges to their capacity to deliver effectively and (with due allowance for American exceptionalism) their ability to resist 'marketisation'.

Chapter 3 demonstrated the continued vitality of the bottom-up approach, building on the smallest units, with gender as an essential ingredient, too often lost to sight. The importance of spontaneous collaboration around a version of the common good runs with the grain of earlier American experience. Where this experience now diverges from that of other societies is over the role of religion, still a major unifying and motive force in the United States – to the point where there is now serious advocacy of handing over welfare to the churches ('charitable choice'). The communitarian agenda's second important prop has been the family, seen as the means of moralising the young but now buckling under the pressures identified in Jane Smiley's acerbic commentary. The

lessons here may run in the opposite direction; through the cohesion of the ethnic diasporas (which combine economic aspirations
with strongly cohesive extended families and communities) – in
sharp contrast to many of those among whom they now live.

The material in Chapter 4 offers another contrast. Twenty-first-
century liberalism's prescription is: 'shrink your politics' – no
need for clashes of first principles, now that all the other major
alternatives are discredited. Politics become simply a matter of
choosing by competence in management. Republicanism sets a
different test – democracy as active participation, citizenship as
involvement in the public sphere, civic virtue as the outcome. The
importance of democratic institutions has been demonstrated by
its continuing centrality as an important determinant of outcomes
in the South. Amartya Sen observes that there is no case yet of
severe famine in a functioning democracy. But what future does it
have in the North? Critical citizens are abandoning the older structures of politics and are increasingly mistrustful of political institutions and politicians. There's no sign of liberation through
technology – reconnecting with public issues by use of media of
electronic communication. There is continued steady decline in
participation measured by voting. An American century may
mean a public sphere in which single issues are promoted by
steadily more sophisticated pressure groups; but with no coherent
sense of a common good.

The liberating potential of an active civil society sphere is
demonstrated by the experience in the former state socialist countries, described for Hungary in Chapter 5 – though the outcomes
across East and Central Europe have differed. Civil society's part in
the initial stages was a necessary but not a sufficient factor in securing change. The role of the market in subsequent transformation has
been more significant, not least in transforming civil society itself.
Events here have exposed with a special clarity the clash between
two wings of liberalism. Political liberalism mandated democracy;
market liberalism required unpopular economic measures.

At the extreme end of the scale lies Russia. With each successive
leader a false dawn of expectations of beneficent transformation to
a functioning market economy has broken and then faded. Now
(November 2000), the country and its immediate neighbours are
perhaps best described as a capitalist dystopia, run by a corrupt
oligarchy behind the façade of a sham democracy, with a population deeply cynical about both politicians and western NGOs.
There is some ironic pleasure to be gained from seeing how the

alibis advanced by believers in the magical transforming powers of the market economy that have somehow mysteriously failed to deliver mirror past apologias for socialism. ('What has been tried is not real capitalism'; 'It will take a generation to produce the necessary cultural changes'; 'What was lacking was an outstanding personality who commanded real respect to promote the changes') and, on this occasion, 'What has been crucial is the absence of an authentic civil society' (Sachs 1999).

Chapters 6 and 7 explored the prospect of the development of an opposition role for new social movements on a global scale. Whether a 'global civil society' actually exists in a coherent form is still a moot point; but the potential for exposing issues clearly now exists; Sen again:

> doubts about global economic relations continue to come from different ends of the globe and there is reason enough to see these doubts about globalisation as global phenomena as well. They are, in this sense, 'global doubts' – not just an ad hoc assortment of localised opposition. (Sen 2000)

But how can they be addressed at the global level? One answer might be to improve the performance and democratic accountability of international bodies. Another, to introduce means of increasing the accountability of multinational corporations operating internationally or the operations of finance capital. But this can't be done without the active participation of the United States, which is not only the hegemonic participant in the new world order but also harbours doubts about the legitimacy of many of the concerns to which Sen refers.

Whatever the attractions of the Internet as a communication device between dissidents and means of telling unwelcome truths to power or even, more ambitiously, a series of 'virtual communities', it is difficult to see it as an effective countervailing force, especially now that it is becoming engulfed by the demands of commerce, however helpful it may be in enabling individuals and groups to 'think globally, act locally'. The utopian potential of technology needs to be balanced (Chapter 8 shows) by the dystopian warnings of the potential for science to pass out of control. Meanwhile, global civil society still risks being written off as Utopia in the sense of somewhere unreal (that is, 'no place').

But to adopt the all prescriptions of neo-liberalism holus-bolus – to put on the golden straight jacket, in Friedman's terminology,

and wear it in every location and circumstance – is to risk impov-
erishing the potential of civil society and setting limits on the variety that ought to be of its essence.

Philanthropy and the good society

Regardless of whether some variety survives or liberal capitalism
becomes effectively the universal form, will the twenty-first century need a new philanthropy? If so, what should the focus and
the objectives of such a new philanthropy be?

Not just as devices for easing the guilt of new money, more easily and more copiously made than ever before. Casual donation,
on whatever scale, can still stink of charity, in the worse sense – a
careless gesture that substitutes for taking thought about the root
causes of the situation it is intended to ameliorate. Or worse, an
attempt to humanise the inhumane or whitewash tarnished repu-
tations. A recent commentary describes contemporary American
philanthropy in unflattering terms:

> There are great tax incentives and a long tradition of philanthropy in
> the US which encourage financial donations and there is no doubt that
> there can be, as one professional put it to me, 'transforming gifts'. So
> few ask 'why do it?'. The soul buy-back still operates, in the manner of
> a medieval banker founding a lay order or a Counter-Reformation
> widow endowing a saint, with one huge donation you can remove
> from your conscience the thousands of hapless souls who have toiled
> in call centres to help make you rich. In this moral economy it is not
> how much you have that defines your worth but how much you give
> away: moral and monetary value sit in inverse relation to one another
> and you pass through the holy portals clothed in virtue but naked of
> wealth. (Stella Tillyard in *Prospect*, March 2000)

If there is scope for a distinctive new philanthropy derived from
turbo-capitalism – what will its particular characteristics be? Will it
be distinctively entrepreneurial? Recent evidence (Council on
Foundations, 2000 reported in *Alliance 5,2*) suggests that venture
philanthropy is evolving in new ways, with a conscious attempt to
apply the principles of venture capital to the field of philanthropy.
There is a focus on the technology that has helped to generate
wealth, using it to distribute resources or to empower. Venture
philanthropists fund organisations, not projects and make fewer,

larger investments, actively supporting their ventures through direct involvement at board level. Staff supporting projects are held directly accountable for their success or failure, and are expected (eventually) to develop exit strategies for the foundation.

Some of the newer philanthropists look in other, more familiar directions and address traditional goals – funding work towards the rediscovery of faith, reinforcement of education systems, or the re-establishment of democracy and preservation of an open society, like George Soros. Two straws in the wind: Bill Gates still can't get rid of enough of his money fast enough (it has to be 5 per cent of your assets to qualify, which in his case means $1bn) and in California 'default philanthropy' (parents ensuring that their children don't have too much money) is now the biggest area of activity.

Is this philanthropy in a different style, producing different results or the same story as before? How far has this new activity begun to help addressing the key issues with which I began – the wealth and poverty of nations; human values in the good society, the promotion of the common good?

There are numerous devices available for measurement of the extent of wealth and the effects of the presence of a healthy civil society (and more to come from the Global Civil Society debate); it is relatively simple to record the existence of the institutions of democracy and civil law or measure the extent of participation in the democratic process.

But ultimately the real test is not objective: it's about feeling good about the future of your own society, having confidence in the ways in which it is changing and developing and in those responsible for setting the course. This subjective sense of what's good is open to abuse and manipulation – in dystopian societies, the citizen body can be pacified with *soma* or multi-channel media offering 'chewing gum for the eyes'. But ultimately real personal satisfaction should lie in the sense, as the French put it, of 'feeling comfortable in your own skin'.

Social possibilities for my grandchildren

Imagining the future at the beginning of the twentieth century, H. G. Wells predicted that the progress of science would generate increased harmony in human relations whose stability would be guaranteed by world government. Wells, his erstwhile critic Aldous Huxley pronounced rather patronisingly, squeaks, but 'squeaks to good effect against stupidity and cupidity' (Bradshaw 1994: 37). But Wells needed a caste of incorruptible administrators – his 'samurai' – and an open conspiracy to bring then to power in order to give substance to his squeaking. J. M. Keynes, another keen reader of Wells, commented in his turn that the idea of the open conspiracy was all very well but it would be difficult to find persons of real substance to join it.

> Why do practical men find it more amusing to make money than to join the Open Conspiracy? I suggest that it is much the same reason which makes them find it more amusing to play bridge on Sunday than to go to church. They lack altogether the kind of motive, the possession of which if they had it, could be expressed by saying they had a creed. They have no creed, these potential open conspirators, no creed whatever. This is why unless they have the luck to be scientists or artists, they fall back on the grand substitute motive, the perfect *Ersatz*, the anodyne for those who, in fact, want nothing at all – Money.'
> (Keynes 1931: 356)

Neo-liberalism believes implicitly in the ersatz, of course: it makes the world of turbo-capitalism go round, with increasing velocity. But I have another reason for rejecting a Wellsian twenty-first century: expressed rather pompously, it is a belief that democracy and civil society should go hand in hand and that civic virtue is not an option but a necessity – but one that must be freely chosen, not imposed. That is why I express my own preference for William Morris's Nowhere as an alternative model of Utopia – and the only one in which I would be at all comfortable for my grandchildren to live.

This may all be theoretical, to some extent. My life over the period in which this book has been written has been measured out in ballpoint pens: each and every institution with which I have had dealings has pressed them on me: a mug-full salutes me every morning at my desk. The opportunities that I have enjoyed for discussing and debating these issues which these pens represent have been invaluable.

These debates have sometimes been abstract and theoretical – and none the less useful for that. But my preference is also rooted in real life experience. Not in dramas, as I have already confessed, but in many encounters. To take only one recent example: the tenants in social housing of my own city, Birmingham, for whom I helped to devise a Millennium Commission scheme. The energies released and the capacities of ordinary people, from a vast range of age groups and backgrounds, when given the opportunity and reassured that it really belonged to them, to take hold of the issues that affect their own lives and do so boldly was deeply impressive.

And if I were one of the Professsors of Foresight that H. G. Wells wanted to appoint, I would want to expand the kind the opportunities that this scheme represents on a miniscule scale with changes to the wider setting – putting in place a society which guarantees proper life chances and a lifelong range of choices for all its citizens. (In other words, attaining the objectives which I describe in my preface.) Frankly, whether this is labelled a civil society or not scarcely matters.

So what I want for my grandchildren is liberty for their imaginations, an education system that preserves and enhances it, and an economy that does not confuse reward with the ersatz but provides opportunities of the kind so nicely captured by David Landes, whom I gratefully quote for the final time:

> The people who live to work are a small and fortunate elite. But it is an elite open to newcomers, self-selected, the kind of people who accentuate the positive. In this world the optimists have it, not because they are always right but because they are positive. Even when wrong, they are positive and that is the way of achievement, correction, improvement, and success. Educated, eyes-open optimism pays; pessimism can only offer the empty consolation of being right. (1998: 523–4)

Appendix: Suggestions for Further Reading and Data Sources

This short note is intended to identify some of the published material that readers wanting to pursue particular topics might find especially helpful. Fuller details of the works mentioned are in the bibliography. I have organised this account along the lines laid out in my own text.

Chapter 1

Readers wanting a simple introduction to the debate around the use of the term civil society and its emergence should, I suggest, try Adam Seligman, John Keane or Cohen and Arato's collection (1992). My own preference for a starting point, as I indicate, is for Michael Walzer's (1995) account – which may have the additional merit of leading readers back to his splendid *Spheres of Justice*. Critics of the use to which the term has been put – or even asserting its essential meaninglessness – are now legion. For the first, Bob Fine (1997) and the Hann and Dunne collection (1996); on the second, Barry Knight (1993) (from the 'Foundation for Civil Society') – I have quoted in the text his recent and highly enjoyable polemic.

For voluntary action, the Johns Hopkins studies are good places to start. There is a summitry of all the reports from the first round of studies in Salamon and Anheier (1997) *Defining the Nonprofit Sector*. The British study, Kendall and Knapp (1996), provides a good balanced account. Other useful collections include Harris and Rochester (2001). Barry Knight's report *Voluntary Action* (1993) (though it was a political fiasco) is very helpful for its definitions – if you can find it.

Chapter 2

The vitality of historical scholarship is one of the striking features of the scene, at least in the Anglo-Saxon countries. For Britain the few but valuable earlier studies (Godsden, Jordan) are now updated by Frank Prochaska (1980, 1988) and the late Geoffrey Finlayson's heroic attempt (1994) at a synthesis. A series of collections (Mandler 1990, Daunton 1996, Cunningham 1998 and Innes 1998) give a good idea of the volume of interesting work now taking place. There is more in the pipeline, I'm glad to say (the Institute for Volunteering Research can provide details).

Chapter 3

The most prolific of the communitarians by far is Amitai Etzioni: a series of books, some drawing on evidence from recent American sociology; others cast in the form of exhortation. These have been supplemented by a number of tracts from think tanks on both left and right (this is a topic that crosses party lines) and have also attracted enthusiastic critics: for example, Stephen Holmes (1993) and for the UK Elizabeth Frazer (1999). Jonathan Sacks' judicially balanced account (1997) would be helpful to non-specialists wanting to stay above the sound of battle. On the detailed evidence, Jeff Bishop and Paul Hoggett (1986) and Ruth Finnegan (1989) both provide fascinating slices of 'thick' evidence on community operating beneath the radar. Robert Putnam's long-awaited *Bowling Alone* (2000) summarises much evidence about the decline of community in the United States and clearly explicates the significance of the concept of social capital; his account falters only when it comes to practical recommendations.

Chapter 4

The debate around political citizenship and its prospects is also controversial. Putnam has things to say here, too. For the United States, the Skocpol (1998) and Norris (1999) collections cast some doubt on both his analysis and prescriptions. In Britain, Paul Hirst (1994) offers a well-argued case for associative democracy; and John Keane (1998) explores the relationship between democracy and civil society. The section on resistance and obedience draws on a number of writers – H. R. Kedward (1999), in particular. (Readers attracted to the subject might like to start there.) Mark Mazower's *Dark Continent* (1998) is invaluable in setting the successes and failure of democracy in Europe, in the twentieth century in a broader context.

Chapter 5

I had better confess at once that I don't read Hungarian and have therefore been wholly dependent on the material that has been translated (the interpretation in my text also draws on interview material, though this is not formally sourced). For general background, the work of Zsuzsa Ferge has been indispensable; for the voluntary sector, that of Eva Kuti and her colleagues at the Hungarian Central Statistical Office. Eva is also the author of the volume (1996) in the Johns Hopkins series – an excellent place for other readers to start. (Both these writers shame natives by the clarity of their English prose.) There are several excellent accounts of the transition from state socialism to liberal capitalism by both Hungarian writers and by outside observers. One of the most useful is presented as a guide book: but Andras Torok's (1999) introduction to Budapest is aptly billed as a 'critical view' and vividly conveys the flavour of the recent past and the distance travelled since. (It's also a first-rate guide to the city.)

Chapter 6

This may be the best point to acknowledge David Landes' *Wealth and Poverty of Nations* (1998), which made much clear to me and justified the risky comparison with Adam Smith implied by the title. Fellow economic (near) illiterates would also benefit from using it, I'm sure. The debate about the influence of the market on voluntary action is bound to run further: Bill Shore's enthusiastic *Cathedral Within* (1999) states a case; others are more cautious (Christopher Lasch 1995). When it comes to the alternatives, like mutualism, and their practical possibilities try Stephen Yeo's work and the Oxford Mutuality Task Force (2000). Demos have also published some useful work here.

Chapter 7

Globalisation needs unpicking (unpacking) as a term: David Held's work is a good place to start: Paul Hirst is sceptical about the originality of the concept. Thomas Friedman is the most recent of the unqualified boosters for globalisation; *The Lexus and the Olive Tree* (1999) is highly (intentionally) provocative: an enjoyable read and influential in certain circles; but already showing some signs of dating. It's curious that there has been so little interconnection between what must be called the NGO world and that of domestic voluntary organisations. Michael Edwards' *Future Positive* (1999) bridges that gap and is a cracking good read. Global civil society provides a possible link: here, too, there is debate about how far the term is meaningful (more work is needed here and is on the way as I write).

Chapter 8

Utopia as a topic has produced a vast literature. Readers wanting to get to grips with it should start, I suggest, with Krishan Kumar (1987) and Barbara Goodwin (1978). A useful collection of snippets from the original texts that will serve as a guidebook for casual visitors is John Carey's anthology of Utopias (1999), though the commentary is disappointingly thin. The experience of utopian experiments in the United States is well caught by Rosabeth Kanter (1972): Christopher Clark's case study *The Communitarian Moment* (1995) is fascinating. The sceptics have a field day in the more recent commentaries.

Data Sources

Readers who want up-to-date factual information about the activities of voluntary bodies (under whatever title) can now obtain it direct by email or on the websites of a number of organisations. In England, such information is provided by the National Council for Voluntary Organisations (NCVO) in cooperation with the equivalent bodies in other countries of the United Kingdom The NCVO (*www.ncvo-vol.org.uk*) produces at regular intervals an *Almanac* of the UK voluntary sector (latest edition 2000). In addition, it publishes a quarterly research bulletin, covering a range of selected issues. The Charities Aid Foundation, (CAF: *www.charitynet.org*) produces in conjunction with the NCVO a review, *Dimensions of the Voluntary Sector* and other publications, like their *Directory of Grant Making Trusts*.

In the United States, Independent Sector in Washington DC (*www.Independentsector.org*) publishes an annual *Non-Profit Almanac* and a regular review of facts and findings from research. Other countries also collect information systematically and make it available regularly. Hungary provides an excellent example: there, the Hungarian Government's Central Statistical Office provides regular reports in English and Hungarian on the development of the non-profit sector there (contact at 26-1-345-6570).

I have referred several times to the Johns Hopkins international comparative studies. The first wave of national studies is now complete and a second one is well underway. Contact through the Center for Civil Society Studies, Institute for Policy Studies, Johns Hopkins University (*www.jhu.edu*). The Center has also inaugurated a series on Global Civil Society (first edition 1999) which aims to provide a country-by-country analysis of the scope, size, composition and financing of the civil society sector throughout the world. Further information on the topic and discussion of key issues will be available from publications of the Centre for Civil Society, Department of Social Policy, London School of Economics (*www.lse.ac.uk/depts/ccs*).

Academic journals published in the field are also useful sources of up-to-date information. Among the most important of these are:

Non-profit Management and Leadership (*www.josseybass.com*)
Non-profit and Voluntary Sector Quarterly (*www.sagepub.com*)
Voluntary Action: The journal of the Institute for Volunteering Research (*instvolres@aol.com*)
Voluntas: International journal of Voluntary and Non-profit Organisations (Kluwer Academic Publications)

There are also a number of active professional associations:

ARNOVA (Association for Research on Non-Profit Organizations and Voluntary Action) (*www.arnova.org*)
Institute for Volunteering Research (*instvolres@aol.com*)
ISTR (International Society for Third Sector Research) (*www.jhu.edu/-istr*)

Bibliography

Addy, T. and Scott, D. (1987) *Fatal Impacts?*, William Temple Foundation: Manchester.

Alinsky, S. (1969) *Reveille for Radicals*, Vintage: New York.

Allen, W. S. (1976) *The Nazi Seizure of Power: The Experience of a Single German Town*, Eyre & Spottiswoode: London.

Almond, G. A. and Verba, S. (1965) *The Civic Culture, Political Attitudes and Democracy in Five Nations*, Little Brown and Company: Boston.

Anheier, H. and Kendall, J. (2000) *Trust and Voluntary Organisations*: Three Theoretical Approaches, London School of Economics, Civil Society Working Papers No 5: London.

Anheier, H. and Seibel, W. (1992) 'The Non-profit Sector and the Transformation of Societies: A Comparative Study of East Germany, Poland and Hungary' in W. W. Powell (ed.) *Private Action and Public Good*, Yale University Press: New Haven.

Annan, N. (1995) *Changing Enemies: The Defect and Regeneration of Germany*, Harper Collins: London.

Arblaster, A. (1994) *Democracy*, Open University Press: Buckingham.

Arruda, M. (1996) 'Globalisation and Civil Society: Rethinking Cooperativism in the Context of Active Citizenship'. A paper presented at the Conference on Globalization and Citizenship, organised by the Institute for the Investigation of Social Development of the United Nations (UNRISD), 9–11 December, 1996: Geneva.

Atkinson, R. (1998) 'Charity Law Conference Paper'. Unpublished paper to the NCVO Conference, September 1998.

Attlee, C. (1920) *The Social Worker*, C. Bell: London.

Aubert, V. (1965) *The Hidden Society*, Bedminster Press: London.

Aves, G. (1969) *The Voluntary Worker in the Social Services*, Allen and Unwin: London.

Becker, M. (1994) *The Emergence of Civil Society in the Eighteenth Century: A Privileged Moment in the History of England, Scotland and France*, Indiana University Press: Bloomington.

Belcham, J. and Hardy N. 'Second Metropolis' in A. Kidd and D. Nicholls (eds) (1998).

Berger, P. (1996) *To Empower People: From State to Civil Society*, American Enterprise Institute: Washington, DC.

Berlin, I. (1991) *The Crooked Timber of Humanity*, Fontana: London.

Berlin, I. (1999) *The Roots of Romanticism*, Chatto and Windus: London.

Beveridge, Sir W. (1942) *Report of the Committee on Social Insurance and Allied Services*, HMSO: London.

Beveridge, Lord (1948*) Voluntary Action,* George Allen and Unwin: London.

Billis, D. and Harris, M. (1996*) Voluntary Agencies: Challenges of Organisation and Management*, Macmillan Press – now Palgrave: London.

Bishop, J. and Hoggett, P. (1986) *Organising Around Enthusiasms*, Comedia London.

Blair, T. (1999) *The Prime Minister's Speech* at the Annual Conference of the National Council of Voluntary Organisations, January.

Boris, E. T. and Steuerle, C. E. (eds) (1998) *Nonprofits and Government Collaboration and Conflict*, The Urban Institute Press: Washington, DC.

Borocz, J (2000) 'Infirmity of Non-profits in ECE Capitalism' *Voluntas*, 11, 2 June.

Bradshaw, D. (ed.) (1994) *The Hidden Huxley*, Faber: London.

Braithwaite, W. J. (1957) *Lloyd George's Ambulance Wagon*, Methuen: London.

Brent, M. G. (1997) *The Political Economy of Civil Society and Human Rights*, Routledge: London.

Bromley, B. and Bromley, K. (2000) 'The Historical Origins of the Definition of Religion in Charity Law', Paper presented to the Fourth International Conference of ISTR, July: Dublin.

Bruce, I. (1994) *Meeting Need: Successful Charity Marketing*, ICSA Publishing: London.

Bryant, C. and Mokrzycki T. (eds) (1995) *Democracy, Civil Society and Pluralism in Comparative Perspective: Poland, Greece and the Netherlands*, IFIS: Warszawa.

Burns, D. and Taylor, M. (1998) *Mutual Aid and Self Help*, The Policy Press: Bristol.

Carey, J. (1999) *The Faber Book of Utopias*, Faber: London.

Checkland, O. and Checkland, S. (1973) *Introduction to The Report of the Poor Law Commission of 1834*, Penguin Books: Harmondsworth.

Clark, C. (1995) *The Communitarian Moment*, Cornell University Press: Ithaca.

Cohen, J. and Arato, A. (1992) *Civil Society and Political Theory*, The MIT Press: Cambridge, MA, and London.

Coogan, T. P. (1995) *The IRA*, Harper Collins: London.

Coote, A. (ed.) (1992) *The Welfare of Citizens: Developing New Social Rights*, IPPR/Rivers Oram Press: London.

Coulson, A. (ed.) (1998) *Trust and Contracts*, The Policy Press: Bristol.

Cox, T. and Furlong, A. (eds) (1995) *Hungary: The Politics of Transition*, Frank Cass: London.

Cox, T. and Vass, L. (1995) 'Civil Society and Interest Representation in Hungarian Political Development' in T. Cox and A. Furlong (eds).

Cunningham, H. and Innes, J. (eds) (1998) *Charity, Philanthropy and Reform*, Macmillan: London.

Dahrendorf, R. (1990) *Reflections on the Revolution in Europe*, Chatto: London.

Dalton R. J. (1999) 'Political Support in Advanced Western Democracies' in P. Norris (ed.).

Davie, G. E. (1981) *The Scottish Enlightenment*, The Historical Association: London.

Daunton, M. (ed.) (1996) *Charity, Self-interest and Welfare in the English Past*, UCL Press: London.

Deakin, N. (1995) 'The Perils of Partnership: The Voluntary Sector and the State, 1945–1992', in Davis Smith, J., Rochester, C. and Hedley, R. (eds) *An Introduction to the Voluntary Sector*, Routledge: London.

De Swaan, A. (1988) *In Care of the State*, Polity Press: Cambridge.

Dichter, T. (1999) 'Globalisation and its Effects on NGOs: Efflorescence or a Blurring of Roles and Relevance', *Non-Profit and Voluntary Sector Quarterly* 28, 4.

Dominique, C. (1997) *Civil Society and Fanaticism: Conjoined Histories*, Stanford University Press: Stanford.

Edwards, M. (1999) *Future Positive*, Earthscan: London.

Edwards, M. and Hulme, D. (eds) (1995) *Non Governmental Organisations Performing and Accountability: Beyond the Magic Bullet*, Earthscan Publications: London.

Elsdon, K. T., Reynolds, J. and Stewart, S. (eds) (1995) *Voluntary Organisations, Citizenship, Learning and Change*, National Institute of Adult Continuing Education: Leicester.

Etherington, S. (1996) 'To the Millenium: The Changing Pattern of Voluntary Organisations' in Hanvey, C. and Philpot, T. (eds) *The Role and Workings of Voluntary Organisations*, Routledge: London.

Etzioni, A. (1995) *The Spirit of Community, Rights, Responsibilities and the Communitarian Agenda*, Fontana Press: London.

Etzioni, A. (1998) *The New Golden Rule*, Profile Books: London.

Etzioni, A. (2000a) *The Third Way to a Good Society*, Demos: London.

Etzioni, A. (2000b) 'Banding Together' *Times Literary Supplement*, 14 June.

Evers, A. (1995) 'Part of the Welfare Mix: The Third Sector as an Intermediate Area' in *Voluntas* 6, 2, 159–82.

Ferge, Z. (1996a) 'The Change of the Welfare Paradigm – the Individualisation of the Social'. Paper for the Annual Conference of the British Social Policy Association, July: Sheffield.

Ferge, Z. (1996b) *The Free Market and the Welfare State: Experiences from the Heart of Europe*, DenUyl Stichting: Amsterdam.

Ferge, Z. (1997) 'Women and Social Transformation in Central-Eastern Europe', *Czech Sociological Review*, 5, 2, 159–78.

Ferge, Z. (1999) 'Report on the World Bank Structural Adjustment Program Loans to Hungary 1988–98', SAPRI Report: Budapest.

Ferguson, A. (1996) An Essay on the History of Civil Society, Cambridge University Press: New York.

Financial Times Management (1998) 'Visions of Ethical Business', *Financial Times* 1 October.

Fine, R. (1997) 'The Concept of Civil Society' in Fine R. and Rai, S. (eds) *Civil Society: Democratic Perspectives*, Frank Cass: London.

Finlayson, G. (1994) *Citizen, State and Social Welfare in Britain 1830–1990*, Clarendon Press: Oxford.

Finnegan, R. (1989) The Hidden Musicians, Cambridge University Press: Cambridge.

Frazer, E. (1999) *The Problems of Communitarian Politics*, Clarendon Press: Oxford.

Friedman, T. (1999) *The Lexus and the Olive Tree*, Harper Collins: London.

Fukuyama, F. (1992) *The End of History and the Last Man*, Penguin: Harmondsworth.

Fukuyama, F. (1995) *Trust: The Social Virtues and the Creation of Prosperity*, The Free Press: New York.

Galbraith, J. K. (1993) *The Culture of Contentment*, Penguin Books: Harmondsworth.

Gellner, E. (1994) *Conditions of Liberty: Civil Society and its Rivals*, Hamish Hamilton: London.

Gellner, E. (1995) 'The Importance of Being Modular' in Hall, J. A. (ed.) *Civil Society Theory History Comparison*, Polity Press: Cambridge.

Gibson, J. L. (1997) 'Social Networks and Civil Society in Processes of Democratization', *Studies in Public Policy 301*. Centre for the Study of Public Policy, University of Strathclyde: Glasgow.

Gilbert, B. B. (1966) *The Evolution of National Insurance in Great Britain*, Michael Joseph: London.

Gladstone, F. (1979) *Voluntary Action in a Changing World*, Bedford Square Press: London.

Goodwin, B. (1978) *Social Science and Utopia*, Harvester Press: Hassocks.

Goodwin, B. and Taylor, K. (1982) *The Politics of Utopia*, Hutchinson: London.

Gramsci, A. (1971) *Selections from the Prison Notebooks*, Lawrence & Wishart Ltd: London.

Gray, B. Kirkman (1908) *Philanthropy and the State*, P. S. King: London.

Green, A. (1999) 'Policy-making Processes and Democratic Development' Paper presented to *Voluntas* conference, October: Prague.

Green, D. G. (1993) *Reinventing Civil Society: The Rediscovery of Welfare Without Politics*, IEA Health and Welfare Unit Choice in Welfare Series, no. 17: London.

Gutman, A. (ed.) (1998) *Freedom of Association*, Princeton University Press: Princeton.

Halfpenny, P. (2000) 'Trust, Charity and Civil Society' in Hems, L., Fenton, N., Passey, A. and Tonkiss, F. (eds) *Trust and Civil Society*, Palgrave: Basingstoke.

Hall, J. A. (ed.) (1995a) *Civil Society: Theory, History, Comparison*, Polity Press: Cambridge.

Hall, J. A. (1995b) 'In Search of Civil Society' in Hall, J. A. (ed.) *Civil Society: Theory, History, Comparison*, Polity Press: Cambridge.

Hall, Peter D. (1982) *The Organisation of American Culture, 1700–1900: Private Institutions, Elites and the Origins of American Nationality*, New York University Press: New York.

Halpern, D. (1998), 'Social Capital, Exclusion and the Quality of Life: Towards a Causal Model and Policy Implications.' Unpublished paper: Faculty of Social and Political Sciences: Cambridge.

Hann, C. and Dunne, E. (1996) *Civil Society: Challenging Western Models*, Routledge: London.

Hanvey, C. and Philpot, T. (eds) (1996) *The Role and Workings of Voluntary Organisations*, Routledge: London.

Harris, M. (1998) *Organising God's Work: Challenges for Churches and Synagogues*, Macmillan: London.

Harris, M. and Rochester, C. (2001) *Voluntary Organisations and Social Policy in Britain*, Palgrave: Basingstoke.

Hartnell, C. (2000) 'Transforming Philanthropy for the Shifting Sands of the Twenty-first Century' *Alliance*, 5, 2–3.

Heater, D. (1990) *Citizenship*, Longmans: Harlow.

Held, D. (1997) 'Democracy and Globalisation' *Global Governance* 3, 251–67.

Himmelfarb, G. (1995) *The Demoralisation of Society*, IEA: London.

Hirsch, F. (1977) *Social Limits to Growth*, Routledge & Kegan Paul: London.

Hirschman, A. O. (1970) *Exit, Voice and Loyalty*, Harvard University Press: Cambridge MA, London.

Hirschman, A. O. (1991) *The Rhetoric of Reaction: Perversion Futility Jeopardy*, Belknap Press of Harvard University Press: Cambridge, MA.

Hirst, P. (1994) *Associative Democracy: New Forms of Economic and Social Governance*, Blackwell Publishers: Oxford.

Hirst, P. and Khilnani, S. (1996) *Reinventing Democracy*, Blackwell Publishers: Oxford.

Hirst, P. and Thompson, G. (1996) *Globalisation in Question*, Polity Press: Cambridge.

Hoggett, P. (1994) *The Future of Civic Forms of Organisation*, Demos: London.

Hoggett, P. and Hambleton, R. (eds) (1987) 'Decentralisation and Democracy Localising Public Services', School for Advanced Urban Studies, University of Bristol Occasional Paper 28: Bristol.

Holmes, S. (1993) *The Anatomy of Anti Liberalism*, Harvard University Press: Cambridge, MA.

Huxley, A. (1932) *Brave New World*, Chatto and Windus: London.

Ignatieff, M. (1986) *The Needs of Strangers*, Chatto and Windus: London.

Inglehart, R. (1999) 'Postmodernisation Erodes Respect for Authority but Increases Support for Democracy' in P. Norris (ed.).

Innes, J. (1998) 'State, Church and Voluntarism' in Cunningham, H. and Innes, J. (eds) *Charity, Philanthropy and Reform*, Macmillan: London.

Jacobs, J. (1961) *The Death and Life of Great American Cities*, Random House: New York.

James, E. (1987) 'The Non-Profit Sector in Comparative Perspective' in W. W. Powell (ed.) *The Non-Profit Sector: A Research Handbook*, Yale University Press: New Haven.

Janowski, T. (1998) *Citizenship and Civil Society: A Framework of Rights and Obligations in Liberal, Traditional and Social Democratic Regimes*, Cambridge University Press: Cambridge.

Jenkins, R. (1995) 'Politics and the Development of the Hungarian Non-profit Sector' *Voluntas*, 6: 2, 183–201.

Kanter, R. M. (1972) *Commitment and Community*, Harvard University Press: Cambridge, MA:

Kateb, G. (1963) *Utopia and its Enemies*, Free Press of Glencoe: New York.

Katz, S. (1999) 'The Idea of Civil society' in *Civil society: A New Agenda for US-Japan Intellectual Exchange* Japan Foundation: Tokyo.

Keane, J. (ed.) (1988) *Civil Society and the State: New European Perspectives*, Verso: London.

Keane, J. (1998a) *Civil Society: Old Images, New Vision*, Polity Press: Cambridge.

Keane, J. (1998b) *Democracy and Civil Society*, University of Westminster Press: London.

Kedward, H. R. (1999) 'The Discourse of Personality' in K. G. Robertson (ed.) *War, Resistance and Intelligence*, Leo Cooper: London.

Kendall, J. and Almond, S. (1998) 'The UK Voluntary Sector in Comparative Perspective: Exceptional Growth and Transformation' Personal Social Services Research Unit, University of Kent.

Kendall, J. and Knapp, M. (1996) *The Voluntary Sector in the United Kingdom*, John Hopkins Non Profit Sector Series 8, Manchester University Press: Manchester.

Keynes, J. M. (1931) *Essays in Persuasion*, Macmillan: London.

Kidd, A. and Nicholls, D. (eds) (1998) *The Making of the British Middle Class*, Sutton Publications: Stroud.

Klink, A., Renn, O. and Lehners, J. P. (eds) (1997) *Ethnic Conflicts and Civil Society: Proposals for a New Era in Eastern Europe*, Aldershot: Ashgate.

Knight, B. (1993) *Voluntary Action*, Home Office, Centris Crown Copyright: London.

Knight, B. and Hartnell, C. (2000) 'Civil Society – Is It Anything More Than a Metaphor for Hope in a Better World?' *Alliance*, vol. 5, no 3, 16–19.

Knight, F. (1854) *The Parochial System versus Centralisation*, Shaw and Sons: London.

Kumar, K. (1987) *Utopia and Anti-Utopia in Modern Times*, Blackwell: Oxford.

Kumar, K. and Bann, S. (eds) (1993) *Utopias and the Millennium*, Reaktion Books: London.

Kuti, E. (1996) *The Non-Profit Sector in Hungary*, Manchester University Press: Manchester.

Kuti, E. (1998a) 'NGO Stocktaking in Hungary' TS: Budapest.

Kuti, E. (1998b) 'Do Foreign NGOs Contribute to Sustainable Development in the Third Sector – the Case of Hungary'. Paper presented to the Third Conference of ISTR, July: Geneva.

Kuti, E. (1999) 'Different Eastern European Countries at Different Crossroads' *Voluntas*, 10, 1 March, 51–60.

Landes, D. (1998) *The Wealth and Poverty of Nations*, Little Brown: London.

Landry, C. *et al.* (1985) *What a Way to run a Railroad*, Comedia: London.

Lansley, J. (2000) 'Changing Concepts of Charity 1700–1900', Paper presented to NCVO Research Conference, September: Birmingham.

Lasch, C. (1995) *The Revolt of the Elites and the Betrayal of Democracy*, W.W. Norton & Co: London.

Laville, J. L. (1998) 'Perspectives for the Social Economy in Europe: From Social Enterprises to a Civil and Solidarity-Based Economy', National Centre of Scientific Research, Paris-France. Paper presented to the Third International Conference of The International Society for Third Sector Research, University of Geneva, July.

Leadbeater, C. and Christie, I. (1999) *To Our Mutual Advantage*, Demos: London.

Lemieux. P. (1988) *L'Anarcho-Capitalisme*, Presses Universitaires de France: Paris.

Lewis, J. (1995) *The Voluntary Sector, the State and Social Work in Britain*, Edward Elgar: London.

Leybourne. K. (ed.) (1997) *Social Conditions, Status and Community*, Sutton Publishing: Stroud.

Lindenberg, M. and Dobel, J. P. (1999) 'The Challenge of Globalisation for Northern International Relief and Development NGOs' *Non-profit and Voluntary Sector Quarterly*, 28, 4, 4–24.

Lipset, S. M. (1984) *Failure of a Dream: Essays in the History of American Socialism*, University of California Press: Berkeley.

Lively, J. (1962) *Social and Political Thought of Alexis de Tocqueville*, Clarenden Press: Oxford.

Lohmann, R. A. (1992) *The Commons: New Perspectives on Non Profit Organisation and Voluntary Action*, Jossey-Bass: San Francisco.

Macadam, E. (1934) *The New Philanthropy: A Study of the Relations between the Statutory and Voluntary Social Services*, George Allen and Unwin: London.

McCarthy, K. D. (1991) *Women's Culture: American Philanthropy and Art 1830–1930*, University of Chicago Press : Chicago.

Macintyre, A. (1985) *After Virtue: A Study in Moral Theory*, Duckworth: London.

Malone, W., Smith, G. and Stoker, G. (1997) 'Social Capital and Urban Governance'. Paper prepared for the ESRC Cities Programme, University of Strathclyde Working Paper: Glasgow.

Mandler, P. (ed.) (1990) *The Uses of Charity*, University of Pennsylvania Press: Pittsburgh.

Mannheim, K. (1936) *Ideology and Utopia*, Routledge and Kegan Paul: London.

Marris, P. (1996) *The Politics of Uncertainty: Attachment in Private and Public Life*, Routledge: London.

Mazower, M. (1998) *Dark Continent: Europe's Twentieth Century*, Penguin Books: Harmondsworth.

Meiskins Wood, E. (1990) 'The Uses and Abuses of Civil Society', *Socialist Register*, 1995, 60–84.

Miszlivetz, F. and Ertsey, K. (1998) 'Hungary: Civil Society in the Post-Soviet World' in A. van Rooey (ed.) *Civil Society and the Aid Industry*, Earthscan: London.

Misztal, B. (1996) *Trust in Modern Societies*, Polity Press and Blackwell Publishers: Cambridge, MA.

Moorehead, C. (1999) *Dunant's Dream*, Harper Collins: London.

Muirhead, J. H. (1909) 'By What Authority?' *The Birmingham Post*.

Mulgan, J. (1995) *The Other Invisible Hand, Remaking Charity for the 21st Century*, Demos: London.

Newton, K. 'Social and Political Trust in Established Democracies' in P. Norris (ed.) 1999.

Nobbio, R. (1995) 'Gramsci' in Hall, J.A. (ed.) *Civil Society Theory History Comparison*, Polity Press: Cambridge.

Norris, P. (ed.) (1999) *Critical Citizens: Global Support for Democratic Governance*, Oxford University Press: Oxford.

Novak, M. (1990) *Morality, Capitalism and Democracy*, IEA Health and Welfare Unit Choice in Welfare Series, 5: London.

Nozick, R. (1974) *Anarchy, State and Utopia*, Blackwell: Oxford.

Ory, P. (1980) *Les Collaborateurs*, Éditions du Seuil, Paris.

Osborne, S. P. (1997) *A Civil Society? Exploring its Meanings in the Context of Post-communist Hungary*, Research Papers Series (Aston Business

School) RP 9712, Aston Business School Research Institute: Birmingham.

Osborne, S. P. (1998) *Voluntary Organizations and Innovation in Public Services*, Routledge: London.

Ousby, I. (1999) *Occupation*, Pimlico: London.

Oxford Mutuality Task Force (2000) *Mutuality: Owing the Solution*, Cooperative Futures: Oxford.

Passey, A., Hems, L. and Jas, P. (2000) *The UK Voluntary Sector Almanac 2000*, NCVO Publications: London.

Pepper, A. and Pepper, L. (1979) *Straight Life*, Schirmer Books: New York.

Philp, F. (1963) *Family Failure*, Faber: London.

Popper, K. (1966) *The Open Society and its Enemies*, Routledge and Kegan Paul: London.

Pickvance, K. (1992) Social Movements and Civil Society', Paper presented to the BSA Sociological Association Conference, Canterbury 6–9 April: University of Kent.

Plant, R. and Barry, N. (1990) *Citizenship and Rights in Thatcher's Britain: Two Views*, IEA Health and Welfare Unit: London.

Potucek, M. (2000) 'The Uneasy Birth of Czech Civil Society', *Voluntas* 11: 2, June, 107–22.

Powell, F. and Guerin, D. (1998) 'The Irish Third Sector and Collaboration with the State: A Case Study on the Redefinition of Civic Virtue'. Paper at International Society for Third Sector Research Annual Conference July: Geneva.

Prochaska, F. K. (1980) *Victorian Women Philanthropists in Nineteenth-century England*, Clarendon Press: Oxford.

Prochaska, F. K. (1988) *The Voluntary Impulse*, Faber: London.

Putman, R. (1993a) *Making Democracy Work*, Princeton University Press: Princeton: NJ, Chichester, West Sussex.

Putnam, R. (1993b) 'The Prosperous Community: Social Goals and Public Affairs' *The American Prospect*, 13, 35–42.

Putnam, R. (2000) *Bowling Alone*, Simon and Schuster: New York.

Rajesh, T. (1991) 'Civil Society, the State and Roles of NGOs', IDR Reports; 8, 3, Institute for Development Research: Boston.

Randle, M. (1994) *Civil Resistance*, Fontana Press: London.

Roberts, D. (1979) *Paternalism in Early Victorian England*, Croom Helm: London.

Roberts, M. (1998) 'Head versus Heart?' in H. Cunningham and J. Innes (eds) *Charity, Philanthropy and Reform*, Macmillan: London.

Rose, R. (1994) 'Distrust as an Obstacle to Civil Society', *Studies in Public Policy*: 226, Centre for the Study of Public Policy: University of Strathclyde.

Ross, E. (1993) *Love and Toil: Motherhood in Outcast London 1870–1918*, Oxford University Press: Oxford.

Ross, E. (1996) 'Hungry Children: Housewives and London Charity 1870–1914' in Mandler, P. (ed.) *The Uses of Charity*, University of Pennsylvania Press: Pittsburgh.

Rowley, K. (ed.) (1997) *Classical Liberalism and Civil Society*, The John Locke series in classical liberal political economy; vol. 7 The Shaftesbury Papers, Edward Elgar: Cheltenham.

Sachs, J. (1999) 'Taking Stock of the Transition' *Central European Economic Review*, VII, 9, November, 6.

Sacks, J. (1997) *The Politics of Hope*, Jonathan Cape: London.

Salaman, L. (1993a) 'The Mutualisation of Welfare: Changing Non-Profit and For Profit Roles in the American Welfare State' *Social Services Review* 67, 1 March, 16–39.

Salaman, L. (1993b) 'The Non-profit Sector and Democracy: Prerequisite, Impediment or Irrelevance', Paper presented to Aspen Institute Symposium, 14 December: Wye, Maryland.

Salamon, L. and Anheier, H. (1997) *Defining the Nonprofit Sector*: *A Cross-national Analysis*, John Hopkins Nonprofit Sector Series 4, Manchester University Press: Manchester.

Salaman, L. and Anheier, H. (1998) Social Origins of Civil Society: Explaining the Nonprofit Sector Cross-Nationally in *Voluntas*, 9: 3, 213–48.

Sassoon, D. (1996) *One Hundred Years of Socialism*, I. B. Tauris: London.

Sebesteny, I. (1999) 'The Non Profit Sector and Local Government: The Hungarian Experience', Paper presented at Charities Aid Foundation Conference, Budapeset, October.

Seidentop, L. (1994) *Tocqueville*, Oxford University Press: Oxford.

Seligman, A. B. (1992) *The Idea of Civil Society*, The Free Press: New York.

Seligman, A. B. (1995) 'Animadversions upon Civil Society and Civic Virtue in the Last Decade of the Twentieth Century' in John A. Hall (ed.) *Civil Society Theory History Comparison*, Polity Press: Cambridge.

Seligman, A. B. (1997) *The Problem of Trust*, Princeton University Press: New Jersey.

Selle, P. and Stromsnes, K. (1997) 'Membership and Democracy: Should We Take Passive Support Seriously?' Paper Presented to the Regional Conference on Social Movements, September 10–12: Tel Aviv.

Selznick, P. (1992) *The Moral Commonwealth*: *Social Theory and a Promise of Community*, University of California Press: Berkeley.

Sen, A. (2000) 'Freedom's Market', *Observer* 25 June.

Sennett, R. (1980) *Authority*, Secker & Warburg: London.

Shapiro, L. (1972) *Totalitarianism*, The Pall Mall Press: London.

Shaw, G. B. (1948) *Man and Superman: The Revolutionist's Handbook* Penguin Books: Harmondsworth.

Shaw Bond, M. (2000) 'A Helping Hand?', *Prospect*, April, 12–13.

Shawcross, W. (1999) *Deliver us from Evil*: *Warlords and Peace-keepers in a World of Endless Conflict*, Bloomsbury: London.

Shils, E. A. (1991) 'The Virtue of Civil Society', *Government and Opposition* 26, 1.3–20: London.

Shils, E. A. (1997) *The Virtue of Civility: Selected Essays on Liberalism, Tradition, and Civil Society*, Liberty Fund: Indianapolis.

Shore, B. (1999) *The Cathedral Within*, Random House: New York.

Siedentop L. (1994) *Tocqueville*, Oxford University Press: Oxford and New York.

Siegel, D. and Yancey, J. (1992) *Rebirth of Civil Society*, Rockefeller Brothers Foundation: Budapest.

Simey, M. (1996) *The Disinherited Society*: *A Personal View of Social Responsibility in Liverpool during the Twentieth Century*, Liverpool University Press: Liverpool.

Simey, T. S. (1937) *Principles of Social Administration*, Oxford University Press: Oxford.

Skinner, B. F. (1976) *Walden Two*, Macmillan: London.

Skocpol, T. and Fiorina, M. (eds) (1998) *Civic Engagement in American Democracy*, Brookings Institution Press: Washington.

Smith, A. (1974) *The Wealth of Nations*, with an introduction by A. Skinner, Penguin: Harmondsworth.

Smith, A. (1976) *Theory of Moral Sentiments*, Clarendon Press: Oxford.

Smith, R. S. and Lipsky, M. (1993) *Nonprofits for Hire: The Welfare State in the Age of Contracting*, Harvard University Press: London.

Soros, G. (1998) *The Crisis of Global Capitalism*, Little Brown: New York.

Spencer, P. (1995–6) Civil Society, Politics and the Revolutions of 1989–1991, Discussion paper, European Research Centre, Kingston University: Kingston.

Stoker, G. (1996) 'Welfare Reform and Local Government in Britain: Exit, Voice but Whatever Happened to Loyalty', Paper presented to *La nova Europa Social I els Municipis* conference, Barcelona, 24–5 October:

Stokes, P. and Knight, B. (1997) *Organising a Civil Society*, Working paper, no 2, Foundation for Civil Society: Birmingham.

Szacki, J. (1995) *Liberalism after Communism*, Central European University Press: Prague.

Szalai, J. (1999) *Post-socialism and Globalisation*, Uj Mandatum: Budapest.

Szeman, Z. and Harsanyi, L. (2000) *Caught in the Net in Hungary and Eastern Europe*, Institute of Sociology of the Hungarian Academy of Sciences: Budapest.

Taylor, B. (1982) *Eve and the New Jerusalem*, Virago: London.

Tester, K. (1960) *Civil Society*, Routledge: London.

Titmuss, R. (1970) *The Gift Relationship: From Human Blood to Social Policy*, Allen and Unwin: London.

Tocqueville, A. de (1998) *Democracy in America* (tr. Henry Reeve) Wordsworth Press: London.

Torok, A. (1999) *Budapest: A Critical Guide*, Corvinus: Budapest.

Uglow, J. (1997) *Hogarth: A Life and a World*, Faber: London.

Vaclav, H. (1994) *Toward a Civil Society: Selected Speeches and Writings*, 1990–94, Lidove Noviny: Prague.

Vajda, A. and Kuti, E. (2000) 'Citizen Votes for Non-profit Causes' in *Forint Votes for Civil Society Organisations*, Non-profit Sector Research series: Budapest.

van Rooey, A. (1998) *Civil Society and the Aid Industry: The Politics of Promise*, Earthscan: London.

Verba, S., Schlozman, K. L. and Brady, H. (1995) *Voice and Equality*, Harvard University Press: Cambridge, MA.

Vienney, C. (1994) *L'économie sociale*, La Découverte: Paris.

Wagner, G. (1987) *The Chocolate Conscience*, Chatto & Windus: London.

Walzer, M. (1983) *Spheres of Justice: A Defence of Pluralism and Equality*, Martin Robertson: London.

Walzer, M. (ed.) (1995) *Toward a Global Civil Society*, Berghahn Books: Providence, MA and Oxford.

Wann, M. (1995) *Building Social Capital: Self Help in a Twenty-first Century Welfare State*, IPRR: London.

Webb, S. and Webb, B. (1911) *The Prevention of Destitution*, Longmans: London.

Wells, H. G. (1903) *A Modern Utopia*, Nelson: London.

Wells, H. G. (1911) *The New Machiavelli*, The Bodley Head: London.

Wells, H. G. (1933) *The Open Conspiracy*, np: London.

Whelan, R. (1996) *The Corrosion of Charity from Moral Renewal to Contract Charity*, IEA Choice in Welfare-Series no. 29: London.

Willhelm, R. (1996) *The Moral Foundations of Civil Society*, Transaction Publishers: New Brunswick, NJ.

Willmott, P. (1989) 'Community Initiatives Patterns and Prospects', Policy Studies Institute Research Report 698, Blackmore Press: Dorset.

Wright, T. (1994) *Citizens or Subjects: An Essay on British Politics*, Routledge: London.

Wolfenden, (Lord) J. (1977) *The Future of Voluntary Organisations*, Croom Helm: London.

Wuthnow, R. (1991) *Acts of Compassion: Caring for Others and Helping Ourselves*, Princeton University Press: Princeton, NJ and Oxford.

Wuthnow, R. (ed.) (1991*) Between States And Markets*: *The Voluntary Sector in Comparative Perspective*, Princeton University Press: Princeton, NJ.

Wuthnow, R. (1996) *Christianity and Civil Society: The Contemporary Debate*, Trinity Press International: Valley Forge, PA.

Young, M. (1961) *The Rise of the Meritocracy*, 1870–2033, Penguin Books: Harmondsworth.

Young, M. and Lemos, G. (1997) *The Communities we have Lost and can Regain*, Lemos and Crane: London.

Yeo, S (1979) 'Working-class Association, Private Capital, Welfare and the State in the Late Nineteenth- and Early Twentieth-Century' in N. Parry *et al.* (eds) *Social Work, Welfare and the State*, Edward Arnold: London.

Yeo, S. (1987) 'Notes on three Socialisms – Collectivism, Statism and Associationalism – Mainly in Late Nineteenth- and Early Twentieth-Century Britain' in C. Levy (ed.) *Socialism and the Intelligentsia, 1880–1914*, Routledge and Kegan Paul: London.

Younghusband, E. (1947) *Report on the Training and Employment of Social Workers*, T & A Constable: Edinburgh.

Glossary

CAF	Charities Aid Foundation
CDP	Community Development Programme
CMEs	Cooperative and mutual enterprises
COMECON	the state socialist equivalent of the Common Market, with membership of all Central and Eastern European countries in the Soviet bloc.
COS	Charity Organisation Society
DfID	Department for International Development
FIDESZ	'Young Democrats' in Hungary
GROs	grass roots organisations
IMF	International Monetary Fund
ISTR	International Society for Third Sector Researchers (US)
LETs	local exchanges by tokens
LSE	London School of Economics
MDF	Hungarian Democratic Forum
MNCs	multinational corporations
MSF	Médecins Sans Frontières
MSZP	'Socialists' in Hungary
NATO	North Atlantic Treaty Organisation
NCSS	National Council of Social Service
NCVO	National Council for Voluntary Organisations
NEM	New Economic Mechanism
NGOs	Non-governmental organisations
OECD	Organisation for Economic Cooperation and Development
OPEC	Organisation of Petroleum Exporting Countries
SZDSZ	'Free Democrats' in Hungary
UN	United Nations
UNDP	United Nations Development Programme
VSO	Voluntary Service Overseas
WRVS	Women's Royal Voluntary Service (from 1981)
WVS	Women's Voluntary Service
WTO	World Trade Organisation

Index

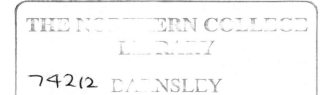